Anonymous

The Habits of Good Society

Handbook for Ladies and Gentlemen

Anonymous

The Habits of Good Society
Handbook for Ladies and Gentlemen

ISBN/EAN: 9783744665216

Printed in Europe, USA, Canada, Australia, Japan

Cover: Foto ©Andreas Hilbeck / pixelio.de

More available books at **www.hansebooks.com**

THE

HABITS OF GOOD SOCIETY:

A Handbook

FOR

LADIES AND GENTLEMEN.

WITH

THOUGHTS, HINTS, AND ANECDOTES CONCERNING SOCIAL OBSERVANCES;
NICE POINTS OF TASTE AND GOOD MANNERS; AND THE ART
OF MAKING ONE'S-SELF AGREEABLE. THE WHOLE INTER-
SPERSED WITH HUMOROUS ILLUSTRATIONS OF SOCIAL
PREDICAMENTS; REMARKS ON THE HISTORY
AND CHANGES OF FASHION; AND THE
DIFFERENCES OF ENGLISH AND
CONTINENTAL ETIQUETTE.

[From the Last London Edition.]

NEW YORK:

RUDD & CARLETON, 130 GRAND ST.

M DCCC LX.

CONTENTS.

PART I.—THE INDIVIDUAL.

CHAPTER I.—THE DRESSING ROOM.   107

Cleanliness.
The Bath : Hot, Cold, and
Tepid.
The Teeth.

The Nails.
Razors and Shaving.
Beards, Moustaches, Whiskers.
The Hair.

CHAPTER II.—THE LADY'S TOILET, ... 127

Early Rising.
Cleanliness.
Exercise.

Rouge and Cosmetics.
The Hair.
Perfumes, Toilet Appliances, &c.

CHAPTER III.—DRESS, ... 138

Fashion ; Appropriateness to
Age ; to Position ; to Place ;
Town and Country ; on the
Continent ; to Climate ; to
Size ; to different occasions.

Extravagance.
Simplicity.
Jewelry.
Maxims for Ornaments.
Orders, &c.

PART. II.—THE INDIVIDUAL IN INDIVIDUAL RELATIONS.

PART III.—THE INDIVIDUAL IN COMPANY.

PREFACE.

I AM the Man in the Club-Window. Which club and which window? you ask, and is it in Pall-Mall or St. James' street? I regret that I must decline to satisfy your very laudable curiosity. But there are other means of doing so: the "clerks" at the army-tailor's, the police-man on beat, even the crossing-sweeper a little lower down will, I fancy, know whom you mean, if you ask for *the* Man in the Club-Window.

I feel less delicacy in explaining to you why I sit in the club-window, and how I come to have sat there for the last ten years. I say "sat," but I may add "stood," for I do vary my position. When day is waning in the west, and the passing populace of the streets fails to interest me any longer, such moments are the drearier ones of my life.

I am a bachelor.

In the year which followed the French Revolution, I was left by a very severe fever, weak, morbid, and incapable of mixing in any society. I could only support the translation from my sick-room to my club. Unable to read, unwilling to talk, and still less inclined to take part

in cards or billiards, my sole amusement was to observe.
I took in the window a seat, which has since by common
consent been reserved for me, and there I have sat ever
since, during three months of the year, from three to
seven P. M. throughout the season. My only change has
been to shift my chair from one side to the other, or to
rise to get nearer to the pane of glass. A very useless
existence, you will say. Pardon me. The present work
will, I think, prove the contrary.

My prospect has been twofold, that without and that
within the club. Let me begin with the former. On the
opposite or non-club side of the street, my view extends
to the following establishments :—First, there is a fashionable hotel at some distance on my right ; next to this
are well-known dining-rooms, celebrated for their cook,
their wines, and their prices. The adjoining house is occupied by several tenants, the principal of whom is a
milliner, who holds the highest place in the estimation of
the London fair, and the execration of their husbands and
fathers. The next house is that of a well-patronized circulating library, certainly more old-fashioned than Mr.
Mudie's, but perhaps on that very account more a favorite with certain classes. Then comes my army-tailor on
the ground floor, and above him a society for the propagation of something, but whether useful knowledge or
fish, I am not in a position to state. Next to the army-
tailor's is a sombre establishment, of which from time to
time we hear in the newspapers as yielding a number of

so-called "fashionable" young men, a green cloth, and a pair of dice-boxes, for the embarrassment of an intelligent magistrate. Beyond this is another sombre mansion, with a large board announcing in the season that the "Exhibition of Painters in Distemper" is there held. and beyond the exhibition I have never succeeded in penetrating.

It will be easily understood that establishments of this varied character bring visitors of a very various description. To the hotel come our country cousins and their boxes; to the dining-rooms the young bachelors of Rotten Row; to the milliner's all the *élite* of London beauty and fashion; to the library a great number of dowagers and elderly females; to the army-tailor's a few young dandies; to the society for propagation a smaller number of clergymen and philanthropists; to the "hell" next to it, various waifs and raffs of the worst description; and to the gallery, when open, half the society of the West End.

With such an ebb and flow of life I might have enough to occupy my four hours of idleness, but this is not all. Between me and these points of attraction there are two side-pavements, and a very broad road. On the former I see specimens from every rank of male life, and the lower ranks of the other sex. The wretched urchin who converts his arms and legs into the spokes of a wheel, and thus runs by your side, presenting at last his bit of a cap for the well-earned halfpenny, has every whit as much interest for me as that stately being in a spotless frock-coat and double-breasted white waistcoat—Lord Charles Starche, I mean—who is stalking from Boodles' to Brookes', and thinks that he does the pavement a great honor by the pressure of his perfect boot.

Then in the road, though we are too *recherché* for omnibuses, we have a graduated scale of vehicles, from the four-wheeled cab up to the yellow chariot, in which Dowager Lady Septuagene is huddled up, while two splendid Mercuries balance themselves behind. There are men of many classes in hansoms, broughams, cabriolets, and curricles, and ladies passing to St. James in barouches and chariots.

What I see, indeed, is what any one may see in the streets of London, but I see it all calmly; and having nothing else to do, I observe in these ordinary outlines details which would escape many others. Indeed, I have arrived at that perfection of observation, that at one glance I can fix the class to which a passer-by belongs, and at a second can tell you whether he or she is an ornament or a disgrace to it.

I must not tell you much of what I see and hear when I turn round. My club was once one of the best in London, but I regret to say it has sadly deteriorated, so much so that when I have finished my studies I shall have to seek another window elsewhere. A number of men have crept into it somehow who ought not to be there. For instance there is Glanderson, who, though he belongs to a good and old family, is nothing more or less than a horse dealer. He vascillates between this and Tattersall's. He comes in from horses, and he goes out to horses. I need not add that he eats, drinks, dresses, and in short lives by horses. Now a horse-dealer may be an excellent man, but if he thinks nothing but horses, he cannot be good society. Glanderson thinks horses. If there is a rumor of war he has nothing to say about it, except that horse-flesh will rise in price. If there is to be a great political movement in a day or two, he only laments that ,it wiil intefere with the " Two Thousand."

Then again there is Trickington, who is simply a card-sharper. It is no matter that his uncle is an earl, and his brother a Member; Trickington would be sent to the treadmill if he practised in a railway carriage what he does here. If these men were away I should not complain of young Moulder, whose father made a fortune by patent candles; for Moulder has been to Eton and Cambridge, and is at least modest.

I am an old bachelor, and have passed a varied life. I have seen and mixed at different times in many grades of society. I have seen hundreds of vulgar, and thousands of ill-bred people. I have lived in the unenviable atmosphere of foreign courts, and in the narrow circles of country villages. As I have sought for *good* rather than *high* society, I have freely disregarded position, and entered where I thought I might find it. I have often been driven back by disgust and disappointment, but sometimes gone to laugh and stayed to enjoy. With this experience I sat down in my club-window, and ruminated on men and manners, classes and company, society and solecisms. In watching from my club-window, I have asked myself, "What makes that man a gentleman, and the other who is passing him a snob?" and I have passsed on to theorize on good-breeding.

Confess, then, that it is magnanimous in me to submit the result of my long cogitations to the critical eye of the public. I have a fancy that any one might be a gentleman if he could watch himself, as I watch him from my club-window. I have often longed to cry out to a man: "In the name of good taste, do give up that habit, take off that coat, or alter that walk." I have often longed to turn Turveydrop, and lecture these people on their manners. It is positively painful to me to see a man who aspires to the name and position of "gentleman," going so very bad a way to become one. I feel convinced that if everybody was well-bred, this world would be far better and far happier. But as I could not cry across the street all day long. and should perhaps do little good if I were to do so. I have had recourse to the printer. But.I had not sat down to my foolscap when a thought of horror rose before my mind. If I, a man, were rash enough to discourse to Crinoline, what a hail of scornful words should I bring down on my head! I therefore bethought me of a device, and rushing off laid all my plan before a lady, of whose judgment in these matters I had the highest opinion, and besought her to assist me. To this excellent and charming person I have now the pleasure to introduce you, that she may speak for herself as to tho share she has taken in this work. If this little book should really improve you, my dear reader, I beg you to take an early opportunity of walking, riding, or driving down this street, and you will soon see from my look and smile how great is the satisfaction of

THE MAN IN THE CLUB-WINDOW.

THE LADY'S PREFACE.

THOSE suggestions which apply peculiarly to the gentler portion of the community differ, in many details, from the advice and rules necessary to be impressed upon the Lords of Creation.

"The Habits of Good Society," as referring to ladies, are here, therefore, treated by "one of themselves."

It is true that certain maxims of politeness, and regulations which are thought to refine and improve the manners of good society, concern both sexes equally. There are, nevertheless, many niceties in conduct, variations in habits, and delicacies of feeling so peculiarly feminine, that the readiest pen of the most observant bachelor, how alive soever he may be to all that should form perfection in the sex whom he adores in dim perspective, can scarcely compass. Even the carefully-turned sentences of an experienced widower would not comprise those details with which a lady is familiar; whilst a married man might be apt to make his model wife the standard of deportment, and thus to copy one style of manners alone.

Men may discriminate and criticise, but woman can alone instruct woman in her every-day habits and conduct, as, we trust may be demonstrated in the course of the following recommendations from

A MATRON.

THE HABITS OF GOOD SOCIETY.

THOUGHTS ON SOCIETY,

AND THE SPIRIT OF SOCIAL OBSERVANCES.

A SERMON and a book of etiquette have been taken as the antipodes of literature. Most erroneously! The one is a necessary appendix to the other; and the missionary of the South Sea Islands would tell you that it is useless to teach the savage religion without the addition of a few rules of courtesy. On manners, refinement, rules of good breeding, and even the forms of etiquette, we are for ever talking, judging our neighbors severely by the breach of traditionary and unwritten laws, and choosing our society and even our friends by the touchstone of courtesy. We are taught manners before religion; our nurses and our parents preach their lay sermons upon them long before they open for us the Bible and the Catechism; our dominies flog into us Greek verbs and English behavior with the same cane; and Eton and Oxford declare with pride, that however little they may teach their frequenters, they at least turn them out gentlemen. Nay, we keep a grand state official, with a high salary, for no other purposes than to preserve the formal etiquette of the Court, and to issue from time to time a series of occasional services in

(23)

which the minutest laws of courtly behavior are codified with majestic solemnity.

Yet with all this and much more deference which we show now to manners in general, now to the arbitrary laws of etiquette which seem to have no object but exclusiveness, we are always ready to raise a titter at the attempt to reduce the former to a system, or codify the latter for the sake of convenience. The polished affect to despise the book of etiquette as unnecessary, forgetting that, in the present day, the circles of good society are growing wider and wider, admitting repeatedly and more than ever, men who have risen from the cottage or the workshop, and have had neither their training nor their experience. What if railway kings and mushroom millionaires had studied their grammars and manner-books in the respites from business, would the noble lords, who, with their wives and daughters, condescended, nay, were proud, to dine with the quondam shop-boy and mechanic, have thus been sneered at by the middle classes for a worship of gold, which could induce them to put up with gross vulgarity, and for a respect for success which could allow the greatest sticklers for etiquette to endure its repeated neglect? Surely it is in the interest of future premiers and noble members of council, that John Smith should know how to behave before they visit him; and how can he possibly learn it without either a tutor, a book, or experience in society?

The first is undoubtedly the best medium; and we constantly find the sons of mannerless millionaires tutored into the habits of good society, but at the same time it is a course which demands youth, time, and the absence of business occupations; but everybody, at first sight, agrees that experience in society is the only good way to acquire the polish it demands. True, maybe; but if it demands that polish in you, how will it take you without it? How can you obtain the *entrée* into good society, when, on the very threshold, you are found deficient in its first rules? How, if you succeed in pushing your way into sets which you believe to constitute good society, can you be sure that they will tolerate you there till you have learned your lesson, which is not one to be known in a day? Your failure, indeed, may be painful, and end in your ejectment for ever from the circles you have taken so much trouble to press into.

I remember an instance of such a failure which occur-red many years ago, in a distant European capital. The English residents had long been without a chaplain, and the arrival of an English clergyman was hailed with such enthusiasm, that a deputation at once attended on him and offered him the post, which he accepted. We soon found that our course was a mistaken one. Slovenly in his dress, dirty in his habits, and quite ignorant of the commonest rules of politeness, our new chaplain would have brought little credit to the English hierarchy even had his manners been retiring and unobtrusive. They were precisely the reverse. By dint of cringing, flattery, and a readiness to serve in no matter what undertaking, he push-ed himself, by virtue of his new position, into some of the highest circles. One evening it happened that the new chaplain and the Pope's nuncio were both at the same evening party. The pontifical legate went out but little, and the lady of the house had used great exertions to procure his presence. The contrast between the repre-sentatives of the two Churches was trying for us.

cardinal, grave, dignified, and courtly, received the ad
vances of those who were introduced to him as his due.
The chaplain, in a frayed and dirty shirt, with holes in
his boots and ill-combed hair, was sneaking up to the
grandees and doing his best to gain their attention by
smiles and flattery.   He had heard somewhere that no introductions were needed in Continental *salons*, and you
can imagine our surprise when we saw him slide sideways
up to the red-stockinged nuncio, tap him familiarly on the
shoulder, and with a full grin exclaim, " Well, *my Lord*,
how did you leave the Pope ? "   The cardinal bowed and
smiled, but could not conceal his astonishment.   The familiarity was not indeed a crime, but it proved that the
offender was not fit for the society into which he had
pushed himself ; and the legate, glad to have a story
against the Protestants, made the most of it, and repeated it until the new chaplain found his *entr'e* to the
drawing-rooms of the great was generally cancelled.

Useful or not useful, it would seem that codes of manners are thought ridiculous.   If the farce-writer wants to
introduce a thoroughly credulous country girl, he makes
her carry a little book of etiquette under her fan into the
hall-room ; and if the heavy-headed essayists of a Quarterly want a light subject to relieve the tedium of their
trimestrial lucubrations, it is almost sure to be the *vade
mecums* of etiquette which come in for their satire.   Poor
indeed, and reduced in honor as well as capital, must be
the man of letters, they tell you, who will condescend to
write on the angle of a bow, or the punctilio of an insult ;
forgetting that these are but some of the details which go
to make an important whole, and that we might as honestly sneer at the antiquarian who revels in a dirty coin

of the size of a farthing, or the geologist who fills his pockets with chips of ugly stone. However, the sneer is raised, and it is our duty to speak of it.

There remain, then, three reasons for holding works of this sort in disrepute: either manners themselves contemptible, or they are not a subject worthy of the consideration of the wise and great; or the books of etiquette themselves are ridiculous in their treatment of the subject.

The value of manners is to be the main theme of this introduction; as regards their value as a subject, I can only point to those who have discoursed or written upon them, and I think it may be affirmed that few moral teachers have not touched on the kindred subject. Indeed the true spirit of good manners is so nearly allied to that of good morals, that it is scarcely possible to avoid doing so. ·Our Saviour himself has taught us that modesty is the true spirit of decent behavior, and was not ashamed to notice and rebuke the forward manners of his fellow guests in taking the upper seats at banquets, while he has chosen the etiquettes of marriage as illustrations in several of his parables. Even in speaking of the scrupulous habits of the Pharisees, he did not condemn their cleanliness itself, but the folly which attached so much value to mere form. He conformed himself to those habits, and in the washing of feet at meals, drew a practical lesson of beautiful humility. His greatest follower has left us many injunctions to gentleness and courteousness of manner, and fine passages on women's dress, which should be painted over every lady's toilet table in the kingdom.

As to the philosophers, who are anything but men of good manners themselves, there are few who have not

taught behavior more or less. To say nothing of the
ugly but agreeable old gentleman, Socrates, who went
about the city asking as many questions as a counsel for
the defendant in a case of circumstantial evidence, we
have his pupil's pupil Aristotle, whose ethics the Oxford
boys are taught to look upon as next in wisdom to the
Bible, and truer than any similar work. We are convinced that the greater part of the ethics might be turned
into a "Guide to the Complete Gentleman." In fact
the Stagyrite's morals are social ones; the morals that
fit a man to shine in the *agora* and the academy. He
has raised the peculiar behavior of the καλὸς κἀγαθὸς
ἀνήρ — alias "gentleman"—to his equals, betters, and
inferiors, into one of the cardinal virtues, and has given
us, besides, several chapters on wit and conversation, in-
timacies, and the proper carriage of a good citizen in
society.   .

But to look nearer home, Lord Bacon himself has devoted an essay to manners, and reminds us that as a precious stone must be of very high value to do without a
setting, a man must be a very great one to dispense with
social observances; and probably Johnson thought himself one of these unset gems, when he made such speeches as, "Sir, you're a fool;" or at Aberdeen, "Yes, sir,
Scotland is what I expected; I expected a savage country, and savage people, and I have found them."

But why multiply instances? If we look to the satirists
of all ages, we find that manners as well as morals came
under their lash, and many taught by ridicule what we
do by precept. Horace, the *Spectator*, and Thackeray
expose the vulgarities and affectations of society; and the
finest wit of his day, Chesterfield, is the patron saint of
the writers on Behavior.

We have, therefore, no lack of precedent; but it is certainly true that too often the office of a teacher of manners has been assumed by retired Turveydreps, and genteel masters of ceremonies, and the laugh that is raised at their hints on propriety is not always without excuse. It would be very bad manners in me to criticise the works of former writers on this subject, and thus put forward my own as the *ne plus ultra* of perfection. I confess, indeed, that I can never aspire to the delicacy and apparently universal acquirements of some of these genteel persons. If I can tell you how to entertain your guests, I cannot furnish a list of *cartes* for dinners, like the author of the *Art of Dining*. If I can tell you how to dance with propriety, I must despair of describing the Terpsichorean inventions of a D'Egville or a Delplanque, or of giving directions for the intricate evolutions of one hundred and one dances, of which in the present day not a dozen are ever performed.

I may, however, be permitted to point out that too many of my predecessors have acted on a wrong principle. I have before me at least a dozen books treating of etiquette of different dates, and I find that one and all, including Chesterfield, state the motive for politeness to be either the desire to shine, or the wish to raise one's self into society supposed to be better than one's own. One of the best begins by defining Etiquette as " a shield against the intrusion of the impertinent, the improper, and the vulgar ;" another tells us that the circles which protect themselves with this shield must be the object of our attack, and that a knowledge of etiquette will secure us the victory ; others of higher character confound good with high society, and as a matter of course declare birth, rank, or distinction as its first requisites. All of them make it appear that the cultivation of manners is not a social duty, but merely a means to the gratification of personal vanity, and on this account they must all appear ridiculous to the man of sense.

Good society is undoubtedly a most desirable accompaniment of the business of life, and with some people it even takes the place of that business itself; but if the reader imagines that he is to put his book of etiquette into his pocket, and, quitting his old friends and acquaintance with disgust, to push himself into sets for which perhaps his position itself does not qualify him, he is much mistaken as to the object of cultivating the habits of good society. His proper objects are these : to make himself better in every respect than he is; to render himself agreeable to every one with whom he has to do; and to improve, if necessary, the society in which he is placed. If he can do this, he will not want good society long. It is in the power of every man to create it for himself. An agreeable and polished person attracts like light, and every kind of society which is worth entering will soon and easily open its doors to him, and be glad to have him in its circle. Exclusiveness is often a proof of innate vulgarity, and the tests applied by the exclusive are generally position, birth, name, or peculiarity, rarely indeed individual merit. Wherever these limitations are drawn, you may be confident of a deficiency in the drawers. My Lady A—, who will have no one under the rank of baronet at her house, can scarcely appreciate the wide diffusion of wit and intelligence among the untitled. Mr. B—, who invites none but literary men to his, must be incapable of enjoying the accomplishments and general knowledge of men of the world. And then, too, it is so easy to be exclusive, if you are content to be dull. My University tailor had a daughter, whose dower he announced as £30,000, and he gave out that none but a gold-tassel should be allowed to cultivate her acquaintance. But the young noblemen never came, and the damsel pined for a couple of years. The father widened the bounds, and gentleman-commoners were admitted, but still the maiden was unwooed. In another three years the suffrage was extended to all members of Christ Church. There may have been wooers now, but no winners. Five years more and the maiden still sat at her window unclaimed. For another five years the ninth part of a man held out resolutely, but by that time youth was gone, and the daughter so long a prisoner was glad to accept the hand of an aspiring cheesemonger.

But the tailor's vulgarity was no greater than that of all exclusive sets, who "draw the line" which preserves the purity of their magic circle, with a measure of rank, wealth, or position, rather than the higher recommendations of agreeable manners, social talents, and elevated character. The dullness of the coteries of the Faubourg St. Germain is equalled in this country only by that of certain sets to be found in most watering-places. A decrepit old lady or gentleman, long retired from fashionable and public life, is always to be found in these localities. Surrounded by a small knot of worshippers, he or she is distinguished by a title, a faultless wig, and a great love of whist, and the playful sallies of "my lord" and "my lady" are hailed as splendid wit, or their petulant tempers endured with affectionate submission. How much Christianity does a nook in the peerage encourage! What a pity there is not a retired nobleman in every set of society, to put our forbearance to a perpetual trial, call forth our broadest charity, and train us at the whist-table to lose our guineas, and not our temper!

Exclusive society, whether the passport for admittance be of rank, birth, wealth, fashion, or even more meritorious distinctions, is not often agreeable society, and not necessarily good. The question at once arises : What is good society? and we proceed to answer it, beginning with an attempt to define society itself.

When the ex-King Ludwig of Bavaria stops, as we have seen him do, to exchange a hearty word with a crossing-sweeper, one of a class which the misnamed " First Gentleman of Europe," while returning punctiliously the marks of respect shown him by every man that he passed, thought it beneath the dignity of a monarch to notice, no one would think of impeaching the sovereign of a love of low society. If, again, a country gentleman chats with his gamekeeper as they come from the fields together, he will, perhaps tell you that he has enjoyed the honest fellow's " society,' but it will be in the tone of a joke. Not so, however, the candidate for the borough, who begs the influential haberdasher he is canvassing, to introduce him to his wife and daughters, whose society " he is most anxious to cultivate." He is quite aware that equality is the first essential of society, and that where it does not exist in reality, it must do so in appearance.

Nor is mere equality of position sufficient. It seems to be a rule in the intercourse of men, that the employer should rank above the employed, and the transaction of business suspends equality for a time. There is no society between a gentleman and his solicitor or physician, in an official visit, and though both hold the same rank, the professional man would never, unless further advances were made, presume on the official acquaintance to consider himself a member of his patient's or client's circle.

Society is, therefore, the intercourse of persons on a footing of equality, real or apparent. But it is more than this. The two thoroughly English gentlemen who, travelling for two hundred miles in the same railway carriage, ensconce themselves behind their newspapers or shilling novels, exchanging no more than a sentence when the one treads upon the other's favorite bunion, cannot, in the widest sense of the phrase, be said to enjoy each other's society. The intercourse must be both active and friendly. Man is a gregarious animal; but while other animals herd together, for the purpose of mutual protection, or common undertakings, men appear to form the only kind who assemble for that of mutual entertainment and improvement. But in society properly so called, this entertainment must address the higher part of man. Never was philosopher more justly put down for narrowness of mind than Plato was by Diogenes. The polished Athenian had the rashness to define man as a biped without feathers. The ill-mannered but sensible philosopher of the tub plucked a cock and labelled it " Plato's Man." Man is not wholly man without his mind, and a game of cricket in which men assemble for mutual entertainment or improvement is not society, since it is the body not the mind which is brought into action.

Indeed we hear people talk of round games being sociable, and it is certain that in most of those which are played in a drawing-room, the mind is made to work as well as the fingers ; but while such games undoubtedly excite sociability with people too shy or too stupid to talk, and be at ease without their assistance, we must beware of

confounding them with sociability itself. The mutual ca-
tertainment of the mind must be *immediate* in society.
In chess and even in whist, the mental working is keen,
and the action is decidedly mutual, if we may not rather
say antagonistic, but no one would think of saying that he
had enjoyed Mr. Morphy's society, because he was one of
his eight opponents in a chess tournament, and none but
doting dowagers would presume to talk of the "society"
of the whist-table. The intercourse must be direct from
mind to mind.

Social intercourse is in fact, the consequence of a necessity felt by men and women for new channels of thought,
and new impulses of feeling. We read books, and we go
to the play for the very same purpose; but that which
constitutes the superior charm of society over these relax-
ations is its variety and uncertainty. The guest could never
have sat through the Barmecide's feast, if he had not expected that each succeeding cover would reveal a dainty
entremets to make up for the shadowy character of the
joints and *hors d'œuvres*, and not even an old maid of
fifty could continue to attend those dreary evening parties
at the vicar's, or those solemn dinners at the hall, if she
did not look forward to meeting some new guest, or at least
having some new idea struck into her.

I have always doubted whether Boswell had not as great
mental capacities of their kind as Johnson. It requires
either a profound mind or a cold heart to feel no necessity
for social intercourse. Bozzy had not the latter. Had he
the former? As the great mind can content itself with
its own reflections, stimulated at most by the printed
thoughts of others, so it carries in itself its power of varying what it takes in, and scorns to look for variety from

without. Most deep thinkers have had one pet book, which
they have read, one bosom-friend whom they have studied,
in a thousand different lights according to the variety which
their own nervous mind would suggest. Had Boswell been
an ordinary man, would he not have wearied of the Doctor's perpetual sameness, of his set answers and anticipated
rebuffs? Lovers weary of one another's minds, and the
cleverest people are incapable of enduring a *tête-à-tête*
for three weeks at a time, and was Boswell more than a
lover?

> " Lean not on one mind constantly,
>   Lest where one stood before, two fall.
> Something God hath to say to thee
>   Worth hearing from the lips of all."*

And it is this feeling which impels men of good sense and
ordinary minds to seek acquaintance as well as friends,
which makes me happy to talk sometimes to the plough-
man coming from the field, to the policeman hanging about
his beat, even to the thief whose hand I have caught in
my pocket. Could I have a professional pickpocket in my
grasp and not seize the rare opportunity of discovering
what view a thief takes of life, of right and wrong, honor,
even manners and the habits of good society? You may
be sure he has something to tell me on all these points, and
for a while I might profit from even his society; though,
as equality is necessary, I should for the time have to let
myself down to his level, which is scarcely desirable.

I have said that there are some minds, universal enough
in themselves to feel no need of society. To such, solitude
is society—of thought. To such the prison-cell is but

---

* Owen Meredith.

little trial. Raleigh was as great in the Tower as out of it, and Michael Angelo desired only to sit for days gazing upon, ay, and communing, with the grand men and wondrous scenes which he found in his own brain.

Other minds again are content with a little society, but it is the weakest class that can never do without it. It will not be difficult to show that the wits and beaux who have lived for society only, were men whom no one need aspire to rival.

I draw this distinction in order that hereafter I may speak more freely of conversation in general society; but it must not be thought, by a converse conclusion, that every common frequenter of society is but a poor-minded being. Socrates and Shakspere, who lived continually with their fellow-creatures, would not thank you for such an inference, and the cleverest men are often the most sociable; though, as La Rochefoucault says " In conversation confidence has a greater share than wit."

Chesterfield says, " there are two sorts of good company; one which is called the *beau-monde*, and consists of those people who have the lead in courts, and in the gay part of life; the other consists of those who are distinguished by some peculiar merit, or who excel in some particular and valuable art or science." If this were not the opinion of my patron saint, I should maintain that the writer knew not what good company was. But in truth in the days of Philip Dormer Stanhope there was little option but between wealth, rank, and fashion, on the one hand, and wi and learning on the other; and his Lordship cannot be blamed for writing thus in the beginning of the eighteenth century, when the middle classes had not learnt manners, if a century later Mr. Hayward, who undertakes to write down books of etiquette, tells us that "rank, wealth, and distinction of some sort," are the elements of success in society.

If the opinion of a man who for twelve years labored to make a graceful gentleman of his son, and, though he failed to do so, certainly thought and wrote more on the manners of good society than any man before and since, is not to be taken as a maxim, I must be allowed some hesitation in putting forward a definition. As Chesterfield himself says, bad company is much more easily defined than good. Let us begin with the bad, then, and see to what it brings us.

Beau Brummel broke off an engagement with a young lady because he once saw her eat cabbage. "Over-nice people," says Dean Swift, "have sometimes very nasty ideas." But George the Le s evidently thought the young lady in question was very bad company. To define exactly where bad manners begin is not easy, but there is no doubt that no society is good in which they are found; and this book will have been written in vain, if the reader after studying it is unable to distinguish between bad and good behavior. In the present day neither Brummel nor his "fat friend," the "greatest gentleman in Europe," would be tolerated in good society. The code of morals is clearly written, whatever may be the traditionary code of manners, and we may at once lay down as a rule, that where morals are openly bad, society must be bad. The badness of morals is soon detected. We may indeed meet in a London ball room a score of young men, whose manners are as spotless as their shirt-fronts, and fail to discover from their carriage and conversation that one requires assistance to undress every third night, another is supported by Hebrews in gambling away his reversionary property, and a third, without Shelley's genius, shares his opinions as to the uselessness of matrimonial vows. But let us pursue their acquaintance, and we shall soon learn from the tone of their conversation what is the tenor of their lives.

Bad society, then, may be divided into three classes: 1. That in which both morals and manners are bad; 2. That in which the manners are bad, be the morals what they will; 3. That in which the manners appear to be good, but the morals are detestable. The first is low, the second vulgar, the third dangerous society.

Few people but undergraduates, young ensigns, and aspiring clerks and shop-boys, will need to be warned against low society. Where vice wears no veil, and decency forever blushes, the man of any self-respect, to say nothing of taste and education, will speedily be disgusted. The first proof of lowness is seen at once in undue familiarity. If there are women in company, you will at once discover their character from the manner in which they allow themselves to be addressed; but if not, you will doubtless ere long be yourself subjected to a freedom of treatment, which you will readily distinguish from ease of manner, and know to be beyond the proper limits. Familiarity, on first introduction, is always of bad style, often even vulgar, and, when used by the openly immoral, is low and revolting. A man of self respect will not be pleased with it even when it comes from the most respectable, or his superiors; he will despise it in his equals, and will take it almost as an insult from those who do not respect themselves. If Brummel really had the impudence to say to his patron prince, " Wales, ring the bell!" we cannot blame the corpulent George for ordering the Beau's carriage when the servant appeared. We can only wonder that he did not take warning by his favorite's presumption to separate himself from the rest of his debauched hangers-on, when he found that respect for the Prince was swamped in contempt for the profligate.

This is a good opportunity for introducing a few words on the subject of familiarity, which, writing as an Englishman, we may at once lay down as incompatible with good society. "You are a race of pokers!" say the French. "You are a race of puppies!" replies the inassailable Englishman; and certainly there is nothing more sublimely ridiculous than the British lion shaking his mane and muttering a growl when the Continental poodle asks him, in a friendly manner, to shake his paw. Dignity has its limits as well as ease, and dignity is extravagant in Spain, and often melodramatic in England. Charles I. never laughed, and his cotemporary, Philip of Spain, never smiled. But it must not be supposed that the English have always been as dignified as the modern towers bristling with cannon, and bearing the motto, "Noli me tangere," who are seen moving in Pall-Mall in the afternoon. Stiffness perhaps came in with Brummell's starched cravat, a yard in height, which took him a quarter of an hour to crease down to that of his neck. In the reigns of the Tudors, familiarity was the order of the day at the Court. There was nothing shocking in Bluff Harry stretching his huge gouty leg upon Catharine Parr's lap; and Queen Elizabeth thought herself only witty when to Sir Roger Williams, presenting a petition which she disliked, she exclaimed, "Williams, how your boots stink!"

"Tut, madame," replied the Welshman, "it is my suit, not my boots which stink." In Ben Jonson's day it was the height of gallantry to chuck a lady under the chin, and make a not very refined compliment to her rosy lips. Even the cavaliers of Charles' court had a freedom of speech and manner which disgusted the puritans; and, if Milton's report be true, the sovereign that never laughed saw no harm in making indelicate remarks before, if not to, the Queen's ladies. But the most curious instances of familiarity, mistaken for wit, are to be found in the reigns of William III. and Anne. When Bath was the most fashionable spot in the kingdom, and Beau Nash the most fashionable man in Bath, the following speeches, interlarded with oaths, were his most fashionable *mots :—*

A lady afflicted with a curvature of the spine, once told him that she had that day come *straight* from London. "Straight, madame!" replied the magnificent master of the ceremonies, "then you've been horribly warped by the way." When, on an another occasion, a gentleman appeared at an assembly in boots, which Nash had interdicted, he called out to him, "Hollo! Hogs Norton, haven't you forgot to bring your horse?" He was well put down, however, by a young lady, whom he once met walking with a spaniel behind her. "Please, madame," asked the Beau, "can you tell me the name of Tobit's dog?" "Yes, sir," answered the damsel; "his name is Nash, and a very impudent dog he is, too."

Familiarity arises either from an excess of friendliness or a deficiency of respect. The latter is never pardonable. We cannot consider that man well-bred who shows no respect for the position, feelings, or even prejudices of others. The youth who addresses his father as "governor," or "come now, paymaster," is almost as blamable as the man who stares at my club-foot, or, because I have a very dark complexion, asks me at first sight when I left India. Still more reprehensible should I be if I exclaimed to a stout lady, "How warm you look!" asked Mr. Spurgeon if he had been to many balls lately; inquired after the wife and family of a Romish priest, or begged the Dean of Carlisle to tell me the odds on the Derby.

Worse, again, is the familiarity which arises from natural coarseness, and which becomes most prominent in the society of elderly men, or where ladies are present. The demeanor of youth to age should always be respectful; that of man to woman should approach even reverence.

> "To thee be all men heroes; every race
> Noble; all women virgins; and each place
> A temple."

And certainly it is better and more comfortable to believe in the worth of all, than by contempt and boldness to leave the impression of impudence and impropriety. It should be the boast of every man that he had never put modesty to the blush, nor encouraged immodesty to remove her mask. But we fear there is far too little chivalry in the present day. If young men do not chuck their partners under the chin, they are often guilty of pressing their hands when the dance affords an opportunity. There is a calm dignity with which to show that the offence has been noticed, but if a lady condescends to reprove it in words, she forces the culprit to defend himself, and often ends by making the breach worse. On the other hand, let a woman once overlook the slightest familiarity, and fail to show her surprise in her manner, and she can never be certain that

it will not be repeated.   There are few actions so atrociously familiar as a wink.   I would rather kiss a lady
outright than wink or leer at her, for that silent movement
seems to imply a secret understanding which may be interpreted in any way you like.   Even between men a wink
should be avoided, however intimate the terms between you,
since it seems to keep the rest of the company in the dark
and is perhaps worse than whispering.

We often hear people complain of the necessity of
" company manners."   As a general rule such people must
be by nature coarse.   A well-bred man has always the
same manners at home and in society, and what is bad in
the former, is only worse in the latter.   It can never be
pardonable to swagger and lounge, nor to carry into even
the family circle the actions proper to the dressing-room.
Even where familiarity has nothing shocking in itself, it
attacks the respect due to the society of others, whoever
they may be, and presents the danger of a further breach
of it.   From familiarity to indecency is but one step.
Thus no part of the dress, not a shoe-string even, should
be arranged in the presence of ladies.   The Hindus, remarkable for the delicacy of their manners, would not allow
kissing, scratching, pinching, or lying down to be represented on the stage, and at least the last three should never
be permitted in a mixed society of men and women.   There
are attitudes too, which are a transition from ease to familiarity, and should never be indulged.   A man may cross his
legs in the present day, but should never stretch them apart.
To wipe the forehead, gape, yawn, and so forth, are only
a shade less obnoxious than the American habit of expec-
toration.   I shall have more to say on this subject, and
must now pass to another.

Familiarity must be condemned or pardoned according to the motive that suggests it. Not unfrequently it arises from over-friendliness or even shyness, and must then be gently and kindly repressed. As for shyness, which is *par excellence* the great obstacle to ease in English society, I, for my part, think it infinitely preferable to forwardness. It calls forth our kindest and best feelings, utterly disarms the least considerate of us, and somewhat endears us to the sufferer. Yet so completely is it at variance with the spirit of society, that in France it is looked on as a sin; and children are brought forward as much as possible that they may early get rid of it, the consequence of whioh is, that a French boy from his *collège* is one of the most obnoxious of his race, while you cannot help feeling that the extreme diffidence of the *débutante* is merely assumed in obedience to *ch're maman.* Give me a boy that blushes when you speak to him, and a girl under seventeen, who looks down because she dares not look up. On the other hand, shyness is trying and troublesome in young people of full age, though a little of it is always becoming on first acquaintance; while in middle-aged people it is scarcely pardonable.

To the young, therefore, who are entering into society I would say, Never be ashamed of your shyness. since, however painful it may be to you, it is far less disagreeable to others than the attempt to conceal it by familiarity.

. The only way to treat familiarity arising from shyness is not to notice it, but encourage the offender till you have given him or her confidence. It is a kindness as much to yourself as to the sufferer from shyness, to introduce merry subjects, to let fly a little friendly badinage at him, until he thinks that you are deceived by his assumed manner, and no longer afraid of being thought nervous, really gets rid of the chief cause of that feeling.

When Brummell was asked by a lady whom he scarcely knew, to come and " take tea" with her, the Beau replied, " Madame, you take a walk, and you take a liberty, but you *drink* tea." It was only one of those many speeches of the Beau's, which prove that a man may devote his whole life to the study of manner and appearance, and, without good feeling to back them up, not be a gentleman. The lady undoubtedly did take a liberty, but the would-be gentleman took a greater in correcting her idiom. The lady erred from a silly admiration of the ex-model of fashion; the broken beau erred from excessive conceit, and an utter want of heart. Let the reader judge between the two. If the object of politeness is to insure harmony to society, and set every one at his ease, it is as necessary to good manners to receive a *well-meant* familiarity in a like spirit, as it is to check one which arises from coarseness.

On the Continent, where diffidence is unknown, and to be friendly is the first object, we find a freedom of manners which in England we should call familiarity. Let a man be of no matter what station, he has there a right to speak to his fellow-man, if good him seems, and certainly the barrier which we English raise up between classes savors very little of Christianity. What harm can it do me, who call myself gentleman, if a horny-handed workman, waiting for the same train as myself, comes up and says, " It is a fine day, sir," evincing a desire for a further interchange of ideas; am I the more a gentleman because I cut him short with a " Yes," and turn away; or because, as many people do, I stare him rudely in the face, and vouchsafe no answer? " Something God hath to say to thee worth hearing from the lips of all," and I may be sure that I shall learn something from him, if I talk to him in a friendly manner, which, if I am really a gentleman, his society can do me no harm.

But of course there is a limit to be fixed. Englishmen respect nothing so much as their purses and their private affairs, and in England you might as well ask a stranger for five pounds as inquire what he was travelling for, what his income was, or what were the names of his six children. But England is an exception in this case, and a foreigner believes that he does himself no harm by telling you his family history at first sight. While, therefore, it is a gross impertinence in this country to put curious questions to a person of whom you know little, while it is reserved for the closest intimacy to inquire as to private means and personal motives, it is equally ridiculous in an Englishman abroad to take offence at such questions, and consider as an impertinence what is only meant as a friendly advance to nearer acquaintance. I certainly cannot understand why an honest man should determine to make a secret of his position, profession, and resources, unless it be from a false pride, and a desire to be thought richer and better than he is; but as these subjects are respected in this country, I should be guilty of great ill-breeding if I sought to remove his secrecy.

I shall never forget the look of horror and astonishment I once saw on the face of an English lady talking to a foreign ambassadress. The latter, thoroughly well-bred, according to native ideas, had admired the former's dress, and touching one of the silk flounces delicately enough, she inquired, " How much did it cost a yard?" Such questions are common enough on the Continent, and our

neighbors see no harm in them. And why should we do
so? Is it anyway detrimental to us to tell how much we
paid for our clothes? Yet, such is the false pride of
English people on matters connected, however slightly,
with money, that even to mention that most necessary article
is considered as bad breeding in this country. We must
respect the prejudice, though, in fact, it is a vulgar one.

The next kind of bad society is the vulgar, in which the
morals may be good, but the manners are undoubtedly bad.
What bad manners are in detail, will be shown in the course
of this work; but I shall now take as the distinguishing
test of this kind of society—a general vulgarity of conduct.
Until the end of the last century, the word vulgarity was
confined to the·low, mean, and essentially plebeian. It
would be well if we could so limit it in the present day,
but the great mixture of classes and the elevation of
wealth, have thrust vulgarity even into the circles of good
society, where, like a black sheep in a white flock, you may
sometimes find a thoroughly vulgar man or woman recommended by little but their wealth. or a position gained by
certain popular qualifications. Where the majority of the
company are decidedly vulgar, the society may be set down
as *bad*.

Apart from coarseness and familiarity, vulgarity may
be defined as pretension of some kind. This is shown prominently in a display of wealth. I remember being taken
to dine at the house of a French corn-merchant, who had
realized an enormous fortune. It was almost a family
party, for there were only three strangers including myself.
The manners of every one present were irreproachable, and
the dinner excellent, but it was *served on gold plate*.
Such a display was unnecessary, inconsistent, and therefore

vulgar. A display of dress in ladies comes under the same head and will be easily detected by inappropriateness. The lady who walks in the streets in a showy dress suitable only to a *fête;* who comes to a quiet social gathering with a profusion of costly jewelry; the man who electrifies a country village with the fashionable attire of Rotten Row, or reminds you of his guineas by a display of unnecessary jewels; the people, in short, who are always over-drest for the occasion, may be set down as vulgar. Too much state is a vulgarity not always confined to wealth, and when a late nobleman visiting a simple commoner at his country house, brought with him a valet, coachman, three grooms, two men servants, a carriage, and half-a-dozen horses, he was guilty of as gross vulgarity as Solomon Moses or Abiathar Nathan, who adorns his fat stumpy fingers with three rings a piece. So completely indeed is modesty the true spirit of good breeding, that any kind of display in poor or rich, high or low, savors of vulgarity; and the man who makes too much of his peculiar excellencies, who attempts to engross conversation with the one topic he is strong in, who having travelled is always telling you " what they do on the Continent;" who being a scholar, overwhelms you with Menander or Manetho, who, having a lively wit. showers down on the whole company a perpetual hail of his own *bon mots*, and laughs at them himself, who, gifted with a fine voice, monopolizes the piano the whole evening, who, having distinguished himself in the Crimea, perpetually leads back the conversation to the theme of war, and rattles away on his own achievements, who, having written a book, interlards his talk with, " As I say in my novel," &c., who being a fine rider. shows his horse off in a score of difficult manœuvres, as Louis Napoleon

did at the Egremont tournament, though not asked to take
part in the lists, who goes to a party with all the medals
and clasps he has perhaps most honorably earned, or who,
being a great man in any line, puts himself prominently
forward, condescends, talks loud, or asserts his privileges,
is a vulgar man, be he king, kaiser, or cobbler.

But there is a form of vulgarity found as much in those
of small as those of large means, and known by the name
of "gentility." I know a man who keeps a poor little
worn-out pony-phæton, and always speaks of it as "my
carriage," taking care to bring it in whenever possible.
My friend Mrs. Jones dines at one o'clock, but invariably
calls it her "lunch." The Rev. Mr. Smith cannot afford
the first-class on a railway, but is too genteel to go in the
second.   Excellent man ! he tells me—and I am bound to
believe it—that he positively prefers the third class to the
first.   "Those first-class carriages are so stuffy," he says,
"and in the second one meets *such* people, it is really unbearable," but he does not let me know that in the third
he will have to sit next to an odoriferous ploughboy, get
his knees crushed by a good woman's huge market-basket,
and catch cold from a draught passing through the ill-
adjusted windows.   There is no earthly reason why he
should not travel in what carriage he likes, but the vulgarity consists in being ashamed of his poverty, and tacitly
pretending to be better off than he is.   Brown, again calls
his father's nutshell of a cottage "our country seat," and
Mrs. Brown speaks of the diminutive buttons as the "man-
servant."   My tailor has his crest embossed on his note-
paper ; Bobinson, the successful stock-broker, covers the
pannels of his carriage with armorial bearings as large as
dishes ; Tomkins, ashamed of his father's name, signs him-

self Tomkyns; and Mrs. Williams, when I call, always discourses on English history that she may bring in John of Gaunt, "an ancestor of ours, you know."

Nor is gentility confined to a pretension to more wealth, letter birth, or greater state than we possess. The commonest form of it, found unfortunately in all classes, is the pretension to a higher position than we occupy. The Johnsons, retired haberdashers, cannot visit the Jacksons, retired linen-drapers, but have moved heaven and earth for an introduction to the Jamesons, who are not retired from anything. The Jamesons receive the Johnsons, but stiffly annihilate them at once by talking of "our friends the Williamsons," who have a cousin in Parliament, and the Williamsons again are for ever dragging the said cousin into their conversation, that the Jamesons may be stupefied. We go higher; the M. P., though perhaps a Radical, will for ever be dogging the steps of the noble viscount opposite, and call the leader of his own party "that fellow so-and-so." The viscount is condescendingly gracious to the commoner, but deferential to the duke, and the duke himself will be as merry as old King Cole, if "the blood" should happen to notice him more than usual. Alas! poor worms, in what paltry shadows we can glory, and forget the end that lays us all in the common comfortless lap of mother earth!

Nothing therefore will more irretrievably stamp you as vulgar in really good society, than the repeated introduction of the names of the nobility, or even of distinguished personages in reference to yourself. It is absurd to suppose that you can reflect the light of these greater orbs; on the contrary, your mention of them naturally suggests a comparison, such as one makes between the unpretending

3

glorious sun, and the pale pitiable moon, when she quits
her proper sphere and forces herself into broad daylight.
When Scribbles of the Seal and Tape Office tells us he
was flirting last night with Lady Adelaide, when the Duke
of —— came up, and "shook hands with me, 'pon honor
he did," I am tempted to think Scribbles either a gross
exaggerator, or a grosser snob. When worthy Mrs.
Midge relates for the thirteenth time how she travelled
down with "Her Grace," and I see how her eyes glow,
and how vainly she attempts to appear indifferent to the
honor (which it is to her), she only proves to me how
small she must feel herself to be, to hope to gain brilliance by such a slight contact. I feel fain to remind her
of the Indian fable of a lump of crystal, which thought
it would be mistaken for gold because it reflected the glit-
ter of the neighboring metal. It was never taken for
gold, but it was supposed to cover it, and got shivered to
atoms by the hammer of the miner.

But when this vulgarity is reduced to practice it becomes actual meanness. The race of panders, parasites,
or "flunkies," as they are now called, is one which has
flourished through all time, and the satire of all ages has
been freely levelled at their servile truculency. But, in
general, they have had a substantial object in view, and
mean as he may be, a courtier who flattered for place or
for money, is somehow less contemptible than the modern
groveller who panders to the great from pure respect of
their greatness, from pure want of self-respect. I am
not one of those who deny position its rights; and as long
as caste is recognised in this country, I would have respect shown from one of a lower to one of a higher class.
But this respect for the position must not be blind; it

should not extend to worship of the man. No rank, no wealth, no distinction, even if gained by merit, should close our eyes to actual unworthiness in its holder. We may bow to the nobility of my lord, but we are truculent slaves if we call it nobleness. We may respect with dignity the accident of birth and wealth, but if the duke be an acknowledged reprobate, or the millionaire a selfish grasper, we are inexcusable if we allow their accidental distinctions to blot out their glaring faults. What we should hate in our friend, and punish in our servant, we must never overlook as a "weakness" in the Duke or Dives. It is not mere vulgarity, it is positive unchristianity, hopeless injustice.

A less offensive but more ridiculous form of vulgar gentility, is that which displays itself in a pretension to superior refinement and sensibility. We have all had our laugh at the American ladies who talk of the "limbs" of their chairs and tables, ask for a slice from the "bosom" of a fowl, and speak of a rump-steak as a "seat-fixing," but in reality we are not far short of them, when we invent the most far-fetched terms for trousers, and our young ladies faint—or try to—at the mention of a petticoat,—*Honi soit qui mal y pense;* and shame indeed to the man, still more to the woman, whose mind is so impure, that the mere name of one common object immediately suggests another which decency excludes from conversation. It is indeed difficult to define in what indelicacy consists and where it begins, but it is clear that nature has intended some things to be hidden; and civilization, removing farther and farther from nature, yet not going against it, has added many more. In this respect, civilization has become a second nature, and what it has once concealed cannot be exposed without indelicacy. For instance, nothing is more beautiful than the bosom of a woman, and to a pure mind there is nothing shocking, but something touching indeed, in seeing a poor woman who has no bread to give it, suckling her child in public. Still civilization has covered the bosom, and the ladies who wear their dresses off their shoulders are, *in the present day*, guilty of an immodesty which was none in the days when Lely painted—on canvas, I mean—the beauties of Charles' court.

But to go beyond the received opinion of the majority is super-refinement and vulgarity, and too often tempts us to fancy that an impure association has suggested the idea of impropriety. I cannot imagine what indelicate fancy those people must have who will not allow us to say " go to bed," but substitute " retire to rest." Surely the couch where dewy sleep drowns our cares and refreshes our wearied forms; where we dream those dreams which to some are the only bright spots of their lives; where we escape for a time from the grinding of the worldly mill, from hunger, calumny, persecution, and dream maybe of heaven itself and future relief;—surely our pure simple beds are too sacred to be polluted with the impure constructions of these vulgar prudes. Or, again, what more beautiful word than woman? woman, man's ruin first, and since then alternately his destroyer and savior; woman, who consoles, raises, cherishes, refines us; and yet I must forget that you are a woman, and only call you a lady. " Lady" is a beautiful name, a high noble name, but it is not dear and near to me like " woman." Yet if I speak of you as a woman, you leap up and tell me you will not stay to be insulted. Poor silly little thing, I gave you the name I loved best, and *you*, not I, connected some horrid idea with it; is your mind or mine at fault? Perhaps the most delightful instance of this indelicate delicacy of terms was in the case of the elderly spinster—of whom I was told the other day—who kept poultry, but always spoke of the cock as the "hen's companion."

In short, it amounts to this. If it be indelicate to mention a thing, let it never be mentioned by any name whatever; if it be not indelicate to mention it, it cannot be so to use its ordinary proper name. If legs are naughty, let us never speak of them; if not naughty, why blush to call them legs? The change of name cannot change the idea suggested by it. If legs be a naughty idea, then no recourse to "limbs" will save you. You have spoken of legs, though, under another name; you thought of legs, you meant legs; you suggested legs to me under that other name; you are clearly an egregious sinner; you are like the French soldier, you will swear by the "sa*p*rement," saving his wretched little conscience by the change of a single letter. That reminds me of a nautical friend who "cured" himself, he said, of the bad habit of swearing, by using, instead of oaths, the words Rotter—, Amster—, Potz—, and Schie—, mentally reserving the final syllable of these names of towns, &c., and fully convinced that he did well.

That same habit of demi-swearing is another bit of pretension, which, if it cannot be called vulgarity, is certainly Pharisaical. The young lady would cut you—properly enough—for using an oath, will nevertheless cry "bother" when her boot-lace breaks, or what not. But "bother" is only the feminine form of your Saxon expletive, and means *in reality* just as much. So, too.

your man who would cut his throat sooner than use a bad word, will nevertheless write it "d—n," as if everybody did not know what two letters were left out. There is great hypocrisy about these things.

- But the worst vulgarity is an assumption of refinement in the choice of language. This is common among servants in England, and in the lower orders in France and Germany, where it is sometimes very amusing to hear fine words murdered and used in any but the right sense. Mrs. Malaprop saves me any trouble of going into details on this point, but I may observe that the best speakers will never use a Latin word where an Anglo-Saxon one will do as well; "buy" is better than "purchase," "wish" than "desire," and so on. The small genteel, you will observe, never speak of rich and poor, but of "those of large and those of small means." Another similar piece of flummery is the expression, "If anything should happen to me," which everybody knows you mean for, "if I should die." As you do not conceal your meaning, why not speak out bravely?

Besides in words, there is an over-refinement in habits. Even cleanliness can be exaggerated, as in the case of the Pharisees, and the late Duke of Queensbury, who would wash in nothing but milk. Our own Queen uses distilled water only for her toilet; but this is not a case in point, since it is for the sake of health, I believe, with her. A sad case, however, was that of the lovely Princess Alex andrina of Bavaria, who died mad from over-cleanliness It began by extreme scrupulousness. At dinner she would minutely examine her plate, and if she saw the slightest speck on it, would send for another. She would then turn the napkin round and round to examine every corner, and often rise from table because she thought she was not served properly in this respect. At last it became a monomania, till on plates, napkins, dishes, table-cloth, and everything else, she believed she saw nothing but masses of dirt. It weighed on her mind, poor thing! she could not be clean enough, and it drove her to insanity.

Anne of Austria could not lay her delicate limbs in any but cambric sheets, and there are many young gentlemen in England who look on you as a depraved barbarian, if you do not wear silk stockings under your boots. Silver-spoonism is, after all, vulgarity; it is an assumption of delicacy superior to the majority; and so too, is prudery, which is only an assumption of superior modesty.

In short, refinement must not war against nature, but go along with it, and the true gentleman can do anything that is not coarse or wrong. Fitzlow, who cannot lift his own carpet-bag into his own cab; Startup, who cannot put a lump of coal on the fire; Miss Languish, who "never touched a needle;" and Miss Listless, who thinks it low to rake the beds in the garden, or tie up a head of roses, are not ladies and gentlemen, but vulgar people. It rather astonishes such persons to find that a nobleman can carry his bag, and stir his fire, and that a noble lady delights in gardening.

But I shall risk the imputation of over-refinement myself, if I say more on this point, and so I come to the third class of bad society in which the manners and breeding are perfect, and the morals bad, which is the most dangerous class there is. Without agreeing at all with the Chartist school in their views of the aristocracy,

I think it must be acknowledged that this class of bad society is found mostly among the upper circles of society, and for the simple reason, that except among them vice is generally accompanied with bad manners. We have historical proofs in any quantity of this class being aristocratic. The vice of courts is proverbial, but courtly manners are reckoned as the best. All the beaux and half the wits on record have led bad lives. Chesterfield himself was a dissolute gambler, and repented bitterly in his old age of his past life, and it is he who says, that the best company is not necessarily the most moral, which determines the value of *his* work on Etiquette. There is, however, something in the vice of this kind of society which at once makes it the most and least dangerous. All vice is here gilded; it is made elegant and covered with a gloss of good-breeding. Men of family have to mix with ladies, and ladies of family have almost public reputations to keep up. All that is done is *sub rosa*. There are none of the grosser vices admitted in the present day. There is no drunkenness, little or no swearing, no coarseness. But there is enough of gambling still to ruin a young man, and the " social evil" here takes its most elegant and most seductive form. While, therefore, on the one hand, you may mix in this kind of society, and *see* and therefore know very little of its immorality, its vices, when known to you, assume a fashionable *prestige* and a certain delicacy which seem to deprive them of their grossness and make them the more tempting. Let us therefore call no society good, till we have sounded its morals as well as its manners; and this brings us to speak of what good society really is.

We cannot do this better than by looking first into

what is generally taken as good society. I shall, therefore, glance over the state of society in different ages in
this country, and in the present day on the Continent.

The real civilization of England can scarcely be dated
earlier than at the Reformation, and even than the tur-
bulent state of the country, setting one man's knife
against another, and leaving when bloodshed was shamed
back, the same deadly hatred showing itself in open reproaches and secret attacks, made social gatherings a difficulty, if not an impossibility. Henry VIII., indeed, had
a somewhat jovial court, but the country itself was far too
unsettled to join much in the merriment. In fact, up to
the time of Charles I., there were but three kinds of society in England : the court, around which all the nobility gathered, making London a Helicon of manners; the
small country gentry who could not come up to London ;
and the country people among whom manners were as yet
as rude as among the serfs of Russia in the present day.
In the court there had succeeded to real chivalry a' kind
of false principle of honor. A man who wore a sword
was bound to use it. Quarrels were made rapidly, and
rapidly patched up by reference to the code of honor.
With the country gentry, the main feature was a rough
hospitality. People spoke their minds in those days without reserve, and a courtier was looked on as a crafty man,
whose words served to conceal rather than express his
thoughts. Among the people was a yet ruder revelry,
and the morality was not of a high kind.

The position of woman is that which has always given
the key to civilization. The higher that position has
been raised, the more influence has the gentleness which
arises from her weakness been felt by the other sex. In

3*

fact, the term "gentleman" only came in when women were admitted into society on a par with men. A "gentleman" was a man who could associate with ladies. And what was the respect exacted by and paid to woman before the time of Charles I., the dramatists of the Elizabethan age tell us in every page. What must have been the education of the Virgin Queen herself, who was not thought very ill of for allowing Leicester to be her lady's-maid, and kiss her without asking leave, and who would have been thought a prude had she objected to the gross scenes in the masks and plays acted before her, and found often enough even in Shakspere. Not only were "things called by their right names," but an insidious innuendo took the place very often of better wit, and was probably enjoyed far more.

The country gentry lived in their moated houses at great distances from one another, and the country lady was rarely more than a good housewife, serving a rough hospitality to her guests ; while the gentlemen drank deep, swore pretty oaths, talked far from reservedly in her presence, and pleased her most with the broadest compliment to her fair form.

The dignity of Charles introduced a rather more noble bearing among the men, and the Puritans did much to cleanse society of its gross familiarities ; but the position of women was still a very inferior one, and it was not till the beginning of the last century that they took a prominent place in society. There had gradually sprung up another class, which gave the tone to manners. Hitherto there had been in London only the Court-circles and the *bourgeoisie*. But as the lesser nobility grew richer and flocked to the large towns, they began to form a large

class apart from the Court, which gradually narrowed its
circle more and more. But good society still meant *high*
society, and Chesterfield was right in recommending his
son to seek out rank and wealth, for those who had it not
were generally badly educated and worse mannered. There
was, however, one class now rising into a separate existence, which the patron of manners has not overlooked.
It is to those men of education and mind, who, lacking
rank and wealth, were still remarkable for the vivacity of
their conversation—in short, to the wits—that we owe the
origin of our modern " middle classes."

The *Spectator*, however, proves what women were at
this period. Little educated and with no accomplishments
save that of flirting a fan, the more fashionable gave themselves up to extravagances of dress, and were distinguished
for the smartness, not the sense of their conversation.
They were still unsuited, perhaps more so than ever, for
the companionship of intellectual men, and it was the
elegant triflers, like Walpole, rather than men of sound
serious minds, who made correspondents of them. The
consequence was that the men gathered together in clubs,
a species of evening society which, while it fostered wit,
destroyed the stage, and made a system of gambling and
drinking. The high society was still the best, and it was
among the nobility chiefly that women began to mix in
the amusements of the other sex. Balls, too, were no
longer an entertainment reserved for Court and the
grandees; and in the balls at Bath, under Beau Nash, we
find the first attempt to mingle the gentry and *bourgeoisie*,
and thus form the nucleus of a middle class. It was now
too that mere wealth, which could never have brought its
owner into the Court-circles, or been a sufficient recom-

mendation to the nobility of the seventeenth century, became an authoritative introduction among the gentry.

If England is the only European country which has a real middle class, where birth is of no account, it is owing to that law of primogeniture which from very remote times caused the formation of a class known as " gentry" which has no equivalent in any Continental country. It was this class, which belonging by connexion to the aristocracy, belonged by necessity to the *bourgeoisie*, from whom they were not distinguished by actual rank. From the *bourgeoisie*, indeed, they kept aloof as long as possible; but wealth, which could give the gentry a footing among the aristocracy, could only come from the mercantile classes, and the rich merchant's daughter who was married to a country gentleman soon succeeded in bringing her relations into his set. Towards the end, therefore, of the last century, we find three classes between the Court and the people, namely, the noble, the "gentle," and the rich; in other words, rank, birth, and wealth were the requisites of society. The higher classes were still the best educated, but the wealthy looked to education to fit them for the circles of the gentry, and women being better educated took a more important place in social arrangements.

In this century these classes began to draw together. The noble sought wives among the rich; the rich became gentle in a couple of generations; and the gentry became rich by marriage.

But if a merchant or successful speculator were admitted in higher circles, the professional man, who could go to Court and had always taken precedence of trade, could not be excluded. Hitherto, the liberal professions and literature had occupied a kind of dependent position. The clergyman was almost a retainer of the squire's, the lawyer was the landowner's agent, the doctor had his great patron, and the writer often lived on the money given for fulsome dedications to those noblemen and others who wished to appear in the light of a Mæcenas. These distinctions, however, were lost in great cities, and the growth of the population gave to at least three of these professions a public which paid as well as, and exacted less adulation than the oligarchy; not indeed giving less trouble, for we have now a thousand tastes to study instead of one, a thousand prejudices to respect; and if we do not write fulsome dedications to the public, we are no less compelled to insert every here and there that artful flattery which makes John Bull appear in the light of— I do not say the best and most noble—but the richest, most powerful, most thriving, most honest, most amiably faulty, but magnanimously virtuous of publics.

But I am not flattering you, Mr. Bull, when I tell you that in respect of your middle classes you have made a vast step in advance of all other nations. For what does the middle-class mean? Not twenty years ago, it was taken to represent only the better portion of the commercial and lower half of professional society. I well remember with what a sneer some people spoke of a merchant, and the gulf that the barrister and physician asserted to exist between them and the lawyer and general practitioner. And how is it now? How many gentlemen of old family would now decline an introduction to a well-educated merchant? How many rather would not recommend their sons to be constant visitors on the merchant's wife and daughters? Is it not the barrister who now flatters the attorney, and where is the distinction between physician and surgeon?   No; the middle-class has an enormous extent now, and even the landed gentry, when brought to town, mingle freely and gladly with commerce and the professions.   In fact, we are more and more widening our range.   The nobleman takes a partnership in a brewery, on the one hand; on the other, the haberdasher sits in Parliament, and sends his son to Oxford.   The gentry, throwing over birth as a useless commodity, rush into commerce and the professions.   Dukes and peers, are delighted to make money by writing, if they do not confess to writing for money.   The merchant is at last received at Court; the banker is a peer; the shop-boy who has worked his way to the Woolsack, brings with him a sympathy for shop-boys (*perhaps*), which lessens the gulf between trade and aristocracy; and beholding these and many other wonders, you exclaim with glee: "It is an age of unity, caste is obliterated, and in another fifty years even the distinction of a title will be gone, and the middle-class will comprise all who are educated.

Softly, softly, my friend; no Utopias, if you please. Caste may be abolished in name, but it will exist in feeling for many an age, though its limitations be not those of rank, birth, and wealth.   We used to say at the university that the larger a college, the smaller its sets, and that you knew more men in a small college than you possibly could in a large one.   It is the same with the middle, or as it is now called the educated class.   The larger it grows, the more it will split up into classes which may have no name, and may be separated by very slight distinctions, but which will in reality, if not in appearance, be as far apart in feeling as the old castes were in every respect. In short, " good society" has substituted for the old distinctions of rank, birth, wealth, and intellectual pre-eminence, one less distinct in appearance, far more subtle, but far more difficult to attain. Indeed, rank and birth were gifts, wealth often came by inheritance, and a man might be born a wit or a genius, but that which has taken their place as a test can be acquired only by education, careful study, and observation, followed up by practice. It goes by the name of "breeding," and when people talk to you of *innate* good breeding, they speak of an impos-sibility. Some of its necessary qualities may be innate, and these may show themselves on occasions, and be mis-taken for good-breeding itself, but a further acquaintance may reveal the possessor in a different light. Good-breed-ing is only acquired, being taught us by our nurses, our parents, our tutors, our school-fellows, our friends, our enemies still more, and our experience everywhere ; and yet not one of these teachers may possess it themselves ; many, as nurses and school-fellows, certainly do not. It is breed-ing which now divides the one class you claim to exist, into so many classes, all of which are educated. One set has no breeding at all, another has a little, another more, another enough, and another too much—for this also is possible—and between that which has none, and that which has enough, there are more shades than in the rainbow.

We can now therefore speak of the principal requisites of good society, of which good-breeding—that is, enough and not too much of it—is the first. I have shown that, until the development of a middle class, the best society (not in a moral, but general point of view) was to be found among the aristocracy. Hence the word " aristo-

cratic" has come to mean " good for society," and therefore
while I premise that the best society is *not* now high society
either by wealth, birth, or distinction, I shall also premise
that good society is essentially aristocratic in the sense in
which we speak of aristocratic beauty, aristocratic bearing,
aristocratic appearance and manners.

The first indispensable requisite for good society is *education*.   By this I do not mean the so-called "finished
education" of a university or a boarding-school.   I think
it will be found that these establishments put their " finish"
somewhere in the middle of the course; they may possibly finish you as far as teachers can, but the education
which is to fit you for good society must be pursued long
after you leave them, as it ought to have been begun long
before you went to them.   This education should have
commenced with developing the mental powers, and especially the *comprehension*.   A man should be able, in
order to enter into conversation, to catch rapidly the
meaning of anything that is advanced ; for instance, though
you know nothing of science, you should not be obliged to
stare and be silent, when a man who does understand it is
explaining a new discovery or a new theory; though you
have not read a word of Blackstone, your comprehensive
powers should be sufficiently acute to enable you to take
in the statement that may be made of a recent cause ;
though you may not have read some particular book, you
should be capable of appreciating the criticism which you
hear of it.   Without such a power—simple enough and
easily attained by attention and practice, yet too seldom
met with in general society—a conversation which departs
from the most ordinary topics cannot be maintained without the risk of lapsing into a lecture ; with such a power

society becomes instructive as well as amusing, and you have no remorse at an evening's end at having wasted three or four hours in profitless banter or simpering platitudes. This facility of comprehension often startles us in some women, whose education we know to have been poor, and whose reading is limited. If they did not rapidly receive your ideas, they could not therefore be fit companions for intellectual men, and it is perhaps their consciousness of a deficiency which leads them to pay the more attention to what you say. It is this which makes married women so much more agreeable to men of thought than young ladies, as a rule, can be, for they are accustomed to the society of a husband, and the effort to be a companion to his mind has engrafted the habit of attention and ready reply.

No less important is the cultivation of taste. If it is tiresome and deadening to be with people who cannot understand, and will not even appear to be interested in your better thoughts, it is almost repulsive to find a man, still more a woman, insensible to all beauty, and immovable by any horror. I remember passing through the galleries of Hampton Court with a lady of this kind in whom I had in vain looked for enthusiasm. "Ah!" I exclaimed, as we passed into a well-known gallery, "we are come at last to Raphael's cartoons."

"Are we?" she asked languidly, as we stood in the presence of those grand conceptions. "Dear me, how high the fountain's playing in the court!"

In the present day an acquaintance with art, even if you have no love for it, is a *sine qua non* of good society. Music and painting are subjects which will be discussed in every direction around you. It is only in bad society that people go to the opera, concerts, and art-exhibitions merely because it is the fashion, or to say they have been there; and if you confessed to such a weakness in really good society, you would be justly voted a puppy. For this, too, some book-knowledge is indispensable. You should at least know the names of the more celebrated artists, composers, architects, sculptors, and so forth, and should be able to approximate their several schools.

" I have just bought a Hobbema," was said to Mrs. B. the other day. " What shall you put into it ?" said she, hoping to conceal her ignorance.

So too, you should know pretty accurately the pronunciation of celebrated names, or, if not, take care not to use them. An acquaintance of mine is always talking about pictures, and asks me how I like *H*annibal Carra*x*i, and G*h*arlanda*go*. It was the same person who, seeing at the bottom of a rare engraving the name "Raphael Mengs," said in a kind of musing rapture, " Beautiful thing, indeed, quite in Raphael's earlier style; you can trace the influence of Perugino in that figure." So, too, it will never do to be ignorant of the names and approximate ages of great composers, especially in London, where music is so highly appreciated and so common a theme. It will be decidedly condemnatory if you talk of the *new* opera, "Don Giovanni," or *Rossini's* " Trovatore ;" or are ignorant who composed " Fidelio," and in what opera occur such common pieces as " Ciascun lo dice," or " Il segreto." I do not say that these trifles are indispensable, and when a man has better knowledge to offer, especially with genius, or " cleverness" to back it, he will not only be pardoned for an ignorance of them, but can even take a high tone and profess indifference or contempt of them. But at the same time such ignorance stamps an ordinary man, and hinders conversation. On the other hand, the best society will not endure dilettantism, and whatever the knowledge a man may possess of any art, he must not display it so as to make the ignorance of others painful to them. We are gentlemen, not picture-dealers. But this applies to every topic. To have only one or two subjects to converse on, and to discourse rather than talk on them, is always ill-bred, whether the theme be literature or horse-flesh. The Newmarket lounger would probably denounce the former as "a bore," and call us pedants for dwelling on it; but if, as is too often the case, he can give us nothing more general than a discussion of the "points" of a mare that perhaps we have never seen, he is as great a pedant in his way.

Reason plays a less conspicuous part in good society, because its frequenters are too reasonable to be mere reasoners. A disputation is always dangerous to temper, and tedious to those who cannot feel as eager as the disputants; a discussion, on the other hand, in which everybody has a chance of stating amicably and unobtrusively his or her opinion, must be of frequent occurrence. But to cultivate the reason, besides its high moral value, has the advantage of enabling one to reply as well as attend to the opinions of others. Nothing is more tedious or disheartening than a perpetual " Yes, just so," and nothing more. Conversation must never be one-sided. Then, again, the reason enables us to support a fancy or opinion, when we are asked *why* we think so and so. To reply, " I don't know, but still I think so," is silly in a man and tedious in a woman. But there is a part of our education so important and so neglected in our schools and colleges, that it cannot be too highly impressed on parents

on the one hand, and young people on the other. I mean
that which we learn first of all things, yet often have not
learned fully when Death cases us of the necessity—the
art of speaking our own language. What can Greek and
Latin, French and German, be for us in our every-day
life, if we have not acquired this? We are often encouraged to raise a laugh at Doctor Syntax and the tyranny
of Grammar, but we may be certain that more misunder-
standings, and therefore more difficulties, arise between
men in the commonest intercourse from a want of grammatical precision, than from any other cause. It was once
the fashion to neglect grammar, as it now is with certain
people to write illegibly, and in the days of Goethe, a
man thought himself a genius if he could spell badly.
How much this simple knowledge is neglected in England,
even among the upper classes, is shown by the results of
the examinations for the army and the civil services; how
valuable it is, is now generally acknowledged by men of
sound sense. Precision and accuracy must begin in the
very outset; and if we neglect them in grammar, we shall
scarcely acquire them in expressing out thoughts. But
since there is no society without interchange of thought,
and since the best society is that in which the best thoughts
are interchanged in the best and most comprehensible manner, it follows that a proper mode of expressing ourselves
is indispensable to good society.

There is one poor neglected letter, the subject of a
poetical charade by Byron, which people in the present
day have made the test of fitness for good society. For
my part, I would sooner associate with a man who dropped
that eighth letter of our alphabet than with one who spoke
bad grammar and expressed himself ill. But if he has

not learned to pronounce a letter properly, it is scarcely
probable that he will have studied the art of speech at all.
It is amusing to hear the ingenious excuses made by
people for this neglect. "Mrs. A—," one person tells
you, "is a woman of excellent education. You must not
be surprised at her dropping her *h's*, it is a Staffordshire
habit, and she has lived all her life in that county." I
fancy that it is not Staffordshire or any other shire that
can be saddled with the fault. It is simply a habit of ill-
bred people everywhere throughout the three kingdoms.
Nor is the plea of dialect any real excuse. It is a peculiarity of Middlesex dialect to put a *v* for a *w*, and a *w*
for a *v*. Would any one on that account present Mr.
Samivel Veller as a gentleman of good education, with a
slight peculiarity of dialect in his speech? Good society
uses the same language everywhere, and dialects ought to
be got rid of in those who would frequent it. The language
of Burns may be very beautiful in poetry, and the ballads of Moore may gain much from a strong Irish brogue,
but if we object to London slang in conversation, we have
as much right to object to local peculiarities which make
your speech either incomprehensible or ridiculous; and
certain it is that the persons whose strong nationality induces them to retain their Scotch or Irish idiom and
accent, are always ready to protest against Americanisms,
and would-be very much bothered if a Yorkshire landowner
were to introduce his local drawl into the drawing-room.
Localism is not patriotism and therefore until the Union
is dissolved, we must request people to talk English in
English society.

The art of expressing one's thoughts neatly and suitably is one which, in the neglect of rhetoric as a study, we

must practice for ourselves. The commonest thought well put is more useful in a social point of view than the most brilliant idea jumbled out. What is well expressed is easily seized and therefore readily responded to; the most poetic fancy may be lost to the hearer if the language which conveys it is obscure. Speech is the gift which distinguishes man from animals, and makes society possible. He has but a poor appreciation of his high privilege as a human being, who neglects to cultivate "God's great gift of speech."

As I am not writing for men of genius, but for ordinary beings, I am right to state that an indispensable part of education is a knowledge of English literature. But *how* to read is, for society, more important than *what* we read. The man who takes up nothing but a newspaper, but reads it to *think*, to deduct conclusions from its premises, and form a judgment on its opinions, is more fitted for society, than he, who, having a large box regularly from Mudie's, and devoting his whole day to its contents, swallows it all without digestion. In fact, the mind must be treated like the body, and however great its appetite, it will soon fall into bad health, if it gorges but does not ruminate. At the same time an acquaintance with the best current literature is necessary to modern society, and it is not sufficient to have read a book without being able to pass a judgment on it. Conversation on literature is impossible, when your respondent can only say, "Yes, I like the book, but I really don't know why." Or what can we do with the young lady whose literary stock is as limited as that of the daughter of a late eminent member of Parliament, whom a friend of mine had once to take down to dinner?

He had tried her on music and painting in vain. She had no taste for either. Society was as barren a theme, for papa did not approve of any but dinner parties.

" Then I suppose you read a great deal ?" asked my friend.

" Oh, yes! we read."

" Light literature ?"

" Oh, yes ! light literature."

" Novels, for instance ?"

" Oh, yes! novels."

" Do you like Dickens ?"

" We don't read Dickens."

" Oh ! I see you are of Thackeray's party."

" We never read Thackeray."

" Then you are romantic, and devoted to Bulwer Lytton ?"

" Never," replied the young lady, rather shocked..

" Then which *is* your favorite novelist ?"

" James," she replied triumphantly.

" Ah !" said my friend, reviving a little, " James is exciting."

" Oh, yes ! we like his books so much ! Papa reads them aloud to us, but then he misses out all the exciting parts."

After that my friend found his knife and fork better company than his neighbor. •

An acquaintance with old English literature is not perhaps indispensable, but it gives a man great advantage in all kinds of society, and in some he is at constant loss without it. The same may be said of foreign literature, which in the present day is almost as much discussed as our own ; but, on the other hand, an acquaintance with

home and foreign politics, with current history, and every
subject of passing interest, is absolutely necessary; and a
person of sufficient intelligence to join in good society cannot dispense with his daily newspaper, his literary journal, and the principal quarterly reviews and magazines
The cheapness of every kind of literature, the facilities
of our well-stored circulating libraries, our public reading-
rooms and numerous excellent lectures on every possible
subject, leave no excuse to poor or rich for an ignorance
of any of the topics discussed in intellectual society. You
may forget your Latin, Greek, French, German, and
Mathematics, but if you frequent good company you will
never be allowed to forget that you are a citizen of the
world.

The respect for *moral character* is a distinguishing
mark of good society in this country as compared with that
of the Continent. No rank, no wealth, no celebrity will
induce a well-bred English lady to admit to her drawing-
room a man or woman whose character is known to be
bad. Society is a severe censor, pitiless and remorseless.
The woman who has once fallen, the man who has once
lost his honor, may repent for years; good society shuts
its doors on them once and for ever. Perhaps this is the
only case in which the best society is antagonistic to Christianity; but, in extenuation, it must be remembered that
there is no court in which to try those who sin against it.
Society itself is the court in which are judged those many
offences which the law cannot reach, and this inclemency
of the world, this exile for life which it pronounces, must
be regarded as the only deterrent against certain sins.
There is little or no means of punishing the seducer, the
cheat, the habitual drunkard and gambler, and men and

women who indulge in illicit pleasures except this one
verdict of perpetual expulsion pronounced by good society
Often is it given without a fair trial, on the report of a
slanderer; often it falls upon the wrong head; often it
proves its injustice in ignoring the vices of one and ful-
minating against those of another; often, by its implaci-
bility, drives the offender to despair, and makes the one
false step lead to the ruin of a life : but it must be remembered what interests society has to protect—the purity of daughters, wives and sisters, the honor of sons; it
must be allowed that its means of obtaining evidence is
very slight; and that, on the other hand, it cannot institute an inquisition into the conduct of all its members,
since the mere suspicion which such an inquiry would ex
cite is sufficient to ruin a character that might prove to
be innocent. Society, then, is forced to judge by common
report, and though it may often judge wrongly, it generally errs on the safe side. What it still wants, and must
perhaps always want, is some check on the slander and
calumny which misleads its judgment. We want some
tribunal which, without blasting a reputation, can call to
account the low sneak who lounges into a club-room, and
actuated by pique, whispers into a frind's ear, " in strict-
est confidence," some silly slur on a lady's character,
knowing that it will pass from mouth to mouth, growing
bigger and bigger, and that it can never be traced back to
the original utterer. We want to put down those old
maids and dowagers who shake their cork-screw ringlets
at the mention of a name, and look as if they knew a
great deal which they would not tell. We want gossip
and scandal to be held a sin, as it is already held bad
taste, and a higher tone which shall reject as inventions

4

the pot-house stories of grooms and lacqueys, and receive with greater caution the gossip of the club-room. How many a fair fame of a virtuous girl is ruined by the man she has rejected; how many an Iago lives and thrives in society to the present day; how many a young man is blackened by a rival; how many a man we meet in the best circles whose chambers are the scene of debauchery, or who carries on an illicit connexion in secret, unexposed. These things make us bitter to the world, but, if we cannot see the remedy, we must endure them silently. Oh! if the calumniator, male or female, could be hanged as high as Haman, if the ninth commandment, like the eighth, could be punished with death, many a hopeful career were not blighted at its outset, many an innocent woman were not driven from her home and thrust into the very jaws of sin, and the world would be happier and far more Christian.

In the meantime good society discountenances gossip, and that is all it can do for the present. Fathers and husbands must be careful whom they introduce to their families, and every one should beware how they *repeat* what has been told them of their neighbors. There is in the church of Walton-on-Thames a kind of iron gag made to fit upon the face, and bearing this inscription:

" Thys is a brydel
For the women of Walton who speake so ydel.'

I know not what poor creature, blasted by a venomous tongue, invented and gave to the church this quaint relic; I only wish that every parish church had one, and that every slanderer might be forced to wear it. One! did I say? we should want a hundred in some parishes, all in use at the same time.

A discourteous but well-merited reply which I heard the other day, reminds me that good temper is an essential of good society. A young lady, irritated because a gentleman would not agree with her on some matter, lost her balance, and irritably exclaimed, " Oh, Mr. A—, you have only two ideas in your head." " You are right," replied the gentleman, " I have only two ideas, and one of them is that you do not know how to behave yourself."

Temper has a great deal to answer for, and it would take a volume to discuss its effect on the affairs of the world. It is a vice of old and young of both sexes, of high and low, even I may say of good and bad, though a person who has not conquered it scarcely merits the name of good, though he should regenerate mankind. Monarchs have lost kingdoms, maidens lovers, and everybody friends, by the irritation of a moment, and in society a display of ill-temper is fatal to harmony, and thus destroys the first principle of social meetings. We pardon it, we overlook it, and sometimes it even amuses us, but, sooner or later, it must chill back love and freeze friendship. In short, it makes society unbearable, and is justly pronounced to be disgustingly vulgar. I used once to frequent the house of a man who had every requisite for being charming but that of a command of temper. He gave dinner-parties which ought to have been most pleasant. He was well-educated, well-informed, well-mannered in every other respect. The first time I dined with him, before I had seen anything of this failing, I was horror-struck by hearing him say to a servant, " Confound you, will you take that dish to the other end !" Of course I paid no attention, but hoping to cover him, talked loudly and eagerly. It was useless. The servant blundered, and the master thundered, till at last there was a dead silence round the table, and we all looked down into our plates. The mistress of the house made the matter worse by putting in at last, "My dear Charles, do be moderate," and the irritable man only increased the awkwardness by an irritable reply. I overlooked this, and dined there again, but only once. This time it was his daughter who offended by some innocent remark. "Really you're quite a fool, Jane," he said, turning savagely upon her, and the poor girl burst into tears. Our appetites were spoiled, our indignation rose, and though we sat through the dinner, we all of us probably repeated Solomon's proverb about a dry morsel where love is, and a stalled ox with contention thereby, which I, for one, interpreted to mean that my chop and pint of ale at home would, for the future, be far more *appetitlich* than my friend's turtle and turbot.

As there is nothing to which an Englishman clings so tenaciously as his opinions, there are few things which rouse the temper so rapidly as an argument. In good society all disputation is eschewed, and particularly that which involves party politics and sectarian religion. It is at least wise to discover what are the views of your company before you venture on these subjects. Zeal, however well-meant, must, as St. Paul warns us, often be sacrificed to peace; and where you cannot agree, and I feel that to reply would lead you into an argument, it is best to be silent. At the same time there are some occasions where silence is servile. No man should sit still to hear sacred things blasphemed, or his friend abused. The gentleman must yield to the Man where an atheist reviles Christianity, a Chartist abuses the Queen, or anybody speaks ill of the listener's friend or relation. Even then he best marks his indignation by rising and leaving the room. Nor need any man fear the imputation of cowardice, if he curbs his anger at direct abuse of himself. "A soft answer turneth away wrath;" and if he cannot check his own feelings sufficiently to reply in a conciliatory tone, no one can blame him if cooly and *politely* he expresses to his antagonist his opinion of his bad manners. The feeling of the company will always go with the man who keeps his temper, for not only does society feel that to vent wrath is a breach of its laws, but it knows, that to conquer one's-self is a far more difficult task than to overcome an enemy; and that, therefore, the man who keeps his temper is really strong and truly courageous. In fact the Christian rule is here (as it should always be) that of society; and the man who offers his left check to the blow, displays not only the rarest Christian virtue, but the very finest politeness, which, while it teems with delicate irony, at once disarms the attacker, and enlists the pity and sympathy, if not the applause, of the bystanders. Of course I speak of blows metaphorically. A blow with the hand is rarely if ever given in good society.

Another case in which the Christian and the social rule coincide, if not in reality at least in appearance, is that of private animosities. Of the "cut," as a necessary social weapon, I shall speak elsewhere, but it now suffices to say, that when given for the first time with a view to breaking off an acquaintance, it should not be done conspicuously, nor before a number of people. Its object is not to wound and cause confusion, but to make known to the person "cut" that your feelings towards him are changed. In good society no one ever cuts another in such a manner as to be generally remarked, and the reason is obvious: It causes awkwardness and confusion in the rest of the company. It is worse. Between a guest and host the relation is supposed to be friendly; if not so, it can always be immediately discontinued; so that generally the ill will must be between one guest and another under the same roof. But what does it then amount to? Is it not a slur upon your host's judgment? Is it not as much as to say, " This man is unfit for me to know; and, since you are his friend, you must be unworthy of me too?" At any rate, it is mortifying to a host to find that he has brought two enemies together, and, with the respect due from a guest to a host you must abstain from making his house a field of battle. There is no occasion for hypocrisy. Politeness, cold and distant if you like it, can cost you nothing, and is never taken to mean friendship. In short, harmony and peace are the rules of good society, as of Christianity, and its denizens can and do throw aside the most bitter enmities when meeting on the neutral ground of a friend's house. Nor is the armistice without its value. Like that between Austria and France, it is not unfrequently followed by overtures of peace; and I have known two people who had not interchanged two words for a score of years, shake hands before they left a house where they had been accidentally brought together. Had they not been well-bred this reconciliation could never have taken place.

The relations of guest to guest are not so well understood in this country as on the Continent. There your host's friends are for the time *your* friends. When you enter a room you have a right to speak to, and be addressed by, everybody present. The friendship of your host, declared, as it were, in his inviting them there, is a sufficient recommendation and introduction to every one of his guests. If you and they are good enough for him to invite, you and they are good enough for each other to know, and it is, therefore, an insult to your host to remain next to a person for a long time without addressing him. In exclusive England we require that our host or hostess shall give a special introduction to every guest, but in the best society this is not absolutely necessary. Exclusiveness is voted to be of bad style; and two people who sat next to one another for a long time, with no one to talk to, would be thought ill-bred as well as ridiculous if they waited for the formal introduction to exchange a few words, at least at a party where conversation was the main object.

As we boast of English hospitality, it is a wonder that we do not better observe the relations of host and guest. On the Continent any man, whether you know him or not, who has crossed your threshold with friendly intent, is your guest, and you are bound to treat him as one. In England a friend must introduce him, unless he has the ingenuity of Theodore Hook, who always introduced himself where there was a dinner going on, and managed to make himself welcome, too; but among ill-bred people even this introduction does not suffice, and the vulgar often take pride to themselves in proving that their houses are their castles. A late neighbor of mine, of somewhat peppery temper, used to tell with glee how he had turned out of his house a gentleman—an innocent but not attractive man—who had been brought there by a common friend, but whom he did not wish to know. I often thought, when I heard the tale repeated, "How little you think you are telling a story against yourself!" So, too, when Arabella, speaking of Charles, with whom she has quarrelled, tells me so proudly, I cut him last night dead, and before the whole party, to his utter confusion," I whisper to myself, "He may richly have deserved the punishment, but I would not have been the executioner." In fact, whether as host or guest, we must remember the feelings of the rest of the company, and that a show of animosity between any of them always mars the sense of peaceful enjoyment, for which all have met. To pick a quarrel, to turn your back on a person, to cut him openly, or to make audible remarks on him, are displays of temper only found in vulgar society.

The other requisites indispensable for good society will be found in various chapters of this work. Confidence, calm, and good habits, are treated in the chapter on carriage. Good manners is, more or less, the subject of the whole book, and appropriate dress, another indispensable, is discussed under that head. Accomplishments, on which I have given a chapter, are not generally considered indispensable, and certainly a man or woman of good education and good breeding could pass muster without them. But they lend a great charm to society, and in some cases are a very great assistance to it. Indeed, there are some accomplishments an ignorance of which may prove extremely awkward. Perhaps, however, the most valuable accomplishment or rather art, especially in persons of full-age, is that of making society easy, and of entertaining. Rules and hints for this will be given in various sections, but. I may here say that it is an art which demands no little labor and ingenuity, and if anybody

imagines that the offices of host and hostess are sinecures,
he is greatly mistaken. The great principle is that of
movement. According to the atomic theory, warmth and
brilliance are gained by the rapidity of the atoms about
one another. We are only atoms in society after all, and
we certainly get both warmth and brilliance when we re-
volve round each other in the ball-room. But it is rather
mental movement that I refer to just now, although the
other is by no means unimportant, and the host and hostess
should, when possible, be continually shifting their places,
easily and gracefully, talking to everybody more or less,
and inducing others to move. But there must be something for the minds of those assembled to dwell upon;
something to suggest thought, and thus generate conversation. If the host or hostess have themselves the talent,
they should do this by continually leading the conversation,
not after the manner of Sydney Smith, who, while dinner
was going on, allowed Mackintosh, Jeffrey, and Stewart, to
fall into vehement discussion, while he himself quietly
made an excellent meal, and prepared for better things.
The moment the cloth was removed, which *was* done in
those days, the jovial wit, happier than his companions
who had had more of the "feast of reason and the flow
of soul" than of beef and mutton, would look up and
make some totally irrelevant and irresistible remark, and
having once raised the laugh, would keep an easy lead of
the conversation to the end. But if they have not this
art, it is highly desirable, that dinner-givers should invite
their regular talker, who, like the Roman parasite, in consideration of a good dinner, will always be ready with a
fresh topic in case of a lull in the conversation, and always
be able to .ntroduce it with something smart and lively

4*

There is a hotel in the city where a certain number of
broken-down ecclesiastics are always "on hand" with a
couple of sermons in pocket. If a clergyman is called
suddenly out of town, or taken ill on the Saturday night,
or hindered from preaching by any accident, he has only to
send down a messenger and a reverend gentleman flies to
him : the sermon is at his service for the sum of one
guinea, or less. Would it not answer to institute a similar
establishment for the benefit of dinner-givers? The only
question the cleric asks is, "High or low?" He has a
sermon in each pocket, "high" in the right, "low" in the
left, and produces the proper article, if he does not by
mistake forget which is in which, and astound an evangel-
ical congregation with the "symbols of the Church," or
a Tractarian one with the "doctrine of election." In
the same way, the *conviva* would be always ready, in full
dress, at six in the evening, and having put the question,
"Serious or gay, Whig or Tory?" bring out his witticisms
accordingly. We do everything now-a-days with money.
Mr. Harker gives out our toasts, our servants carve and
give out the wine for us. The host sits at the head or side
of his table, and only smiles and talks. The next generation will make a further improvement, and the host will
hire a gentleman to do even the smiling and talking, or,
like the Emperor Augustus, he will just look in on his
guests at the middle of dinner, ask if the *entremets*
are good, and go to his easy-chair again in the library.
Of the art of entertaining on various occasions I shall
treat under the proper heads, and we come now to the dis-
pensables of good society, which I take to be wealth, rank,
birth, and talent.

Of birth there is little to say, because, if a man is fit

for good society, it can make very little difference wnether
his father were a chimney-sweep or a chancellor, at least to
sensible people.   Indeed, to insist on good birth in England would not only shut you out from enjoying the society
of people of no ordinary stamp, but is now generally considered as a cowardly way of asserting your superiority.
A young lady said to me the other day, "I wonder you
can visit the C.'s; their mother was a cook."   "Well,"
said I, "it is evident she did not bring them up in the
kitchen."   My interlocutrix wore the name of a celebrated
poet, and was of one of the oldest families in England,
but I confess that I thought her remark that of a snob,
the more so as the C.'s happened to be the most agreeable
people I knew.

The advantages of wealth are considerable in the formation of society.   In this country, where hospitality
means eating and drinking, it demands money to receive
your friends; and in London, where a lady can with difficulty walk in the streets unaccompanied, a carriage of
some sort, in which to visit them, becomes almost a necessity if you are to mix much in the world.   But good
society would be very limited if every man required his
l rougham or cabriolet.   In the metropolis, again, a man-
servant is almost indispensable, though not quite; and if
you have the moral courage to do without one you will
find that your small dinners—always better than large
ones—will be more quietly served by women than by men.
Londoners have still to learn that large pompous "feelings" are neither agreeable nor in good taste, and that
evening meetings, for the purpose of conversation, with as
little ceremony as possible, are far less tedious, less bilious,
and less expensive.

They do these things better in Paris, where the dinner-party is an introduction of the *nouveaux riches*. There the £300 a year does not exclude its owners from the enjoyment of the best, even the highest society. They may be asked to every ball and dinner of the season, and are not expected to return them. A *voiture de remise* is good enough to take them even to the Tuileries. The size of their apartment is no obstacle to their assembling their friends simply for tea and conversation. If the rooms are elegantly furnished and arranged, and the lady of the house understands the art of receiving, and selects her guests rather for their manners and conversational powers than for position or wealth, their reception may become fashionable at no further expense than that of a few simple refreshments which are handed about. Even dances are given without suppers, and no one cares whether your household consists of a dozen lacqueys or a couple of maid-servants.

"Mere wealth," says Mr. Hayward, truly enough, "can do little, unless it be of magnitude sufficient to constitute celebrity." He might have added, that wealth, without breeding, generally draws the attention of others to the want of taste of its possessor, and gives envy an object to sneer at. I remember an instance of this in a woman who had recently, with her husband, returned from Australia, with a large fortune. I met her at a ball in Paris: she was magnificently, almost regally dressed, and as she swept through the rooms people whispered, "That is the rich Mrs.——." I had not been introduced to her, and had no desire to be so, but I could not escape her vulgarity. On going to fetch a cup of chocolate from the buffet for my partner, I had to pass within a yard of Mrs. ——, who was gorging ices amid a crowd of rather inferior Frenchmen; there was not the slightest fear of my spilling the chocolate, and I was too far from her to spoil her dress, had I been awkward enough to do so; but as I passed back, she suddenly screamed out, in very bad French, " Monsieur, Monsieur quoi, faites-vous, vous gâtery mon robe !" Of course everybody looked round. I bowed low, and begged her pardon, assuring her that there was not the slightest cause for alarm; but she was not satisfied, and while I beat a retreat I heard her loud voice denouncing me as a " stupid fellow," and so forth, and I soon found that Mrs. —— was pronounced to be " atrociously vulgar" as well as immensely rich.

I cannot think that rank is a recommendation to a man with any but vulgar people. Not every nobleman is a gentleman, and fewer still perhaps bear that character that would entitle them to a free *entrée* among the well-bred. On the other hand, rank is a costly robe, which must be worn as modestly as possible, not to spoil that feeling of equality which is necessary to the ease of society. Some deference must be paid to it, and the man of rank who cannot forget it, will find himself as much in the way in a party of untitled people, as an elephant among a troop of jackals. If titles were as common in England as on the Continent, there would be less fear of a host devoting himself to My Lord to the neglect of his other guests, or of those guests centering their attention on the one star. In Paris, it is only in the vulgar circles of the Chaussée d'Autin, that " Monsieur le Comte," or " Monsieur le Marquis," is shown off as a lion; and in the well-bred circles in this country, the nobleman must be content with precedence, and the place of honor, and for the rest be as

one of the company. In Southern Germany, the distinction is the other way; the simple *Herr* is almost as remarkable as the man of title in England. In fact, everybody admitted to what is there called good society, has
some title, whether by birth or office; and a man must be
highly distinguished by talents or achievements to have
the *entrée* of the Court. I found that the Esquire after
my name was generally translated by Baron; the tradesmen raised it to Graf, or Count; and the people who
" knew all about it," called me " Herr Esquire von ——."
Something in the same way are military titles allotted to
civilians in some parts of America. A store-keeper becomes " Major;" a merchant, " Colonel;" and a man of
whom you are to ask a favor, is always a " General."

Nothing can be more ill-judged than lion-hunting. If
the premise with which I set out, that society requires
real or apparent equality, be true, anything which raises
a person on a pedestal unfits him for society. The men
of genius are rarely gifted with social qualities, and the
only society suited to them is that of others of the same
calibre. If Shakspere were alive, and I acquainted with
him, I would not ask him to an evening party; or, if I
did so, it should be with huge Ben, and half-a-dozen more
from the " Mermaid," and they should have strict injunctions not to engross the conversation. If you must have
a literary lion at your receptions, you should manage to
have two or three, for you may be sure that they will behave less arrogantly in one another's presence; or perhaps a better plan still, is to invite a score of critics to
meet him; you will then find your show beast as tracta-
ble and as quiet as his name-sake in the caresses of Van
Amburg or Wombwell. The man of science again, has

too lofty a range of thought to descend to the ordinary topics of society; and the bishop and distinguished general usually bear about with them the marks of their profession, which, for perfect ease and equality, should be concealed. Distinguished foreigners, if they are clean, and can talk English well, may be very agreeable, but your guests will often suspect them, and their names must be known in England to make them desirable in any point of view.

Of rank and distinction, however, it may be said, in preference to wealth and mere birth, that they are, when seconded by character, absolute passports to good society. A title is *presumed* to be a certificate of education and good breeding, while a celebrity will often be pardoned for the want of both, in virtue of the talents and perseverance by which he has raised himself. Of the two, the latter excuses more our adulation. Rank is rarely gained by merit, and when it is so, it is swamped by it. Macaulay and Brougham have not gained a single step in the estimation of well-bred people by being raised to the peerage, and no one would hesitate for a moment between them and the untitled son of a Duke or Marquis. While, too, we naturally fear the epithet of " toady," if we cultivate noblemen only for the sake of their rank, we may well defend ourselves for the admiration which genius, perseverance, and courage excite. To women, again, distinction is less trying, since it takes them less out of their ordinary sphere. They are still women, still capable of enjoying society, with two exceptions, the blue-stocking and the *esprit fort*, neither of which should ever be admitted into good society.

But while genius is scarcely a recommendation in social

meetings, there are mental qualities nearly allied to it, which are the best we can bring to them; I mean a thinking mind and a ready wit. The most agreeable men and women are those who think out of society as well as in it; those who have mind without affectation, and talents without conceit; those who have formed, and can form fresh opinions on every subject, and to whom a mere word serves as the springing-board from which to rise to new trains of thought. Where people of this kind meet together, the commonest subjects become matters of interest, and the conversation grows rapidly to brilliance, even without positive wit. The man to whose mind everything is a suggestion, and whose words suggest something to everybody, is the best man for a social meeting.

We have now seen what are, and what are not the requisites for good society. High moral character, a polished education, a perfect command of temper, good breeding, delicate feeling, good manners, good habits, and a good bearing, are indispensable. Wit, accomplishments, and social talents are great advantages, though not absolutely necessary. On the other hand, birth is lost sight of, while wealth, rank, and distinction, so far from being desirable, must be carefully handled, not to be positively objectionable. We are now therefore enabled to offer a definition of good society. It is, the meeting on a footing of equality, and for the purpose of mutual entertainment, of men, of women, or men and women together, of good character, good education, and good breeding.

But what is the real spirit of the observances which this society requires of its frequenters for the preservation of harmony and the easy intercourse of all of them? Certainly, one may have a spotless reputation, a good education, and good breeding, without being either good in reality, or a Christian. But if we examine the laws which good society lays down for our guidance and governance, we shall find without a doubt, that they are those which a simple Christian, desiring to regulate the meetings of a number of people who lacked the Christian feeling, would dictate. I am, of course, quite aware that good society will never make you a Christian. You may be charming in a party, and every one may pronounce you a perfect and agreeable gentleman ; but you may go home and get privately intoxicated, or beat your wife, or be cruel to your children. If society finds you out, be sure it will punish you ; but society has no right to search your house, and intrude upon your hearth, and, as you say, it may be long before it finds you out. But, *as far as its jurisdiction extends*, good society can compel you, if not to be a Christian, at least to act like one. The difference between the laws of God and the laws of men, is, that the former address the heart from which the acts proceed, the latter, which can only judge from what they see, determine the acts without regard to the heart. The one waters the root, the other the branches.

The laws of society are framed by the unanimous consent of men, and, in all essential points, they differ very little all over the world. The Turk may show his politeness by feeding you with his fingers, the Englishman by carving your portion for you ; but the same spirit dictates both—the spirit of friendliness, of goodwill. Thus, though the laws of society are necessarily imperfect, are moulded by traditional and local custom, and are addressed to the outer rather than the inner man, their *spirit* is invariably the same. The considerations which dictate them are reducible to the same law, and this law proves to be the fundamental one of Christian doctrine. Thus, what the heathen arrives at only by laws framed for the comfort of society, we possess at once in virtue of our religion. And it is a great glory for a Christian to be able to say, that all refinement and all civilization lead men— as far as their conversation is concerned—to the practice of Christianity. It is a great satisfaction to feel that Christianity is eminently the religion of civilization and society.

The great law which distinguishes Christianity from every other creed, that of brotherly love and self-denial, is essentially the law which we find at the basis of all social observances. The first maxim of politeness is to be agreeable to everybody, even at the expense of one's own comfort. Meekness is the most beautiful virtue of the Christian; modesty the most commendable in a well-bred man. Peace is the object of Christian laws; harmony that of social observances. Self-denial is the exercise of the Christian; forgetfulness of self that of the well-bred. Trust in one another unites Christian communities; confidence in the good intentions of our neighbors is that which makes society possible. To be kind to one another is the object of Christian converse; to entertain one another, that of social intercourse. Pride, selfishness, ill-temper, are alike opposed to Christianity and good-breeding. The one demands an upright life; the other requires the appearance of it. The one bids us make the most of God's gifts and improve our talents; the other will not admit us till we have done so by education. And to go a step farther; as a Christian community excludes sinners and unbelievers from its gatherings, so a social community excludes from its meetings those of bad character, and those who do not subscribe to its laws.

But society goes farther, and appears to impose on its members a number of arbitrary rules, which continually restrict them in their actions. It tells them how they must eat and drink and dress, and walk and talk, and so on. We ought to be very thankful to society for taking so much trouble, and saving us so much doubt and confusion. But if the ordinances of society are examined, it will be found that while many of them are merely derived from custom and tradition, and some have no positive value, they all tend to one end, the preservation of harmony, and the prevention of one person from usurping the rights, or intruding on the province of another. If it regulates your dress, it is that there may be an appearance of equality in all, and that the rich may not be able to flaunt their wealth in the eyes of their poorer associates. If, for instance, it says that you are not to wear diamonds in the morning, it puts a check upon your vanity. If it says you may wear them on certain occasions, it does not compel those who have none to purchase them. If society says you shall eat with a knife and fork, it is not because fingers were not made before forks, but because it is well known that if you were to use the natural fork of five prongs instead of the plated one of four, you would want to wash your hands after every dish. If she goes farther and says you shall not put your knife into your mouth, it is because she supposes that you, like ninety-nine out of every hundred of civilized beings, can taste the steel when you do so, and is surprised at your bad taste, and since she demands good taste she cannot think you fit for her court. Of course, she cannot stop to hear you explain that you find a particular enjoyment in the taste of steel, and that therefore on your part it is good not bad taste. She is by necessity forced to judge from appearance. If again she forbids you to swing your arms in walking, like the sails of a windmill, it is not because she finds any pleasure in pinioning you, but because beauty is a result of harmony, which is her first law, and she studies beauty, adopts the beautiful, and rejects the inelegant. That motion of the arms is not lovely, confess it. Society is quite right to object to it. Once more, if she dubs you vulgar for speaking in a loud harsh voice, it is because whatever be your case, other people have nerves which may be touched and heads which can ache, and your stentorian tones set the one vibrating and the other throbbing. In short, while she may have many an old law that needs repealing, you will find that the greater number of her enactments are founded on very good and very Christian considerations. You will find that the more religious a man is, the more polite he will spontaneously become, and that too in every rank of life, for true religion teaches him to forget himself, to love his neighbor, and to be kindly even to his enemy, and the *appearance* of so being and doing, is what society demands as good manners. How can it ask more? How can it rip open your heart and see if with your bland smile and oily voice you are a liar and a hypocrite? There is One who has this power—forget it not!—but society must be content with the semblance. By your works men do and must judge you.

Before I quit the demands of society, I must say a few words on the distinction she makes between people of different ages and different domestic positions; to wit, how she has one law for the bachelor, another for the bene-

dict; one for the maid, another for the matron; one law,
I mean, to regulate their privileges and to restrict their
vagaries.

Let us begin with that awful, stately, and majestic
being, Paterfamilias Anglicanus; the same who, having
reached the age of perpetual snow, exacts our reverence
and receives our awe; the same who, finding his majesty
lost on the vagabond Italian with the monkey and organ,
resolves to crush him in a column of *The Times;* the
same before whom not Mamma herself dares open that
same newspaper; the same who warns her against encouraging the French count, for whom Mary Anne has
taken such a liking,—who pooh-poohs the idea of a
watering-place in summer, who frowns over the weekly
bills, and talks of bankruptcy and ruin over the milliner's little account, who is Mamma's excuse with the
sons, the daughters, and the servants—"your papa wishes
it," she says, and there is not a word more,—who with a
mistaken dignity raises up an impassable barrier between
himself and his children, chilling back their tenderest advances, receiving their evening kiss as a cold formality;
and who, ah, human heart! when one of them is laid low,
steals to the chamber of death privily and ashamed of his
grief, turns down the ghastly sheet, and burying his head
there pours out the only tears he has shed for so many a
year. Poor father! bitter, bitter is the self-reproach
over that cold form now. What avails now the stern
veto that bade her reject the handsome lover who had so
poor a fortune, and broke—ay, broke her heart that beats
no more? Of what use was that cold severity which
drove him to sea, who lies there now past all recal?
Ah! stern, hard, cold father; so they thought you, so

you seemed, and yet you meant it for the best, and you
say you loved your children too well. Well, well, it is
not all fathers who are like this. There is another species of the genus Paterfamilias Anglicanus, who is a jovial, and merry, and blithe by his fireside, whose children nestle round his knees, and who has a kiss and a
word, and a kind, soft smile for each.

But what is the position of Paterfamilias in society?
Where is his place? Certainly not in the ball-room. If
he comes there, he must throw aside his dignity, and delight in the pleasure of the young. He must be young
himself. In his own house he must receive all comers
merrily—the *bal folâtre* is to be a scene of mirth; he
must not damp your gaiety with his solemn gravity. He
is as little missed from his wife's ball-room, as a mute
from a wedding procession; and yet he must be there to
talk to chaperons, to amuse the elderly beaux, and, if
necessary, to spread the card-table and form the rubber.
At all events, he never dances unless to make up a set in
a quadrille. He is still less at home in the pic-nic, the
matinée, and the *fête,* but he is great at the evening
party, and all-important at the dinner. But even here
there is a dignity proper to Paterfamilias, which, while it
should avoid stateliness, should scarcely descend to hilarity. He must not be a loud laugher or an inveterate
talker. He is seen in his most trying light in his conduct to the young. While we excuse his antique fashion,
which rather becomes him, and would laugh to see him in
the latest mode of the day, while we are pleased with his
old-fashioned courtesy, and would not have him talk slang
or lounge on the sofa, we expect from him some consideration for the changes that have taken place since he

courted his worthy spouse. Paterfamilias is too apt to insist that the manners and fashions of his spring were better than those of his winter are. He should be smiling to young women, and even a little gallant, and he should rejoice in their youthful mirth. But too often he is tempted to set down his younger brethren, too often he is a damper, and wished away. The dignity of Paterfamilias should never interfere with the ease, though it may well check the impudence of youth.

The Matron is tender to her own. How much I wish she was as tender to the pride of others. But one hen will always kill another's chickens if she has the opportunity, and Mrs. Jones will always pick to pieces Mrs. Brown's daughters. The Matron has many more social duties than Paterfamailias. It is she who arranges everything; who selects the guests; who, with her daughter's pen, invites them; who receives their visits; who looks after their comforts; who, by her active attentions, keeps up the circulation in evening parties; who orders dinner, and distributes the guests at it; who introduces partners at balls with her daughter's assistance; who engages the chaperons; who herself must go, willing or not, to look after her Ada and her Edith at the ball, and sit unmurmuring to the end of the dance. But she is well repaid by their pleasure, and when Ada talks of the Captain's attention, and Edith tells her what the curate whispered, she is perfectly happy. The matron without children is a woman out of her sphere, and until her children are grown up, she is a young married woman, and not a matron. It is only when Ada "comes out" that her office commences. She must then in society be an appendage to her daughter, and forget herself. But in the evening

party and the dinner-party she takes a higher place, and
in fact the highest, and whether as guest or host, it is to
her that the most respect is shown; she has a right to it,
and it is her duty to keep it up. Still the matron appears
more in her relation to her children than any other position, and in this her place in society is one that demands
care. Great as her pride may be in her family, she has
no right to be continually asserting their superiority to all
other young people. This is particularly remarkable in
her treatment of her grown-up sons; and a mother should
remember that when fully fledged, the young birds can
take care of themselves. She has no right to tie them to
her apron-string, and her fondness becomes foolish when
she fears that poor Charles will catch cold at eight-and-
twenty, or shrieks after James, because he will stroll
away to his club. But when she assumes the dress and
airs of youth, she becomes ridiculous. When once she
has daughters presentable, she must forget to shine herself; she should never, even if a widow, risk being her
daughter's rival, and her conduct to young men must be
that of a mother, rather than of a friend.

It is very different in France, where the married woman
is *par excellence* the woman of society, no matter what
her age. But in England, the bearing of the married
woman with grown-up children must be the calm dignity
and affability of the matron. The French have a proverb, " *Faire la cour à la mère pour avoir la fille ;*" and
I should strongly recommend the young man who wishes
to succeed with a damsel, to show particular attentions to
her mamma. A mother indeed does not expect you to
leave her daughter's side in order to talk to her; but be
sure that such an act gains you much more good will than

all the pretty speeches you could have made in that time
to the daughter. And it is only kind too. As I have
said, the mother's and chaperon's position is secondary
when the daughter or *protégée* is present, at least in England; but a good-natured man will take care that she does
not feel it to be so. A good girl is always pleased to see
proper respect and attention shown to her mother; and
when at breakfast the next morning, mamma says, " My
dear, I like Mr. Jones very much; he is a well-bred and
agreeable young man; I recommend you to cultivate
him." And when Arabella exclaims, " Oh, mamma, the
idea! Mr. Jones indeed!" you may be sure the maternal
praise is not lost upon her, and the idea is precisely one
that she will allow to return to her mind. One of the
most fattening dishes on which Master Cupid feeds, is that
same praise bestowed by others. But whether you have
an eye to Arabella or not, the chaperon ought not to be
neglected.

Now, what part young Benedict shall take in society
depends on his young wife. If she be wise, she will not
fret when he dances with pretty girls, and if he be kind
he will not let the dance lead him into a flirtation. But
Benedict may go everywhere, and need not sigh over the
days of his celibacy. Only he must remember, that while
he has gained some privileges, he has lost others. In the
meetings of the young, for instance, he is less wanted than
Cœlebs, while, since he cannot be invited without his wife,
he can no longer expect to fill the odd seat at dinner. On
the other hand, he takes precedence of the bachelor, and
is naturally a man of more weight, so that when he has
passed his head under the yoke, he must be calmer, more
sober, less frivolous, though not less lively than he was in

5

the old "chambers" days. A great deal is forgiven to
Cœlebs on account of his position. If he talks nonsense
occasionally, it is his high spirits; if he dances incessant-
ly the whole evening, it is that he may please "those
dear girls;" if he dresses *au point de vice* now and then,
he is Claudio in love, lying sleepless for the night, "carving out a new doublet;" if he hurries to the drawing-
room after dinner, or is marked in his attention to ladies,
he is only on his promotion; and if he has a few fast
lounging habits, "it is all very well for the boys," says
Paterfamilias, and in short, "a young fellow like that"
may do a thousand things that Benedict the married man
must abstain from. Greater than any change, however,
is that of his relations to his own sex. Some married
men throw all their bachelor friends overboard, when they
take that fair cargo for which they have been sighing so
long; but I would not be one of such a man's friends.
At the same time, I must expect to see less of Benedict
than before. "Adieu the *petit souper*," he murmurs,
"the flying corks, the chorused song, the trips to Rich-
mond and Greenwich, the high dog-cart, and the seat on
the box of my friend's drag!" Adieu the fragrant weed,
the cracking hunting-whip, the merry bachelor-dinner,
and the late hours! Shall I sigh over them? No. indeed! Mrs. Jones is not only an ample compensation for
such gaieties, but I am thankful to her for keeping me
from them. Why, that little baby-face of hers, that pouts
so prettily for a kiss when I come home, is worth a hundred dozens of champagnes, a thousand boxes of Hudson's
best, and a score of the longest runs after reynard we
ever had." Yes, Benedict I envy thee, and if Beatrice
be wise, she will not draw the reins too tight all at once;

and whatever she may say to hunting, she will see no
harm in a mild havana and a couple of bachelor friends
to dinner now and then. But Benedict has not only
changed his manner and his habits, he has got new duties,
and where his wife goes he may go, and ought to go.
He can no longer claim exemption from solemn dinners,
from weary muffin-worries, and witless tea-parties. On
the other hand, he will never be made use of, and his
wife will furnish a ready excuse for refusing invitations
which he had better not accept. Lastly, the young married man should never assume the gravity of Paterfamilias,
and though he is promoted above Coelebs, he will take
care not to snub him.

What a happy man is Coelebs! The more I sit in my
club-window the more I feel convinced of this. It is true
that I have never been married, and therefore know nothing
of the alternative, but will make you a little confession,
priestly reader—I have been once or twice *very near it*.
Free from incumbrance. Coelebs is as irresponsible as a
butterfly; he can choose his own society, go anywhere,
do anything, be early or late, gay or retired, mingle with
men or with ladies, smoke or not, wear a beard or cut it
off, and, if he likes, part his hair down in the middle.
What a happy man is Coelebs! free and independent as he
is, he is as much courted as a voter at an election; he is
for ever being bribed by mammas and feasted by papas;
nothing is complete without him; he is the wit at the dinner, the "life" of the tea-fight, an absolute necessity in
the ball-room, a *sine quâ non* at f te and pic nic, and welcome everywhere. Indeed, I don't know what society can
do without him. The men want him for their parties, the
ladies, I suppose I must not say, "still more" for theirs.

The old like him because he is young, the young like him
because he is not old; and in short he is as much a necessity as the refreshments, and must be procured somehow
or other. Then, too, if he does not care for these things
he can come and sit here in the club-window; or he can
travel, which Benedict seldom can; or he can take an occupation or an art, while the married man has no choice,
and must work, if he work at all, to keep quiet the
mouths of those blessed cherubim in the perambulator.

But that which makes Cœlebs a happy man is, that he
can enjoy society so much. If it be the bachelor-party,
he is not there against his conscience with fear of a Cau-
dle lecture to spoil his digestion. If it is among ladies,
he has the spice of *galanterie* to curry his conversation
with, and as for dancing, he at least enjoys it as an introduction to flirtation. But perhaps his greatest privilege
is the power of falling in love, for as long as that power
lasts—which, heigh-ho! is not for ever—there is no innocent pleasure which is greater. But Cœlebs has not
always the privilege of falling out of love again, and if
the married man has a wife to look after his doings, the
bachelor is watched by chaperons, and suspected by papas.
Poor Cœlebs, do not leave the matter too late; do not say,
" Hang me in a bottle like a cat, and shoot at me," if ever
I lose my heart. Believe me, boy, the passion must be
enjoyed when young. When you come to my age, Cupid
won't waste an arrow on you, and if he did so, it would
only make you ridiculous. Yes, the young bachelor is a
happy man, but the old bachelor—let me stop, if I once
begin on that theme, I shall waste three quires of paper,
and tire you out. But if much is allowed to Cœlebs,

much is expected of him. He has not the substance of
Benedict to back him up, not the respectability of wedded
life, not the charms of his young wife to make amends
for his deficiencies. The young bachelor is more than any
man a subject for the laws of etiquette. Less than any
will he be pardoned for neglecting them. He has no excuse to offer for their non-observance. He must make
himself useful and agreeable, must have accomplishments
for the former, and talents for the latter, and is expected
to show attention and respect to both sexes and all ages.

Happier still is the young lady, for whom so many allowances are made, and who, in society, is supposed to do
nothing wrong. To her the ball is a real delight, and the
evening party much more amusing than to any one else.
On the other hand, she must not frequent dinner-parties
too much, particularly if she is very young, and in all
cases she must consider modesty the prettiest ornament she
can wear. She has many privileges, but must beware how
she takes advantage of them. To the old her manner must
always be respectful and even affectionate. If she lacks
beauty, she will not succeed without conversational powers; and if she has beauty, she will soon find that wit is
a powerful rival. With the two she may do what she
will; all men are her slaves. She must, however, have
a smile as well, for every person and every occasion.
Dignity she seldom needs, except to repel familiarity.
Without a good heart her mind and her face will only
draw envy and even dislike upon her. In England, the
young lady is queen; in France, the young married woman
takes her place; and though society can do without her,
there is, in my opinion, no more charming companion than

a young married woman. She has left off nonsense, and forgotten flirtation, and she has gained from the companionship of her husband a certain strength of mind, which, tempered by her modest dignity, enables her to broach almost any subject with a man. She is at home everywhere, may dance in the ball-room, and talk at the dinner table, and the respect due to her position enables her to be more free in her intercourse without fear of remark. In short, if a man wishes for sensible conversation, with gentleness and beauty to lend it a charm, he must look for it in young married women.

Of the elderly unmarried lady—for of course there is no such thing as an " old maid"—I decline, from a feeling of delicacy, to say anything.

I shall conclude this *pi`ce de résistance* with a few parting remarks on the art of making one's self agreeable. I take it that the first thing necessary is to be in good spirits, or at least in the humor for society. If you have any grief or care to oppress you, and have not the strength of will to throw it off. you do yourself an injustice by entering the society of those who meet for mutual entertainment. Nay, you do them too a wrong. for you risk becoming what is commonly known as a " damper." The next point is to remember that the mutual entertainment in society is obtained by conversation. For this you require temper, of which I have already spoken : confidence, of which I shall speak elsewhere ; and appropriateness, which has been treated under the head of ."Conversation." I have already said. that that man is the most agreeable to talk to, who thinks out of society as well as in it. It will be necessary to throw off all the marks and feelings of your profession and occupation, and surround yourself, so to speak, with a purely social atmosphere. You must remember that society requires equality, real or apparent and that all professional or official peculiarities militate against this appearance of equality. You must, in the same way, divest yourself of all feeling of superiority or inferiority in rank, birth, position, means, or even acquirements. You must enter the social ranks as a private. If you earn your laurels by being agreeable, you will, in time, get your commission. Having made this mental preparation, having confidence without pride, modesty without shyness, ease without insolence, and dignity without stiffness, you may enter the drawing-room, and see in what way you may best make yourself agreeable.

The spirit with which you must do so is one of general kindliness and self-sacrifice. You will not, therefore, select the person who has the most attractions for you, so much as any one whom you see neglected, or who, being not quite at his or her ease, requires to be talked into confidence. On the same principle, you will respect prejudices; you will take care to ascertain them, before coming, on subjects on which people feel strongly. Then you will not open a conversation with a young lady by abusing High or Low Church, nor with an elderly gentleman by an attack on Whig or Tory. You will not rail against babies to a married woman, nor sneer at modern literature to a man with a beard, for if he is not a Crimean officer, he is sure to be an author.

In like spirit you will discover and even anticipate the wants of others, particularly if you are a man. On first acquaintance you will treat every one with particular

respect and delicacy, not rushing at once into a familiar
joke, or roaring like a clown. Your manner will be calm—
because if you have no nerves, other people have them—
and your voice gentle and low. Oh ! commend me to an
agreeable voice, especially in a woman. It is worth any
amount of beauty. The tone, too, of your conversation
and style of your manner will vary with the occasion.
While it will be sensible and almost grave at table, it will
be merry and light at a pic-nic.

Your attention, again, must not be exclusive. However
little you may enjoy their society, you will be as attentive
to the old as to the young ; to the humble as to the grand ;
to the poor curate, for instance, as to the M. P. ; to the
elderly chaperon as to her fair young charge. In this
manner you not only evince your good-breeding, but often
do a real kindness in amusing those who might otherwise
be very dull. On some occasions, particularly when a
party is heavy and wants life, you will generalize the conversation, introducing a subject in which all can take an
interest, and turning to them all in general. On the other
hand, when, as in a small party, the conversation is by
necessity general, you will particularly avoid talking to
one person exclusively, or mentioning people, places, or
things, with which only one or two of them can be acquainted. For instance, if at a morning call there happen
to be two or three strangers at the same time, it is bad
taste to talk about Mr. this or Mr. that. It is far better
to have recourse to the newspapers, which every body is
supposed to have read, or to public affairs, in which everybody can take more or less interest.

But it is not in your words only that you may offend

against good taste. Your manners, your personal habits, your very look even may give offence. These, therefore, must not only be studied, but if you have the misfortune to be with people who are not accustomed to refined manners, and to find that insisting on a particular refinement would give offence, or cast an imputation on the rest, it is always better to waive a refinement than to hurt feelings, and it sometimes becomes more ill-bred to insist on one than to do without it. For instance, if your host and his guest dine without dinner napkins, it would be very bad taste to call for one, or if, as in Germany, there be no spoons for the salt, you must be content to use your knife or fork as the rest do. " To do in Rome as the Romans do," applies to every kind of society. At the same time, you can never be expected to commit a serious breach of manners because your neighbors do so. You can never be called on in America to spit about the room, simply because it is a national habit.

But what you should do, and what not, in particular cases, you will learn in the following chapters. I have only now to say, that if you wish to be agreeable, which is certainly a good and religious desire, you must both study how to be so, and take the trouble to put your studies into constant practice. The fruit you will soon reap. You will be generally liked and loved. The gratitude of those to whom you have devoted yourself will be shown in speaking well of you; you will become a desirable addition to every party, and whatever your birth, fortune, or position, people will say of you, " He is a most agreeable and well-bred man," and be glad to introduce you to good society. But you will reap a yet better reward. You will

5*

have in yourself the satisfaction of having taken trouble
and made sacrifices in order to give pleasure and happiness
for the time to others.   How do you know what grief or
care you may not obliterate, what humiliation you may
not alter to confidence, what anxiety you may not soften,
what—last, but really not least—what intense dullness
you may not enliven ?   If this work assist you in becoming an agreeable member of good society, I shall rejoice
at the labor it has given me.

PART I.—THE INDIVIDUAL.

CHAPTER I.

INSIDE THE DRESSING-ROOM.

THERE are several passages in Holy Writ which have been shamefully, I may almost say, ludicrously misapplied. Thus when we want a scriptural authority for making as much money as possible in an honest way, we quote St. Paul, "Not slothful in business," forgetting that the word "business" had once a far wider meaning, and that the Greek, for which it is placed, means really "zeal," that is, in God's work. But the most impudent appropriation is that of cleanliness being next to godliness, and the apostle is made to affirm that if you cannot be religious, you should at least wear a clean shirt. Of course, a reference to the Greek would show in a moment that purity of mind and heart are meant, and that "cleanliness" was once the proper English for "purity."

Though we have no right to claim scriptural authority for soap and water, we cannot agree with Thomas of Ely, who tells us that Queen Ethelreda was so clean of heart as to need no washing of the body; nor can we believe that the loftiness of Lady Mary Wortley Montague's sentiments at all replaced the brush and comb, towel and ba-

sin, to which the liveliest woman of her day had such a
strange aversion.   It was she who, when some one said to
her at the opera, " How dirty your hands are, my lady!"
she replied with *naïve* indifference, " What would you
say if you saw my feet?"

Genius, love, and fanaticism, seem partial to dirt.
Every one knows what a German philosopher looks like,
and Werther showed his misery by wearing the same coat
and appendices for a whole year.   As to the saints, they
were proud of their unchanged flannel, and the monk was
never made late for matins by the intricacy of his toilet.
St. Simeon of the Pillar is an instance of the common
opinion of his day, that far from cleanliness being next
to godliness, the nearest road to heaven is a remarkably
dirty one.   Perhaps, however, he trusted to the rain to
cleanse him, and he was certainly a user of the shower-
bath, which cannot be said of many a fine gentleman.
Religion, however, is not always accompanied with neglect
of the person.   The Brahman bathes twice a day, and
rinses his mouth seven times the first thing in the morning.   It is strange that Manu, while enumerating the
pollutions of this world, should have made the exception
of a woman's mouth, which he tells us is always clean.
Probably the worthy old Hindu was partial to osculation,
but it is certain that there can be no Billingsgate in India.

In the beginning of the present century, it was thought
proper for a gentleman to change his under garment three
times a day, and the washing bill of a beau comprised
seventy shirts, thirty cravats, and pocket-handkerchiefs
à discrétion.   What would Brummell say to a college chum
of mine who made a tour through Wales with but one
flannel shirt in his knapsack?   The former's maxim was,

" linen of the finest quality, plenty of it, and country washing." Fine linen has always been held in esteem, but it did not save Dives.

Cleanliness is a duty to one's self for the sake of health, and to one's neighbor for the sake of agreeableness. Dirtiness is decidedly unpleasant to more than one of the senses, and a man who thus offends his neighbor is not free from guilt, though he may go unpunished. But if these reasons were not sufficient, there is another far stronger than both. St. Simeon Stylites may have preserved a pure mind in spite of an absence of ablutions, but we must not lose sight of the influence which the body has over the soul, an influence, alas, for man! sometimes far too great. We are convinced that bad personal habits have their effect on the character, and that a man who neglects his body, which he loves by instinct, will neglect far more his soul, which he loves only by command.

There is no excuse for Brummell's taking more than two hours to dress. It was in his case mere vanity, and he was—and was content to be—one of the veriest showthings in the world, as useless as the table ornaments on which he wasted the money he was not ashamed to take from his friends. On the other hand, when a young lady assures me that she can dress in ten minutes, I feel confident that the most important part of the toilet must be neglected. The morning toilet means more than a mere putting on of clothes, whatever policemen and French *concierges* may think.

The first thing to be attended to after rising is the BATH. The vessel which is dignified, like a certain part of lady's dress, with a royal Order, is one on which folios might

be written. It has given a name to two towns—Bath and
Baden—renowned for their toilets, and it is all that is left
in three continents of Roman glory. It is a club-room in
Germany and the East, and was an arena in Greece and
Rome. It was in a bath that the greatest destroyer of
life had his own destroyed, when he had bathed all France
in blood. But Clarence, I am convinced, has been much
maligned. He has been called a drunkard, and people
shudder at his choosing that death in which he could not
but die in sin ; but for my part, so far as the Malmsey is
concerned, I am inclined to think that he only showed
himself a gentleman to the last. He was determined to
die clean, and he knew, like the Parisian ladies—which
we should perhaps spell *laïdes*—who sacrifice a dozen of
champagne to their morning ablutions, that wine has a
peculiarly softening effect upon the skin. Besides Champagne, the exquisites of Paris use milk,* which is supposed to lend whiteness to the skin. The expense of this
luxury is considerably diminished by an arrangment with
the milkman, who repurchases the liquid after use. I
need scarcely add, that in Paris I learned to abjure *café
au lait*, and to drink my tea simple.

The bath deserves an Order, and its celebrity. It is of
all institutions the most unexceptionable. Man is an amphibious animal, and ought to pass some small portion of
each day in the water. In fact, a large, if not the larger
proportion of diseases arises from leaving the pores of
the skin closed, whether with natural exudation or matter from without, *alias* dirt. It is quite a mistake to

---

*The late Duke of Queensbury had his milk-bath every day. It is
supposed to nourish as well as whiten and soften the skin.

suppose, and the idea must at once be done away with, that one is to wash because one is dirty. We wash because we wear clothes; in other words, because we are obliged to remove artificially what would otherwise escape by evaporation. We wash again, because we are never in a state of perfect health, although with care we might be so. Were our bodies in perfect order—as the Swedenborgians inform us that those of the angels are—we should never need washing, and the bath would chill rather than refresh us, so that, perhaps, man is by necessity and degradation—not by destination—an amphibious creature.

However this may be, we must not suppose, because a limb looks clean, that it does not need washing, and however white the skin may appear, we should use the bath once a day at least, and in summer, if convenient, twice.

The question now arises, What kind of a bath is best? and it must be answered by referring to the person's constitution. If this is weak and poor, the bath should be strengthening; but at the same time it must be remembered, that while simple water cleanses, thicker fluids are apt rather to encumber the skin, so that a tonic bath is not always a good one. This is the case with the champagne, milk, mud, snake, and other baths, the value of which entirely depends on the peculiar state of health of the patient, so that one person is cured, and another killed by them. The same is to be said of sea-bathing, and the common bath even must be used with reference to one's condition.

The most cleansing bath is a warm one from 96° to 100°, into which the whole body is immersed. If cleansing alone be the aim, the hotter the water the better, up to 108°. It expands the pores, dives well into them, and increases the circulation for the time being. But since it is an unnatural agent, it exhausts the physical powers, and leaves us prostrate. For health, therefore, it should be sparingly indulged in, except in persons of rapid and heated circulation. Even with such, it should be used with discretion, and the time of remaining in the bath should never exceed a few minutes.

The cold bath of from 60° to 70°, on the other hand, cleanses less, but invigorates more. It should therefore be avoided by persons of full temperament, and becomes really dangerous after eating, or even after a long rest following a heavy meal. If you have supped largely over night, or been foolish, perhaps I may say wrong enough, to drink more than your usual quantity of stimulating liquids, you should content yourself with passing a wet sponge over the body.

A tepid bath, varying from 85° to 95°, is perhaps the safest of all, but we must not lose sight of health in the desire for comfort. The most healthy, and one of the handsomest men I ever saw, and one who at sixty had not a single grey hair, was a German, whose diet being moderate, used to bathe in running water at all seasons, breaking the ice in winter for his plunge. Of the shower bath, I will say nothing, because I feel, that to recommend it for general use, is dangerous, while for such a work as this, which does not take health as its main subject, it would be out of place to go into the special cases.

The best bath for general purposes, and one which can do little harm, and almost always some good, is a sponge bath. It should consist of a large flat metal basin, some four feet in diameter, filled with cold water. Such a vessel may be bought for about fifteen shillings. A large

coarse sponge—the coarser the better—will cost another
five or seven shillings, and a few Turkish towels, complete the " properties." The water should be plentiful
and fresh, that is, brought up a little while before the
bath is to be used; not placed over night in the bed-room.
Let us wash and be merry, for we know not how soon the
supply of that precious article which here costs nothing
may be cut off. In many continental towns they buy
their water, and on a protracted sea voyage the ration is
often reduced to half a pint a day *for all purposes*, so
that a pint per diem is considered luxurious. Sea-water,
we may here observe, does not cleanse and a sensible man
who bathes in the sea will take a bath of pure water immediately after it. This practice is shamefully neglected,
and I am inclined to think, that in many cases a sea-bath
will do more harm than good without it, but if followed
by a fresh bath, cannot but be advantageous.

Taking the sponge bath as the best for ordinary purposes, we must point out some rules in its use. The
sponge being nearly a foot in length, and six inches broad,
must be allowed to fill completely with water, and the
part of the body which should be first attacked is the
stomach. It is there that the most heat has collected
during the night, and the application of cold water quick-
ens the circulation at once, and sends the blood which has
been employed in digestion round the whole body. The
head should next be soused, unless the person be of full
habit, when the head should be attacked before the feet
touch the cold water at all. Some persons use a small
hand shower bath, which is less powerful than the common shower bath, and does almost as much good. The
use of soap in the morning bath is an open question. I

confess a preference for a rough towel or a hair glove
Brummell patronized the latter, and applied it for nearly
a quarter of an hour every morning.

The ancients followed up the bath by anointing the
body, and athletic exercises.   The former is a mistake;
the latter an excellent practice shamefully neglected in
the present day.   It would conduce much to health and
strength if every morning toilet comprised the vigorous
use of the dumb-bells, or, still better, the exercise of the
arms without them.   The best plan of all is, to choose
some object in your bedroom on which to vent your hatred,
and box at it violently for some ten minutes, till the
perspiration covers you.   The sponge must then be again
applied to the whole body.   It is very desirable to remain
without clothing as long as possible, and I should therefore
recommend that every part of the toilet which can conveniently be performed without dressing, should be so.

The next duty, then, must be to clean the TEETH.
Dentists are modern inquisitors, but their torture-rooms
are meant only for the foolish.   Everybody is born with
good teeth, and everybody might keep them good by a
proper diet, and the avoidance of sweets and smoking.
Of the two the former are perhaps the more dangerous.
Nothing ruins the teeth so soon as sugar in one's tea, and
highly sweetened tarts and puddings, and as it is *le pre-
mier pas qui coûte*, these should be particularly avoided in
childhood.   When the teeth attain their full growth and
strength it takes much more to destroy either their enamel or their substance.

It is upon the teeth that the effects of excess are first
seen, and it is upon the teeth that the odor of the breath
depends.   What is more repulsive than a woman's smile

discovering a row of black teeth, unless it be the rank smell of the breath? Both involve an offence of your neighbor's most delicate senses, and neither can therefore be pardoned. If I may not say that it is a Christian duty to keep your teeth clean, I may at least remind you that you cannot be thoroughly agreeable without doing so. Ladies particularly must remember that men love with their eyes, and perhaps I may add with their noses, and that these details do not escape them. In fact, there are few details in women that do escape their admirers, and if Brummell broke off his engagement because the young lady ate cabbages, there are numbers of men in the present day who would be disgusted by the absence of refinement in such small matters as the teeth. Let words be what they may, if they come with an impure odor, they cannot please. The butterfly loves the scent of the rose more than its honey.

The beau just mentioned used a red root, which is of oriental origin. It is not so penetrating as a good hard tooth-brush, with a lather of saponaceous tooth-powder upon it. The Hindus, who have particularly white teeth, use sticks of different woods according to their caste; but perhaps a preparation of soap is the best thing that can be employed. The teeth should be well rubbed inside as well as outside, and the back teeth even more than the front. The mouth should then be rinsed, if not seven times, according to the Hindu legislator, at least several times, with fresh cold water. This same process should be repeated several times a day, since eating, smoking, and so forth, naturally render the teeth and mouth dirty more or less, and nothing can be so offensive, particularly to ladies, whose sense of smell seems to be keener than that of the other sex, and who can detect at your first approach whether you have been drinking or smoking. But if only for your own comfort, you should brush your teeth both morning and evening, which is quite requisite for the preservation of their soundness and color; while if you are to mingle with others, they should be brushed, or at least the mouth well rinsed after every meal, still more after smoking, or drinking wine, beer or spirits. No amount of general attractiveness can compensate for an offensive odor in the breath; and none of the senses is so fine a gentleman, none so unforgiving if offended, as that of smell. The following reproof was well-merited, if not polite. " I have had the wind in my teeth all the way," said an Irishman, after a brisk walk on a breezy morning, before which he had been indulging his propensity to onions. " Well, sir," replied his friend, who at once perceived how he had breakfasted, " I must say that the wind had the worst of it."

The custom of allowing the nails to grow as a proof of freedom from the necessity of working, which is most absurdly identified with gentility, is not peculiar to China. In some parts of Italy the nails of the left hand are never cut till they begin to break, and a Lombard of my acquaintance once presented me a huge nail which he had just cut, and which I must do him the justice to say was perfectly white. I admired it, and threw it away. " What!" cried he indignantly, " is that the way you receive the greatest proof of friendship which a man can give you?" and he then explained to me that in his native province the nail held the same place as a lock of hair with us. I really doubt which has the preference, and whether a Lothario's desk filled with little oily packets of different colored hair is at all more romantic than a box of beloved finger nails. Certainly there is beauty in a long silken tress, the golden tinge reminding us of the fair head of some lost child so like its mother's, or in the rich dark curl that, in the boldest hour of love, we raped from her head, who was then so confidently ours, and now—What is she now? But even this fancy can take a very disagreeable form, and what can we say of an ardent hopeless lover whom I once knew, and who I was assured gave a guinea to a lady's maid for the stray hairs left in her mistress' comb!

But though we may not be cultivating our nails either to tear a rival's face with, or to confer with a majestic condescension on some importunate admirer, we are not absolved from paying strict attention to their condition, and that both as regards cleaning and cutting. The former is best done with a liberal supply of soap on a small nail-brush, which should be used before every meal, if you would not injure your neighbor's appetite. While the hand is still moist, the point of a small pen-knife or pair of stumpy nail-scissors should be passed under the nails so as to remove every vestige of dirt; the skin should be pushed down with a towel, that the white half-moon may be seen, and the finer skin removed with the knife or scissors. Occasionally the edges of the nails should be filed, and the hard skin which forms round the corners of them cut away The important point in cutting the nails is to preserve the beauty of their shape. That beauty even in details is worth preserving I have already remarked, and we may study it as much in paring our nails, as in the grace of our attitudes, or any other point. The shape, then, of the nail should approach as nearly as pos-

sible to the oblong. The oriental ladies know this and
allow the nail to grow to an enormous length, and bend
down towards the finger. But then they cultivate beauty
in every detail, for, poor things, they have none but personal attractions to depend on ; and they give to the pink
nail a peculiar lustre by the little speck of purple henna,
just as Parisian beauties pass a line of blue paint under
the lower eyelash ; perhaps, too, they keep their fingers
thus well armed to protect themselves from angry pashas,
or even—but let us hope not—to spoil the beauty of some
more favored houri. However this may be, the length of
the nail is an open question. Let it be often cut, but always long, in my opinion. Above all, let it be well cut,
and *never* bitten. Had Brummell broken off his engagement because the young lady bit her nails, I think I could
not have blamed him.

Perhaps you tell me these are childish details. Details,
yes, but not childish. The attention to details is the true
sign of a great mind, and he who can in necessity consider
the smallest, is the same man who can compass the largest
subjects. Is not life made up of details ? Must not the
artist who has conceived a picture, descend from the dream
of his mind to mix colors on a palette? Must not the
great commander who is bowling down nations and setting
up monarchies care for the health and comfort, the bread
and beef of each individual soldier ? I have often seen a
great poet, whom I knew personally, counting on his
fingers the feet of his verses, and fretting with anything
but poetic language, because he could not get his sense
into as many syllables. What if his nails were dirty ?
Let genius talk of abstract beauty, and philosophers dog-
matize on order. If they do not keep their nails clean, I

shall call them both charlatans. The man who really loves beauty will cultivate it in everything around him. The man who upholds order is not conscientious if he cannot observe it in his nails. The great mind can afford to descend to details; it is only the weak mind that fears to be narrowed by them. When Napoleon was at Munich he declined the grand four-poster of the Witelsbach family, and slept, as usual in his little camp-bed. The power to be little is a proof of greatness.

For the hands, ears, and neck we want something more than the bath, and as these parts are exposed and really lodge fugitive pollutions, we cannot use too much soap, or give too much trouble to their complete purification. Nothing is lovelier than a woman's small white shell-like ear; few things reconcile us better to earth than the cold hand and warm heart of a friend; but to complete the charm, the hand should be both clean and soft. Warm water, a liberal use of the nail-brush, and no stint of soap, produce this amenity far more effectually than honey, cold cream, and almond paste. Of wearing gloves I shall speak elsewhere, but for weak people who are troubled with chilblains, they are indispensable all the year round. I will add a good prescription for the cure of chilblains, which are both a disfigurement, and one of the *petites mis'res* of human life.

" Roll the fingers in linen bandages, sew them up well, and dip them twice or thrice a day in a mixture, consisting of half a fluid ounce of tincture of capsicum, and a fluid ounce of tincture of opium."

The person who invented razors libelled Nature, and added a fresh misery to the days of man. " Ah !" said Diogenes, who would never consent to be shaved, " would

you insinuate that Nature had done better to make you a
woman than a man?" As for barbers, they have always
been gossips and mischief-makers, and Arkwright, who
invented spinning by rollers, scarcely redeemed his trade
from universal dishonor. They have been the evil spirits
of great men too, whom they shaved and bearded in their
private closets. It was a barber who helped the late
King of Oude to ruin the country he governed; and it
was a barber who, at the beginning of the present century, was the bottle-imp of a Bishop of Hereford. Who in
fact can respect a man whose sole office is to deprive his
sex of their distinctive feature?

It is said that Alexander the Great introduced shaving,
to prevent his soldiers being caught by the beard by their
enemies, but the conqueror of Asia must be absolved of
priority in this iniquitous custom, which he probably
found prevalent in the countries he invaded. At any
rate it would appear that the Budhist priests of India
were ashamed of their locks at least a century before, and
this reminds me that shaving and fanaticism have always
gone together. The custom of the clergy wearing a
womanish face is purely Romanist, and I rejoice to see
that many a good preacher in the present day is not
afraid to follow Cranmer and other fathers of our Church
in wearing a goodly beard. The Romish priests were
first ordered to shave when transubstantiation was established, from a fear that the beard might fall into the cup.
It is clear that a Protestant chin ought to be well covered

Whatever be said of the clergy, the custom of shaving
came to this country like many other ugly personal habits,
with the foreign monarchs. As long as we had Planta-
genets, Tudors, and Stuarts on the throne, we were men

as to the outward form. William of Orange was ashamed of that very appendage which it is a disgrace to a
Mussulman to be without. Peter the Great had already
proved that barber and barbarian are derived from the
same root, by laying a tax on all capillary ornaments.

In England there has always been a great distinction
between civil and military men, and this is the only country in the world where the latter have been held in such
dislike, as to compel them to abandon their uniform in
everyday life. Perhaps it was on this account that civilians in general adopted the *coutumes* of the learned
professions, lest they should be thought to belong to that
of the sword. The beard and the rapier went out together at the beginning of the last century. In the present day many a young shop-boy joins " the moustache
movement" solely with a hope of being mistaken for a
" captain."

Whatever *Punch* may say, the moustache and beard
movement is one in the right direction, proving that men
are beginning to appreciate beauty and to acknowledge
that Nature is the best valet. But it is very amusing to
hear men excusing their vanity on the plea of health, and
find them indulging in the hideous " Newgate frill" as a
kind of compromise between the beard and the razor.
There was a time when it was thought a presumption and
vanity to wear one's own hair instead of the frightful
elaborations of the wig-makers, and the false curls which
Sir Godfrey Kneller did his best to make graceful on
canvas. Who knows that at some future age some *Punch*
of the twenty-first century may not ridicule the wearing
of one's own teeth instead of the dentist's? At any rate
Nature knows best, and no man need be ashamed of show-

ing his manhood in the hair of his face. Of razors and
shaving therefore I shall only speak from necessity, because, until everybody is sensible on this point, they will
still be used.

Napoleon shaved himself. "A born king," said he,
"has another to shave him. A made king can use his
own razor." But the war he made on his chin was very
different to that he made on foreign potentates. He took
a very long time to effect it, talking between whiles to his
hangers-on. The great man, however, was right, and
every sensible man will shave himself, if only as an exercise of character, for a man should learn to live in every
detail without assistance. Moreover, in most cases we
shave ourselves better than barbers can do. If we shave
at all, we should do it thoroughly, and every morning.
nothing, except a frown and a hay-fever, makes the face
look so unlovely as a chin covered with short stubble.
The chief requirements are hot water, a large soft brush
of badger hair, a good razor, soft soap that will not dry
rapidly, and a steady hand. Cheap razors are a fallacy.
They soon lose their edge, and no amount of stropping
will restore it. A good razor needs no strop. If you
can afford it, you should have a case of seven razors, one
for each day of the week, so that no one shall be too much
used. There are now much used packets of papers of a
certain kind on which to wipe the razor, and which keep
its edge keen, and are a substitute for the strop.

I may here remark, that the use of violet-powder after
shaving, now very common among well-dressed men, is
one that should be avoided. In the first place, it is almost always visible, and gives an unnatural look to the
face. I know a young lady, who, being afflicted with a

redness in a feature above the chin, is in the habit of powdering it. For a long time I thought her charming, but since I made the discovery I can never look at her without a painful association with the pepper-castor. Violet-powder also makes the skin rough, and enlarges the pores of it sooner or later.

Beards, moustaches, and whiskers, have always been most important additions to the face. Italian conspirators are known by the cut of those they wear; and it is not long since an Englishman with a beard was set-down as an artist or a philosopher. In the present day literary men are much given to their growth, and in that respect show at once their taste and their vanity. Let no man be ashamed of his beard, if it be well kept and not fantastically cut. The moustache should be kept within limits. The Hungarians wear it so long that they can tie the ends round their heads. The style of the beard should be adopted to suit the face. A broad face should wear a large full one; a long face is improved by a sharp-pointed one. Taylor, the water poet, wrote verses on the various styles, and they are almost numberless. The chief point is to keep the beard well-combed and in neat trim.

As to whiskers, it is not every man who can achieve a pair of full length. There is certainly a great vanity about them, but it may be generally said that foppishness should be avoided in this as in most other points. Above all, the whiskers should never be curled, nor pulled out to an absurd length. Still worse is it to cut them close with the scissors. The moustache should be neat and not too large, and such fopperies as curling the points thereof, or twisting them up to the fineness of needles—though patronized by the Emperor of the French—are decidedly a proof of vanity. . If a man wear the hair on his face which nature has given him, in the manner that nature distributes it, keeps it clean, and prevents its overgrowth, he cannot do wrong. If, on the other hand, he applies to Marie Coupellé, and other advertisers, because he believes that "those dear silky whiskers" will find favor in the eyes of the fair, he will, if unsuccessful, waste much money—if successful, incur the risk of appearing ridiculous. All extravagancies are vulgar, because they are evidence of a pretence to being better than you are; but a single extravagance unsupported is perhaps worse than a number together, which have at least the merit of consistency. If you copy puppies in the half-yard of whisker, you should have their dress and their manner too, if you would not appear doubly absurd.

The same remarks apply to the arrangment of the hair in men, which should be as simple and as natural as possible, but at the same time a little may be granted to beauty and the requirements of the face. For my part I can see nothing unmanly in wearing long hair, though undoubtedly it is inconvenient and a temptation to vanity, while its arrangement would demand an amount of time and attention which is unworthy of a man. But every nation and every age has had a different custom in this respect, and to this day even in Europe the hair is sometimes worn long. The German student is particularly partial to hyacinthine locks curling over a black velvet coat; and the peasant of Brittany looks very handsome, if not always clean, with his love-locks hanging straight down under a broad cavalier hat. Religion has generally taken up the matter severely. The old fathers preached and railed against wigs, the Calvinists raised an insurrection in Bordeaux on the same account, and English Roundheads consigned to an unmentionable place every man who allowed his hair to grow according to nature. The Romans condemned tresses as unmanly, and in France in the middle ages the privilege to wear them was confined to royalty Our modern custom was a revival of the French revolution, so that in this respect we are now republican as well as puritanical.

If we conform to fashion we should at least make the best of it, and since the main advantage of short hair is its neatness, we should take care to keep ours neat. This should be done first by frequent visits to the barber, for if the hair is to be short at all it should be very short, and nothing looks more untidy than long, stiff, uncurled masses sticking out over the ears. If it curls naturally so much the better, but if not it will be easier to keep in order. The next point is to wash the head every morning, which, when once habitual, is a great preservative against cold. I never have more than one cold per annum, and I attribute this to my use of the morning bath, and regular washing of my head. A pair of large brushes, hard or soft, as your case requires, should be used, not to hammer the head with, but to pass up under the hair so as to reach the roots. As to pomatum, Macassar, and other inventions of the hairdresser, I have only to say that, if used at all, it should be in moderation, and never sufficiently to make their scent perceptible in company. Of course the rrangment will be a matter of individual taste, but as the middle of the hair is the natural place for a parting, it is rather a silly prejudice to think a man vain who parts his hair in the centre. He is less blamable than one who is too lazy to part it at all, and has always the appearance of having just got up.

Of wigs and false hair, the subject of satires and sermons since the days of the Roman emperors, I shall say nothing here except that they are a practical falsehood which may sometimes be necessary, but is rarely successful. For my part I prefer the snows of life's winter to the best made peruke, and even a bald head to an inferior wig.

When gentlemen wore armor, and disdained the use of their legs, an esquire was a necessity; and we can understand that, in the days of the Beaux, the word "gentleman" meant a man and his valet. I am glad to say that in the present day it only takes one man to make a gentleman, or, at most, a man and a ninth—that is, including the tailor. It is an excellent thing for the character to be neat and orderly, and, if a man neglects to be so in his room, he is open to the same temptation sooner or later in his person. A dressing-case is, therefore, a desideratum. A closet to hang up cloth clothes, which should never be folded, and a small dressing-room next to the bed-room, are not so easily attainable. But the man who throws his clothes about the room, a boot in one corner, a cravat in another, and his brushes anywhere, is not a man of good habits. The spirit of order should extend to everything about him.

CHAPTER II.

THE LADY'S TOILET.

IN no particular has the present generation become more fastidious than in what is requisite for the use of ladies in their own dressing-rooms. Essences, powders, pastes, washes for the hair, washes for the skin, recal the days of one's grandmother, when such appurtenances were thought essential and were essential : for our great-grandmothers were not rigid in points of personal cleanliness; and it is only uncleanliness that requires scents to conceal it, and applications to repair its ravages. Our great-grandmothers wore powder and pomatum, and had their hair dressed three times a week; going to bed in the cushioned structure, after suffering torture for some hours lest they should, in the weakness of human infirmity, lean back in their chairs. Our great-grandmothers, too, had their white kid gloves sewn to the bottom of each sleeve, lest they should incur the calamity of a sun-burnt arm. Our great-grandmothers were afraid of cold water, and delicately *wiped* their faces with the corner of a towel no larger than a pocket handkerchief. There were those amongst them who boasted that they had never washed their faces in their whole span of existence, lest it should spoil their complexions, but had only passed a cambric handkerchief over the delicate brow and cheeks, wetted with elderflower water or rose water. I believe the nearest ap-

proach to the ablution we now diurnally practise was the
bathing their lovely countenances in May-dew, esteemed
the finest thing in the morning for the skin by our belles
of the last century: so they turned out betimes in high-
heeled shoes and *négligés*, trotted down the old avenues
of many a patriarchal home to the meadow, and saturat-
ing their kerchiefs in May-dew, refreshed with it the cheeks
flushed over-night at quadrille or great cassino, and went
home contented that a conscientious duty had been performed!

Nor were they wrong. Some wise fairy of old must
have inspired the nymph whom she loved with the belief
in May dew; tradition handed down the counsel from one
generation to another, the fairy, or gnome, smiling all the
while as she saw the lovely procession of the squires' young
daughters steal out and bend down amid the butter-cups
and ladies'-smock in the meadow: she smiled, and, as she
smiled, wafted to them good health, good spirits, and their
type—bloom. She had induced them by a stratagem—
Heaven pity her pious fraud!—to take a preliminary step
to beauty and its preservation; she had beguiled them into
early rising.

For, gentle ladies, you may wash, may bathe your forms
and faces, curl your locks, and shake out your crinoline;
use every essence Atkinson has, wherewith to arrest the
attention of wistful passers-by; you may walk by the
hour, eat by rule, take beauty-sleep before midnight, yet,
if you are very long after the

" Sanguine sunrise with his meteor eyes"*

in coming out and abroad from your chambers, youth will

---

*·Shelley.

not stay with you out his time, but, like an ill-behaved apprentice, will break his indentures, and vow that he cannot abide with you. It is true that rules for habitual early rising cannot be laid down for every one, without especial reference to other habits; very early rising, after late parties, or great fatigue on the previous day, or extreme delicacy of the lungs or throat, might even be pernicious, and its use or abuse must be regulated by the physician. In those cases the advice that is now given is for persons in an ordinary condition of health. For them, and even with some exceptions for invalids, there can be no habit of the day or life so important, as far as good looks are concerned, as early rising.· All other animals whose health is of importance to man are forced to rise early. The horse, on whose good condition his beauty, and therefore his value depends, is exercised as early as possible. Our cattle on the uplands scent the morning breeze as it brings the odors of the woodbine; the little house-dog pants till he can rush forth from the pent-up heated chamber to the fresh lawn; and why is this obvious law of nature of so great importance to these objects of preference or of value? The morning air is more strengthening, has a great proportion of oxygen, be it replied, than any other breeze that refreshes us by day, or when "the pale purple even" warns us that our enjoyment of its delicious sensations are not devoid of danger. No one catches cold in the morning air, at least with the ordinary prudence of sufficient clothing. Fortified by sleep, the change of atmosphere is most salubrious. To the careless and happy, what can be more delightful than to feel all the freshness of nature soothing every sense, whilst the great world and its interests and troubles is silent and slumbers? And it is this fresh breeze, this emancipation from the pent-up chamber, this reviving influence, that combine to form a restorative, such as neither medicine nor regimen can offer; that preserves looks, appetite for food, and bloom and delicacy of complexion.

An aged clergyman who had known not one day's illness was asked his secret: "Dry feet and early rising," was his reply; "these are my only two precautions."

With regard then to what a French author calls "a whole Cyclopædia of narcotics," young women forget that there is no royal road to health and beauty. They must take the right path if they wish to reap the reward. No person in good health should remain in bed after seven o'clock, or half-past seven, in the spring and summer; that may, in the present century, when the daughters of England are reproached with self-indulgence, be termed early rising. She may then be down stairs at eight, and without taking a long and fatiguing walk, saunter in the garden a little; or, if in a large town, have time to practise, supposing that the opportunity of going out into the air is denied. By this means, that vigor which is the very soul of comeliness, the absence of hurry and the sense of self-reproach incurred by late rising, and the hunger felt for breakfast, will all conduce to arrest Time, as she hovers over his wholesale subjects, and to beguile him into sparing that process with his scythe by which he furrows the brow of the indolent with wrinkles, whilst he colors the poor victim, at the same time, with his own pet preparation of saffron.

Suppose then that this first and vital standing order for the toilet be stringent, and that refreshed, and therefore energetic, buoyant, and conscious of one duty being at least

performed, the lady leaves her bed and prepares to dress.
L. E. L. used to say, for she was no early riser, that " we
begin every day with a struggle and a sacrifice." But the
struggle is soon changed by habit into an eager desire to
get up; and the sacrifice, to the habitual early riser, is to
be in bed. She rises : if in summer, throws open the
window for a quarter of an hour, whilst the bath is being
prepared, then closes it again, until the ablutions are completed. The nature of these must be guided in a great
measure by the general health. Of all bracing processes,
to a sound constitution, that of the shower-bath is the
greatest. It should be used however only with the sanction of the physician. The nervous energy is invigorated
by it, the digestion, a great desideratum for the complexion,
is improved ; the balance of circulation between the viscera
and skin is maintained ; and taking cold, that enemy of
the graces, rheums, catarrhs, and sore throats are kept
off; swelling glands are prevented, and the whole powers
of the frame increase. But, since the reaction is not in
some delicate constitutions sufficient to make the use of
the shower-bath desirable, the hip-bath, half filled with
tepid water at first, and with cold afterwards, or the spong-
ing bath, are admirable modifications of the shower-bath.
Thus fortified, the lady who has courage to conquer a
shower-bath, or to plunge into a hip-bath, can face the
morning air, and go forth with the self-earned coat-of-
mail, as a defence against all that ugly family of catarrhal
affections.

We now come to the toilet-table. This, in a lady's as
well as in a gentleman's room, should be always neatly
set out, and every article placed where it can be most conveniently used. In former times, vast expense used to be

bestowed on china, and even on gold and silver toilet-
services; then came the war, and the national poverty,
and those luxurious appliances were let down, if not abandoned. We have now resumed them with a degree of expense that is hardly wise or consistent. The secrets of
the toilet were, indeed, no fancied mysteries in former
days. Until the first twenty years of this century had
passed away, many ladies of *bon ton* thought it necessary,
in order to complete their dress, to put a touch of rouge
on either cheek. The celebrated Mrs. Fitzherbert was
rouged to the very eyes; those beautiful deep blue eyes
of hers. The old Duchess of R— enamelled, and usually
fled from a room when the windows were opened, as the
compound, whatever formed of, was apt to dissolve and
run down the face. Queen Caroline (of Brunswick) was
rouged fearfully; her daughter, noble in form, fair but
pale in complexion, disdained the art. Whilst the rouged
ladies might have sung or said,

> " We are blushing roses,
>   Bending with our fulness,"

that gifted and lamented princess might have answered,

> " We are lilies fair,
>   The flower of virgin light,
>   Nature held us forth, and said,
>   Lo ! ' my thoughts of white.' " *

And it was certainly remarkable, that after the Princess
Charlotte's introduction at Court, rouge, which had been
the rule, became the exception, and that young people generally never used it.

---

* Hunt.

Still there were other means resorted to for attaining the whiteness of skin which medical men dread, but which is certainly a very striking and beautiful characteristic of an English woman. I once knew a lady who was bled from time to time to keep the marble-like whiteness of her complexion; others, to my knowledge, rub their faces with bread-crumbs as one should a drawing. But, worst of all, the use of pearl powder, or of violet powder, has been for the last half century prevalent.

Independent of all sorts of *art* being unpleasant, no mistake of the fair one is greater than this. She may powder, she may go forth with a notion that the pearly whiteness of her brow, her neck, will be deemed all her own; but there are lights in which the small deception will be visible, and the charm of all coloring is gone when it proves to be artificial. We tremble to think what is underneath.

There is another inconvenience attached to the use of pearl powder, its great unwholesomeness. It checks the natural relief of the skin, perspiration; and though it may not always injure the health, it dries up the cuticle, and invites as it were age to settle. Where pearl powder has been made an article of habitual use, wrinkles soon require additional layers to fill it up, just as worn out roads have ruts, and must be repaired; but the macadamising process cannot be applied to wrinkles.

Still more fatal is the use of cosmetics; its extravagance, in the first place, is an evil; but I treat not of the moral question, but of its physical effects. Some women spend as much on essences and sweet waters as would enable them to take a journey, and thus do more for their looks than all that a bureau full of cosmetics could insure.

Many an eruptive disease has arisen from the desire to make the skin clear ; above all, avoid specifics. Your friends are in the habit of saying, such a thing " is good for the complexion ;" but remember that complexion is the dial of constitution, and that no two constitutions are alike. What is salutary in one case, may produce serious mischief in another.

For instance, when abroad, a lady who had been very much sunburnt was told that cucumbers cut into slices and put into cream, produce a decoction that would take off the burning effects of the sun. It is, in fact, a remedy used by German ladies, who must however have skins differently constituted than ours to bear it. The lady used this very powerful specific, and her face was blistered. Nothing, indeed, but time and cold weather will take away the effects of the sun : butter-milk, from its gentle · acid, has some efficacy on certain skins, but it is a disagreeable remedy.

The softest possible water ought, however, to be resorted to in washing the face ; and rain-water, filtered, is incomparably the best. Great care should be taken not to check perspiration by washing when heated ; these are precautions consistent with nature, and therefore valuable. The water should be dashed freely over the face several times, and the process be pursued in the middle of the day, as well as in the morning and at dinner-time : it is true, the face may, without that, be *clean* all day, but it will not be *fresh*. The Turkish towels now used so much are excellent for wiping, as they do that important operation not only thoroughly, but without irritating the skin ; the body, on the other hand, should be dried with a coarse huckaback, an article unknown in France, but excellent for promoting quick circulation in the frame after bathing. To complete, then, the toilet so far as the person is con‐ cerned; with few or no cosmetics, with nothing but the use of soap (the old brown Windsor being still, in spite of all modern inventions, far the best for the skin,) to have the water brought in fresh in the morning, as that in the room is seldom, except in winter, really cool, these are the simple preservatives of the skin, which it is very easy to injure and irritate, and very difficult to restore to a healthy condition. It must, however, be remembered that a healthy condition of the skin depends far less on external than on internal causes; and that good health, maintained by early rising, and a simple, nutritive diet, is the great originator of a clear and blooming complexion. In cases of eruption, however, do nothing without good advice. Many an eruption which poisons the comfort even of the strongest-minded woman, has been fixed beyond cure by dabblings of Eau-de-Cologne on the face—thus exciting instead of allaying the fiery enemy—milk of roses, essences, and cosmetics, whose name is Legion. Such is the effect of desperation on the female mind, that it has been even tried whether raw veal cutlets being put on the face would not soften and improve the skin; an act of folly which can only be characterized as disgusting.

Banish, therefore, if free from any cutaneous disease, every essence, cosmetic, or sweet-water from your toilet; and remember that to keep the skin smooth and clean, all rubbing and touching should be avoided; fresh air, when the heat of the sun is not intense, and pure water, are the best and only cosmetics that can be used without pre‐ judice.

There are many alleviations to eruptive complaints;

among the best is a solution of sulphur; but even this should never be resorted to without advice, and in the proper proportions. In many cases, however, it almost immediately removes an eruption, by cooling the skin; hence it will be seen how very injurious are all essences with spirit in them, which have a tendency to heat and inflammation.

" Do you want luxuriant hair ?" is a question we see daily in the papers, answered, of course, by a specific. If possible, the skin of the head requires even more tenderness and cleanliness than any other portion of the body, and is very soon capable of being irritated into disease. In respect of this, as of the complexion, people err generally, from doing too much. In the first place, the most perfect cleanliness must be enjoined; formerly the use of a fine-tooth comb was considered essential, and abroad it is still resorted to, and is in some cases salutary. But, in general, to the *careful* brusher the comb is not essential. I say the careful brusher, for great harm is often done to the hairs by rude, sharp, irregular brushing. The hairs should be separated with a comb, so that the head and not the hairs be brushed. The brush should not be too hard; it may slightly redden the skin, but no more; the use of pomatum should be sparing, and confined to that of which the ingredients are known—marrow and bear's grease are the best, and the former is most easily obtained genuine. All scents are more or less injurious to the hair, and they should be used in the slightest possible proportion. To wash the roots of the hair from time to time with weak vinegar and water, or with a solution of ammonia, cleanses it effectually, whilst a yolk of an egg beaten up and mixed with warm water is excellent for the skin and hair;

but it is troublesome to wash out, and must be done by a careful maid. There is no risk, but great benefit, in washing even the "luxuriant hair" of a person in health, if done in warm weather, and well dried, or by a fire; and a small quantity of ammonia insures from catching cold. It is quite a mistake to suppose that washing the hair makes it coarse; it renders it glossy and flexible; the washing cools the head, the heat of which is the great source of baldness and grey hairs; it prevents all that smell from very thick hair which is detected in persons who trust to the brush only; lastly, it is one of the most refreshing personal operations, next to the bath, that can be devised.

A lady's hair should, in ordinary life, be dressed·twice a day, even if she does not vary the mode. To keep it cool and glossy, it requires being completely taken down in the middle of the day, or in the evening, according to the dinner-hours. The taste in dressing it in the morning should be simple, without pins, bows, or any foreign auxiliary to the best ornament of nature. I do not mean to deprecate the use of the pads, as they are called, or supports under the hair used at this time, because they supersede the necessity of frizzing, which is always a process most injurious to the hair; but I own I object much to the ends of black lace, bows of ribbon, &c., used by many young women in their morning coiffure: of course, for those past girlhood, and not old enough to wear caps, the case is different.

CHAPTER III.

DRESS.

"A STORY," says an eminent writer, "is never too old to tell, if it be made to sound new." If this be true, I may be excused for narrating the following veritable history:—In an Indian jungle there once resided a tawny jackal, a member, as all those animals are, of a jackal club which met at night in the said jungle. It was the custom for the different subscribers to separate early in the evening on predatory excursions, and on one occasion the individual in question having dined very sparingly that day on a leg of horse, ventured, in hopes of a supper, within the precincts of a neighboring town. It happened that while employed in the prowling distinctive of his kind, he fell into a sunken vat filled with indigo, and when he had contrived to struggle out again, discovered, by the light of the moon, that his coat had assumed a brilliant blue tinge. In vain he rolled himself on the grass, in vain rubbed his sides against the bushes of the jungle to which he speedily returned. The blue stuck to him, and so, with the acuteness for which jackals are renowned, he determined to "stick to" it. Shame indeed would have overcome him, ridicule have driven him to despair, when he rejoined his club, but for this resolution. That very morning he appeared among his kind, whisking his tail with glee, and holding his head erect. A titter, of course, welcomed him, and, before long, you

(138)

would have thought that every jackal present had been turned into a laughing hyæna. Our hero was nothing abashed. "Gentlemen," said he, in the dialect of Hindustani peculiar to his kind, "I have been to town, and bring you the last new fashion." The laughter changed to respectful admiration. One by one the members of the club stole up to him and inquired where he had met with the coloring, just as George IV. asked Brummell what tailor had made *that* coat. The address was imparted, and if on the following evening not all of the prowling beasts appeared in a blue coat, it was only because three of them had been drowned in the attempt to procure it.

The fable, which is a real Sanskrit one, will at once remind us of one concerning that sharp-nosed quadruped which farmers denounce, and squires combine to run to death. But it has a moral as well as a satirical bearing, and we believe that this moral has not been done justice to. Fashion is called a despot; but if men, like the jackals and foxes, are willing, nay, eager to be its slaves, we cannot, and ought not, to upbraid fashion. Its crowning is, in short, nothing more than the confession that vanity makes of its own weakness. We must be vain; we *are* weak; all we ask is to be guided in our vanity.

The worst of it is, that the man who rebels against fashion, is even more open to the imputation of vanity than he who obeys it, because he makes himself conspicuous, and practically announces that he is wiser than his kind. There cannot be greater vulgarity than an affectation of superior simplicity. Between the two it is left to the man of sense and modesty only to follow fashion so far as not to make himself peculiar by opposing it.

Dress and sin came in together, and have kept good fellowship ever since. If we could doubt, as some have done, the authenticity of the Pentateuch, we should have to admit that its author was at least the shrewdest observer of mankind, inasmuch as he makes a love of dress the first consequence of the Fall. That it really was so, we can be certain from the fact that it has always accompanied an absence of goodness. The best dressers of every age have always been the worst men and women. We do not pretend that the converse is true, and that the best people have always dressed the worst. Plato was at once a beau and a philosopher, and Descartes was the former before he aspired to be the latter. But the love of dress, take it as you will, can only arise from one of two closely allied sins, vanity and pride; and when in excess, as in the miserable beaux of different ages, it becomes as ridiculous in a man as the glee of a South Sea islander over a handful of worthless glass beads. No life can be more contemptible than one of which the Helicon is a tailor's shop, and its paradise the Park; no man more truly wretched than he whose mind is only a mirror of his body, and whose soul can fly no higher than a hat or a neck-tie; who strangles ambition with a yard-measure, and suffocates glory in a boot. But this puny peacockism always brings its own punishment. The fop ruins himself by his vanity, and ends a sloven, like Goodman, first a well-dressed student of Cambridge, then an actor, then a highwayman, who was at last reduced to share a shirt with a fellow-fool, and had to keep his room on the days when the other wore it.

But we must not suppose that this vanity lies in the following more than in the outraging of fashion; and if there were no such thing as a universal rule of dress, we may be confident that there would be just as much, if not more foppery, where each could dress as he liked. When it could not glory in the roll of a coat-collar or the turn of a hat-brim, it would show itself in richness of stuffs and splendors of ornaments; and while fashion has to be blamed for many extravagances, the gold chains of one age, the huge wigs of another, and the crinoline of a third, we must rejoice that it holds so severe a sway over men's minds, when we find that at another period it decrees simplicity, and legislates to put down superfluous ornament. The wise man, therefore, who frets at its follies, will attempt not to subvert, but rather to reform it; not to tear from his throne a monarch elected by universal suffrage, who will instantly be reinstated, but to lead him by his own example, and, if possible, by his voice, to make simple and sensible enactments. Better a wise despot than a silly republic.

When kings were the ministers of fashion, dress was generally costly and showy; when philosophers were its counsellors, it became slovenly and untidy; and when, as in the present day, it is led by private gentlemen and private ladies, it is often absurd a in bad taste, but generally tends towards simplicity. It is certainly amusing, when looking back at the history of dress, to see how often the story of the blue jackal may be cited. Wigs were inflicted on our forefathers by a bald monarch, and we were tortured by stiff cravats and high shirt-collars, because another had the king's evil in his neck. Long skirts probably came in to hide a pair of ungainly feet, and hoops were introduced to make a queenly waist look smaller than it was.

There is, however, a difference between the prerogative of fashion and that of other despots. While we are bound to yield a general obedience to his laws, we have the right, without a loss of caste, to disregard any which are manifestly absurd and inconvenient. If, for example, a fashionable of the present day, to whom nature had given an ugly foot, were to follow the example of Fulk, Duke of Anjou, and introduce such long peaks to our boots that we could not walk in them, we may be certain that their use would not survive a season, and would be confined to a class who have little to do but look ornamental. It is certainly a consolation to find that in the present day the fashions of male attire are restricted, not as they once were, by royal edicts, but by the common sense of men who know that dress ought to be convenient as well as elegant. With ladies it is otherwise. Woman is still too generally believed to have no higher mission than that of pleasing the senses rather than the judgment of men, and so many women of all classes are idle, that a fashion, however preposterous, is more readily accepted and more universally adopted by them than by the stronger sex. And this is the case even when the reform proposed is obviously most advantageous. How difficult, for instance, has it been to abolish the stiff black hat and the throat-cutting collar, though the wide-awake and the turned-down collar were at once more graceful and more comfortable. How completely has the attempt to establish the "peg-top" been a failure, though every man of sense who values his health must feel that a loose covering is both more comfortable and more healthy than a tight sheathing of cloth. The fact is, that there is a conservatism in fashion which has the appearance of being respectable, but is really slavish and

silly; and the weekly satirists who undertake to laugh
down its extravagances have not always the sense to appreciate its wisdom. Those in fact who are most eager in
the blind attack on fashion, are often really its more ab-
ject and least sensible servants. To condemn a new fashion only because it is new, is contemptibly short-sighted;
and the old wise gentlemen who sneer at " new-fangled fancies" should first ascertain whether the innovation is for
the better or the worse.

But, after all, the changes of fashion are not sufficiently
rapid or violent in respect of men's dress, to make even
our grandfathers uncomfortable on account of their peculiarity. If the hat-brim and coat-collar have lost what
was once considered a graceful curl, if huge shirt-collars
and stiff cravats have given way to a freer arrangement
for the neck, if blue swallow-tailed coats and brass buttons
have been succeeded by blue frocks without them, and buff
waistcoats with painfully tight appendices, by white waistcoats and the liberty of the leg, the change is not great
enough to require a new race of tailors, or make old men
ridiculous even in our streets. But while an old man in
an old fashion not only passes muster, but seems to acquire
additional respectability from the antiquity of his style, a
young man can scarcely adopt his grandfather's wardrobe
without risking a smile. I remember once taking a friend
of mine—a country squire of one-and-twenty—to dine
with some extremely fashionable but not very well-bred
bachelors. The appearance of my companion was decidedly antique; for, conservative to the back and its covering, he prided himself on maintaining the style of his
worthy progenitor. I saw that the eye-glasses were turned
on him with a look of mingled pity and contempt, and in

the course of dinner heard the following remarks pass between the host and a guest :—

" Pray, G—," asked a lisping bewhiskered exquisite of the former, " who is your fine old English gentleman ? What style do you call it ? Rather George the Fourth —eh !"

" Yes, rather," replied the host ; "but," he added in a whisper, " he has just come in to £12,000 a year and B— Hall."

" Oh !—aw, indeed ! Then of course he can afford to be eccentric."

This brings me to speak of certain necessities of dress : the first of which I shall take is appropriateness. The age of the individual is an important consideration in this respect; and a man of sixty is as absurd in the style of nineteen as my young friend in the high cravat of Brummell's day. I know a gallant colonel who is master of the ceremonies in a gay watering-place, and who, afraid of the prim old-fashioned *tournure* of his *confrères* in similar localities, is to be seen, though his hair is grey and his age not under five-and-sixty, in a light cut-away, the " peg-top" continuations, and a turned-down collar. It may be what younger blades will wear when they reach his age, but in the present day the effect is ridiculous. We may, therefore, give as a general rule, that after the turning-point of life a man should eschew the changes of fashion in his own attire, while he avoids complaining of it in the young. In the latter, on the other hand, the observance of these changes must depend partly on his taste and partly on his position. If wise, he will adopt with alacrity any new fashions which improve the grace, the ease, the healthfulness, and the convenience of his gar-

ments.   He will be glad of greater freedom in the cut of
his cloth clothes, of boots with elastic sides instead of
troublesome buttons or laces, of the privilege to turn down
his collar, and so forth, while he will avoid as extravagant, elaborate shirt-fronts, gold bindings on the waistcoat, and expensive buttons.   On the other hand, whatever his age, he will have some respect to his profession
and position in society.   He will remember how much
the appearance of the man aids a judgment of his character, and this test, which has often been cried down, is
in reality no bad one; for a man who does not dress appropriately evinces a want of what is most necessary to
professional men—tact and discretion.   I could not, for
instance, feel confidence in a young physician dressed as
I am accustomed to see a guardsman; while, if my lawyer were a dandy in his office, I should be inclined to
think he knew more of gay society than of Coke upon
Lyttleton.   The dress of the clergy is not an arbitrary
matter, yet I have seen ecclesiastics, who, abandoning the
white choker, lounge in an easy costume, little different
from that of their undergraduate days, and though it is
certainly hard to condemn a man for life to the miseries
of black cloth, we have a right to expect that he should
be proud rather than ashamed of the badge of his high
calling.

Position in society demands a like appropriateness.
Well knowing the worldly value of a good coat, I would
yet never recommend a man of limited means to aspire to
a fashionable appearance.   In the first place, he becomes
thereby a walking falsehood; in the second, he cannot,
without running into debt, which is another term for dis-
honesty, maintain the style he has adopted.   As he can-

7

not afford to change his suits as rapidly as fashion alters, he must avoid following it in varying details. He will rush into wide sleeves one month, in the hope of being fashionable, and before his coat is worn out, the next month will bring in a narrow sleeve. We cannot, unfortunately, like Samuel Pepys, take a long cloak now-a-days to the tailor's, to be cut into a short one, "long cloaks being now quite out," as he tells us. Even when there is no poverty in the case, our position must not be forgotten. The tradesman will win neither customers nor friends by adorning himself in the mode of the club-lounger, and the clerk, or commercial traveller, who dresses fashionably, lays himself open to inquiries as to his antecedents, which he may not care to have investigated. In general, it may be said that there is vulgarity in dressing like those of a class above us, since it must be taken as a proof of pretension.

I remember going to church in a remote little village on the borders of Wales, and being surprised to see enter, among the clodhoppers and simple folk of the place, a couple of young men dressed in the height of fashion, and wearing yellow kid gloves and patent leather boots. On inquiry I found them to be the sons of a rich manufacturer, who had himself been once a working man, and was residing in the neighborhood. I was not surprised, for vulgar pretension was here carried out to the worst extreme. Better-bred men would have known that, whatever their London costume, a difference must be made in the country. The rule may be laid down that wherever we are we should assimilate, as far as convenient, to the customs and costumes of the place. While I had no wish to see the sons of the *parvenu* appear in smock-frocks

and high-lows, I was reasonable in thinking that a rough
er style of dress would have been better, and this may be
said for the country generally. As it is bad taste to flaunt
the airs of the town among provincials, who know nothing
of them, it is worse taste to display the dress of a city in
the quiet haunts of the rustics. The law which we have
enunciated, that all attempts at distinction by means of
dress is vulgar and pretentious, would be sufficient argument against wearing London fashions in the country; but
if this is not sufficient, we may picture the inconvenience
of such a measure under certain circumstances. Had a
shower of rain descended at the conclusion of the service, our two young sprigs of gentility would have looked
superbly ridiculous in their thin boots and light gloves,
and no London hansom to take refuge in, to say nothing
of spoiling one's boots and catching cold.

While in most cases a rougher and easier mode of dress
is both admissible and desirable in the country, there are
many occasions of country visiting where a town man
finds it difficult to decide. It is almost peculiar to the
country to unite the amusements of the daytime with
those of the evening: of the open air with those of the
drawing-room. Thus, in the summer, when the days are
long, you will be asked to a pic-nic or an archery party,
which will wind up with dancing in-doors, and may even
assume the character of a ball. If you are aware of this
beforehand, it will always be safe to send your evening
dress to your host's house, and you will learn from the
servants whether others have done the same, and whether,
therefore, you will not be singular in asking leave to
change your costume. But if you are ignorant how the
day is to end, you must be guided partly by the hour of

invitation, and partly by the extent of your intimacy with the family. I have actually known gentlemen arrive at a large pic-nic at mid-day in complete evening dress, and pitied them with all my heart, compelled as they were to suffer, in tight black clothes, under a hot sun for eight hours, and dance after all in the same dress. On the other hand, if you are asked to come an hour or two before sun-set, after six in summer, in the autumn after five, you cannot err by appearing in evening dress. It is always taken as a compliment to do so, and if your acquaintance with your hostess is slight, it would be almost a familiarity to do otherwise. In any case you desire to avoid singularity, so that if you can discover what others who are invited intend to wear, you can always decide on your own attire. On the Continent there is a convenient rule for these matters; never appear after four in the afternoon in morning dress; but then grey trousers are there allowed instead of black, and white waistcoats are still worn in the evening. At any rate, it is possible to effect a compromise between the two styles of costume, and if you are likely to be called upon to dance in the evening, it will be well to wear thin boots, a black frock-coat, and a small black neck-tie, and to put a pair of clean white gloves into your pocket. You will thus be at least less conspicuous in the dancing-room than in a light tweed suit.

Englishmen are undeniably the most conservative men in the world, and in nothing do they show it more universally than in maintaining their usual habits in any country, climate, or season. *L'Anglais en royaye* has been a fruitful subject of ridicule both to our own and foreign writers, and I shall therefore content myself with saying that, while I would not have an Englishman adopt every

local habit or every fantastic costume of those among whom
he finds himself, I would fain see him avoid that distinctiveness in both which is set down by our neighbors to
pride and obstinacy. Excellent, for instance, is the custom of shaking hands, but it has on the Continent generally a much more friendly and particular signification, and
is permitted between the sexes only after a long intimacy.
In fact, a French *jeune fille* never takes a gentleman's
hand unless he is quite an *emi de la maison*, so that for
an Englishman at a first visit to shake hands all round
amounts to a familiarity. I shall never forget the deep
crimson on the cheeks of a charming girl to whom I once
introduced an English friend, and who was too well-bred not
to touch his proffered hand, but did so with an air of un-
mistakable surprise. " Qu'est-ce que c'est que votre ami,"
she asked me afterwards; " est-ce qu'il veut donc m'em-
brasser?" To impose the manners of one's country on
the people of another, is as bad as to revive those of a
past century.

In the middle of the last century it was the custom for a
gentleman on entering a room, to kiss the ladies all round
on the cheek. Had not my French friend as much right
to blush, as any English young lady would if I were to
subject her to the practice of the charming but obsolete
custom?

Can anything be more painfully ridiculous than an Englishman wearing a black silk hat and frock-coat of cloth
under the sun of the equator? Yet such is our want of
sense, or our love of national costumes, however hideous.
that it is the etiquette in our colonies, whether in the tro-
pics or the arctic regions, to wear precisely the same stiff
hot court dress as at St. James'. However this might be

excused on the plea of uniformity in official dress, it is no
excuse for the fashion which imposes the coat, &c. of Pall
Mall on the gentleman of Calcutta or Colombo; and the
same may be said of our own fashion of wearing cloth
clothes throughout the year.   There is many a summer's
day in England as hot as any in Italy, and in general the
difference between our summer and that of France and
America is, that there the heat is glaring and clear, with
us, if less powerful, close and oppressive.   Why then
should my Lord Fashion permit the Frenchman and Yan-
kee to wear whole suits of white linen, and condemn us to
black cloth?   Nothing can be neater or prettier, as modern dress goes, than the white coat, waistcoat, *et cetera*,
with a straw hat and a bright blue tie; but it is something to say against it, that London smoke would necessi-
tate a clean suit per diem, which would materially aug-
ment the washing expenditure of our metropolitan Beaux
Tibbses.   The nearest approach we are allowed to make
to a sensible costume, on days when we should like to follow Sidney Smith's advice, by the removal of our flesh
and sitting in our skeletons, is that of light thin tweeds,
but even these are not countenanced in St. James' and the
Park, and we must be content to take refuge in a white
waistcoat and the thinnest possible material for our frock-
coat.   On the other hand, as our winters are never very
severe, we have only to choose thicker tweeds of a darker
color for that season, and the wrapper or great coat then
becomes not nearly so important an article as the indis
pensable umbrella.   In this country, therefore, as present
fashions require, appropriateness to the season will be
easily acquired by a change of material and color rather
than of form, in our apparel.

Not so the distinction to be made according to size. As a rule, tall men require long clothes—some few perhaps even in the nurse's sense of those words—and short men short clothes. On the other hand, Falstaff should beware of Jenny Wren coats and affect ample wrappers, while Peter Schemihl, and the whole race of thin men, must eschew looseness as much in their garments as their morals.

Lastly we come to what is appropriate to different occasions, and as this is an important subject, I shall treat of it separately. For the present it is sufficient to point out that while every man should avoid not only extravagance, but even brilliance of dress on ordinary occasions, there are some on which he may and ought to pay more attention to his toilet, and attempt to look gay. Of course, the evenings are not here meant. For evening dress there is a fixed rule, from which we can depart only to be foppish or vulgar; but in morning dress there is greater liberty, and when we undertake to mingle with those who are assembled avowedly for gaiety, we should not make ourselves remarkable by the dinginess of our dress. Such occasions are open air entertainments, *fêtes*, flower-shows, archery-meetings, *matinées*, and *id genus omne*, where much of the pleasure to be derived depends on the general effect on the enjoyers, and where, if we cannot pump up a look of mirth, we should at least, if we go at all, wear the semblance of it in our dress. I have a worthy little friend, who, I believe, is as well-disposed to his kind as Lord Shaftesbury himself, but who, for some reason, perhaps a twinge of philosophy about him, frequents the gay meetings to which he is asked in an old coat and a wide-awake. Some people take him for a wit, but he soon shows that he does not aspire to that character; others for a philoso-

pher, but he is too good-mannered for that; others poor
man! pronounce him a cynic, and all are agreed that
whatever he may be, he looks out of place and spoils the
general effect. I believe in my heart that he is the mild-
est of men, but will not take the trouble to dress more
than once a day. At any rate, he has a character for eccentricity, which, I am sure, is precisely what he would
wish to avoid. That character is a most delightful one for
a bachelor and it is generally Cœlebs who holds it, for it
has been proved by statistics that there are four single to
one married man among the inhabitants of our mad-houses ;
but eccentricity yields a reputation which requires something to uphold it, and even in Diogenes of the Tub it was
extremely bad taste to force himself into Plato's evening
party without sandals, and nothing but a dirty tunic on
him.

Another requisite in dress is its simplicity, with which
I may couple harmony of color. This simplicity is the
only distinction which a man of taste should aspire to in
the matter of dress, but a simplicity in appearance must
proceed from a nicety in reality. One should not be
simply ill-dressed, but simply-well dressed. Lord Castle-
reagh would never have been pronounced the most distinguished man in the gay court of Vienna, because he wore
no orders or ribbons among hundreds decorated with a profusion of those vanities, but because besides this he was
dressed with taste. The charm of Brummell's dress was
its simplicity; yet it cost him as much thought, time, and
care, as the portfolio of a minister. The rules of simplicity, therefore, are the rules of taste. All extravagance,
all splendor, and all profusion, must be avoided. The colors,
in the first place, must harmonize both with our complexion

and with one another; perhaps most of all with the color of our hair. All bright colors should be avoided, such as red, yellow, sky-blue, and bright green. Perhaps only a successful Australian gold digger would think of choosing such colors for his coat, waistcoat, or trousers; but there are hundreds of young men who might select them for their gloves and neck-ties. The deeper colors are, somehow or other, more manly, and are certainly less striking. The same simplicity should be studied in the avoidance of ornamentation. A few years ago it was the fashion to trim the evening waistcoat with a border of gold lace. This is an example of fashions always to be rebelled against. Then, too, extravagance in the form of our dress is a sin against taste. I remember that long ribbons took the place of neck-ties some years ago. At an Oxford' commemoration, two friends of mine determined to cut a figure in this matter, having little else to distinguish them. The one wore two yards of bright pink; the other the same quantity of bright blue ribbon round their necks. I have reason to believe they think now that they both looked superbly ridiculous. In the same way, if the trousers are worn wide, we should not wear them as loose as a Turk's; or if the sleeves are to be open, we should not rival the ladies in this matter. And so on through a hundred details, generally remembering that to exaggerate a fashion is to assume a character, and therefore vulgar. The wearing of jewelry comes under this head. Jewels are an ornament to women, but a blemish to men. They bespeak either effeminacy or a love of display. The hand of a man is honored in working, for labor is his mission: and the hand that wears its riches on its fingers, has rarely worked honestly to win them. The best jewel a man can wear is

his honor. Let that be bright and shining, well set in prudence, and all others must darken before it. But as we
are savages, and must have some silly trickery to hang
about us, a little, but very little concession may be made
to our taste in this respect. I am quite serious when I
disadvise you from the use of nose-rings, gold anklets, and
hat-bands studded with jewels; for when I see an incred-
ulous young man of the nineteenth century, dangling from
his watch-chain a dozen silly "charms" (often the only
ones he possesses), which have no other use than to give
a fair coquette a legitimate subject on which to approach
to closer intimacy, and which are revived from the lowest
superstitions of dark ages, and sometimes darker races. I
am quite justified in believing that some South African
chieftain, sufficiently rich to cut a dash in London, might
introduce with success the most peculiar fashions of his
own country. However this may be, there are already
sufficient extravagances prevalent among our young men
to attack.

The man of good taste will wear as little jewelry as
possible. One handsome signet-ring on the little finger
of the left hand, a scarf-pin which is neither large nor
showy nor too intricate in its design, and a light, rather
thin watch-guard with a cross-bar, are all that he ought to
wear. But if he aspires to more than this, he should observe the following rules:—

1. Let everything be real and good. False jewelry is
not only a practical lie, but an absolute vulgarity, since
its use arises from an attempt to appear richer or grander
than its wearer is.

. 2. Let it be simple. Elaborate studs, waistcoat-buttons,
and wrist-links, are all abominable. The last particularly

should bo as plain as possible, consisting of plain gold ovals, with at most the crest engraved upon them. Diamonds and brilliants are quite unsuitable to men, whose jewelry should never be conspicuous. If you happen to possess a single diamond of great value you may wear it on great occasions as a ring, but no more than one ring should ever be worn by a gentleman.

3. Let it be distinguished rather by its curiosity than its brilliance. An antique or bit of old jewelry possesses more interest, particularly if you are able to tell its history, than the most splendid production of the goldsmith's shop.

4. Let it harmonize with the colors of your dress.

5. Let it have some use. Men should never, like women, wear jewels for mere ornament, whatever may be the fashion of Hungarian noblemen, and deposed Indian rajahs with jackets covered with rubies.

The precious stones are reserved for ladies, and even our scarf-pins are more suitable without them. English taste has also the superiority over that of the Continent in condemning the wearing of orders, clasps, and ribbons, except at court or on official occasions. If these are really given for merit, they will add nothing to our fame; if, as in nine cases out of ten, they are bestowed merely because the recipient has done his duty, they may impose on fools, but will, if anything. provoke only awkward inquiries from sensible men. If it be permitted to flaunt our bravery or our learning on the coat-collar, as much as to cry, like little Jack Horner, "See what a good boy am I!" I cannot for my part, discover why a curate should not carry his silver teapot about with him, or Mr. Morison enlarge his phylacteries with a selection from the one million cases of "almost miraculous cures."

The dress that is both appropriate and simple can never offend, nor render its wearer conspicuous, though it may distinguish him for his good taste. But it will not be pleasing unless clean and fresh. We cannot quarrel with a poor gentleman's thread-bare coat, if his linen be pure, and we see that he has never attempted to dress beyond his means or unsuitably to his station. But the sight of decayed gentility and dilapidated fashion may call forth our pity, and at the same time prompt a moral: " You have evidently sunken," we say to ourselves; " but whose fault was it? Am I not led to suppose that the extravagance which you evidently once revelled in has brought you to what I now see you?" While freshness is essential to being well-dressed, it will be a consolation to those who cannot afford a heavy tailor's bill, to reflect that a visible newness in one's clothes is as bad as patches and darns, and to remember that there have been celebrated dressers who would never put on a new coat till it had been worn two or three times by their valets. On the other hand, there is no excuse—except at Donnybrook— for untidiness, holes in the boots, a broken hat, torn gloves, and so on. Indeed, it is better to wear no gloves at all than a pair full of holes. There is nothing to be ashamed of in bare hands if they are clean, and the poor can still afford to have their shirts and shoes mended, and their hats ironed. It is certainly better to show signs of neatness than the reverse, and you need sooner be ashamed of a hole than a darn.

Of personal cleanliness I have spoken at such length that little need be said on that of the clothes. If you are economical with your tailor, you can be extravagant with your laundress. The beaux of forty years back put on three shirts a day, but except in hot weather one is sufficient. Of course, if you change your dress in the evening you must change your shirt too. There has been a great outcry against colored flannel shirts in the place of linen, and the man who can wear one for three days is looked on as little better than St. Simeon Stylites. I should like to know how often the advocates of linen change their own under-flannel, and whether the same rule does not apply to what is seen as to what is concealed. But while the flannel is perhaps healthier as absorbing the moisture more rapidly, the linen has the advantage of *looking* cleaner, and may therefore be preferred. As to economy, if the flannel costs less to wash, it also wears out sooner; but, be this as it may, a man's wardrobe is not complete without half a dozen or so of these shirts, which he will find most useful, and ten times more comfortable than linen in long excursions, or when exertion will be required. Flannel, too, has the advantage of being warm in winter and cool in summer, for, being a non-conductor, but a retainer of heat, it protects the body from the sun, and, on the other hand, shields it from the cold. But the best shirt of all, particularly in winter, is that which wily monks and hermits pretended to wear for a penance, well knowing that they could have no garment cooler, more comfortable, or more healthy. I mean, of course, the rough hair-shirt. Like flannel, it is a non-conductor of heat; but then, too, it acts the part of a sham-poor, and with its perpetual friction soothes the surface of the skin, and prevents the circulation from being arrested at any one point of the body. Though I doubt if any of my readers will take a hint from the wisdom of the merry anchorites, they will per-

haps allow me to suggest that the next best thing to wear
next the skin is flannel, and that too of the coarsest description.

Quantity is better than quality in linen. Nevertheless
it should be fine and well spun. The loose cuff, which we
borrowed from the French some four years ago, is a great
improvement on the old tight wrist-band, and, indeed, it
must be borne in mind that anything which binds any part
of the body tightly impedes the circulation, and is therefore unhealthy as well as ungraceful. Who more hideous
and unnatural than an officer of the Russian or Austrian
army—compelled to reduce his waist to a certain size—
unless it be a dancing-master in stays? At Munich, I remember there was a somewhat corpulent major of the
Guards who, it was said, took two men to buckle his belt
in the morning, and was unable to speak for about an
hour after the operation. His face, of course, was of a
most unsightly crimson.

The necessity for a large stock of linen depends on a
rule far better than Brummell's, of three shirts a day,
viz. :—

Change your linen whenever it is at all dirty.

This is the best guide with regard to collars. socks,
pocket-handkerchiefs, and our under garments. No rule
can be laid down for the number we should wear per week.
for everything depends on circumstances. Thus in the
country all our linen remains longer clean than in London :
in dirty, wet, or dusty weather, our socks get soon dirty
and must be changed : or, if we have a cold, to say nothing
of the possible but not probable case of tear-shedding on
the departure of friends, or of sensitive young ladies over
a Crimean engagement, we shall want more than one

pocket handkerchief per diem. In fact, the last article of modern civilization is put to so many uses, is so much displayed, and liable to be called into action on so many various engagements, that we should always have a clean one in our pockets. Who knows when it may not serve us in good stead? Who can tell how often the corner of the delicate cambric will have to represent a tear which, like difficult passages in novels, is " left to the imagination." Can a man of any feeling call on a disconsolate widow, for instance, and listen to her woes, without at least pulling out that expressive appendage? Can any one believe in our sympathy if the article in question is a dirty one? There are some people who, like the clouds, only exist to weep; and King Solomon, though not one of them, has given them great encouragement in speaking of the house of mourning. We are bound to weep with them, and we are bound to weep elegantly.

A man whose dress is neat, clean, simple, and appropriate, will pass muster anywhere. But he cannot always wear the same clothes, like Werther. The late Mr. Fountayn Wilson, notorious for his wealth and stinginess, thought otherwise. When Napoleon the First was threatening England, and there was the same mania for volunteer corps as now, he bought up an immense quantity of grey cloth, in the hope that the government would give a good price for it later. He was disappointed, and to make use of his purchase, determined to wear nothing else himself for the rest of his life. Future biographers may perhaps invent a similar story, to account for Lord Brougham's partiality to checked trousers.

A well-dressed man does not require so much an extensive as a varied wardrobe. He wants a different costume

for every season and every occasion ; but if what he selects
is simple rather than striking, he may appear in the same
clothes as often as he likes, as long as they are fresh and
appropriate to the season and the object.   There are four
kinds of coats which he must have : a morning-coat, a
frock-coat, a dress-coat, and an over-coat.   An economical
man may do well with four of the first, and one of each
of the others per annum.   George the Fourth's wardrobe
sold for £15,000, and a single cloak brought no less than
£800.   But George was a king and a beau, and in debt
to his tailor.   The dress of an English gentleman in the
present day should not cost him more than the tenth part
of his income on an average.   But as fortunes vary more
than position, if his income is large it will take a much
smaller proportion, if small a larger one.   But generally
speaking, a man with £300 a year should not devote more
than £30 to his outward man.   The seven coats in question will cost about £18.   Six pairs of morning, and one
of evening trousers, will cost £9.   Four morning waistcoats, and one for evening, make another £4.   Gloves,
linen, hats, scarves and neck-ties, about £10, and the important item of boots, at least £5 more.   This, I take it,
is a sufficient wardrobe for a well-dressed man who employs
a moderate tailor, and the whole is under £50.   It is quite
possible to dress decently for half that sum, and men of
small means should be content to do so.   If a man, however, mixes in society, and I write for those who do so,
there are some things which are indispensable to even
proper dressing, and every occasion will have its proper
attire.

In his own house, then, and in the morning, there is
no reason why he should not wear out his old clothes.

Some men take to the delightful ease of a dresssing-gown and slippers; and if bachelors, they do well. If family men, it will probably depend on whether the lady or the gentleman wears the pantaloons. The best walking-dress for a non-professional men is a suit of tweed of the same color, ordinary boots, gloves not too dark for the coat, a scarf with a pin in winter, or a small tie of one color in summer, a respectable black hat, and a cane. The last item is perhaps the most important, and though its use varies with fashion, I confess I am sorry when I see it go out. The Englishman does not gesticulate when talking, and in consequence has nothing to do with his hands. To put them in his pockets is the natural action, but this gives an appearance of lounging *insouciance*, or impudent determination, which becomes very few men, if any. The best substitute for a walking-stick is an umbrella, *not* a parasol unless it be given you by a lady to carry. The main point of the walking-dress is the harmony of colors, but this should not be carried to the extent of M. de Maltzan, who some years ago made a bet to wear nothing but pink at Baden-Baden for a whole year, and had boots and gloves of the same lively hue. He won his wager, but also the soubriquet of " Le Diable enflammé." The walking dress should vary according to the place and hour. In the country or at the sea-side a straw hat or wide-awake may take the place of the beaver, and the nuisance of gloves be even dispensed with in the former. But in London, where a man is supposed to make visits as well as lounge in the Park, the frock coat of very dark blue or black, or a black cloth cut-away, the white waistcoat, and lavender gloves, are almost indispensable. Very thin boots should be avoided at all times, and whatever clothes

one wears they should be well brushed. The shirt,
whether seen or not, should be quite plain. The shirt collar should never have a color on it, but it may be stiff or
turned down according as the wearer is Byronically or
Brummellically disposed. The scarf, if simple and of modest colors, is perhaps the best thing we can wear round the
neck; but if a neck-tie is preferred it should not be too
long, nor tied in too stiff and studied a manner. Brummell made his reputation by the knot of his cravat, and
even in so tiny a trifle a man may show his taste or his
want of it. The cane should be extremely simple, a mere
stick in fact, with no gold head, and yet for the town not
rough, thick, or clumsy; nor of the style beloved of Cor-
poral Shanks of the Fusileers. The frock-coat should be
ample and loose, and a tall well-built man may throw it
back. At any rate, it should never be buttoned up.
Great-coats are so little worn in this country that I need
say little about them. If worn at all they should be buttoned up, of a dark color, not quite black, longer than the
frock coat, but never long enough to reach the ankles.
If you have visits to make you should do away with the
great-coat, if the weather allows you to do so. On the
Continent it is always removed before entering a drawing-
room, but not so in England. The frock-coat, or black
cut-away, with a white waistcoat in summer, is the best
dress for making calls in.

It is certainly very hard that a man may not wear what
he likes, and that if I have a fancy to grandeur, and a
fine pair of shoulders, I may not be allowed to strut along
Pall Mall in a Roman toga ; or having lost a seventeenth
cousin removed, am forbidden by the laws—at least those
of Policeman Z 500, who most certainly would insist on

my "moving on"—to array myself in a paletot of sack-
cloth, with a unique head-dress of well-sifted cinders : but
so it is, and if my relatives did not commit me to the
walls of some delightful suburban " Retreat," patronized
by Doctor Conolly, and make the toga an excuse for ap-
propriating my small income,—even if the small boys
would let me alone, and I could walk without a band of
self-appointed and vociferous retainers, there would still
be that terrible monosyllable, *snob*, to cure me in a moment of a weakness for classical attire. I will not en-
lighten you as to the amount of horror I feel at the mere
mention of that title ; I will only say that those who do
not care whether the title is given them or not, can afford
to dress in any style they like. Those who do, on the
other hand, must avoid certain articles of attire which are
either obsolete or peculiar to a class. Thus unless a man
is really a groom, why should he aspire to be like
one ? Why should he compress his lower limbs into the
very tightest of garments, made for a man of seven feet
high, and worn by one of five, necessitating in consequence
a peculiar wrinkling from the foot to the knee, which
seems to find immense favor in the eyes of the stable-boy.
Unless you are a prize-fighter, again, why should you pa-
tronize a neck-tie of Waterloo blue with white spots on it,
commonly known as the " bird's eye" pattern, and much
affected by candidates for the champion's belt. If your
lot has not been cast behind the counter of a haberdasher,
can there be any obvious reason why you should clothe
your nether man in a stuff of the largest possible check.
and the most vivid colors? Or if fortune did not select
you for a " light" in some sect, or at any rate for the position of a small tradesman, can you on any plausible

grounds defend the fact that you are seen in the morning
in a swallow-tail black cloth coat, and a black satin tie?
Nay, if like Mr. Fountayn Wilson, you have been specu-
lating in cloth, black instead of grey, and had twenty
thousand yards on your hands, you must on no consideration put any of them on your legs before a certain hour
of the evening. Of course you may, if you please, wear
jockey trousers, broad patterns, bird's-eye handkerchiefs,
tail-coats, and black cloth, at any hour of the day, and in
any portion of the civilized world, but it will be under
pain and penalty of being dubbed by that terrible monosyllable, which nothing could induce me to repeat. No,
it *must* be a shooting coat of any cut or color, or a frock-
coat that is dark, or in winter an over-coat, but it may
never be a tail-coat, and so on with the rest. You may
dress like a bargee, in shorts and grey stockings. like a
chimney-sweep in the deepest mourning, like a costermonger, a coalheaver, a shoeblack, or as M. de Maltzan
did, like " Sa Majesté d'en bas," and you will either be
taken for a bargee, chimney-sweep, costermonger, coalheaver, shoeblack, or demon, or you will be set down as
eccentric ; but if, while not discarding your ordinary attire, you adopt some portion peculiar to a class below you,
you will, I regret to say, be, certainly most uncharitably,
entitled only a snob.

So much for morning dress.

It is simple nonsense to talk of modern civilization, and
rejoice that the cruelties of the dark ages can never be
perpetrated in these days and this country. I maintain
that they are perpetrated freely, generally, daily, with
the consent of the wretched victim himself, in the com-
pulsion to wear evening clothes. Is there anything at

once more comfortless or more hideous ? Let us begin
with what the delicate Americans call limb-covers, which
we are told were the invention of the Gauls, but I am inclined to think, of a much worse race, for it is clearly an
anachronism to ascribe the discovery to a Venetian called
Piantaleone, and it can only have been Inquisitors or demons who inflicted this scourge on the race of man, and
his ninth-parts, the tailors, for I take it that both are
equally bothered by the tight pantaloon. Let us pause
awhile over this unsightly garment, and console ourselves
with the reflection that as every country, and almost every
year, has a different fashion in its make of it, we may at
last be emancipated from it altogether, or at least be able
to wear it *à la Turque.*

Whenever I call at a great house, which, as I am a
writer on etiquette, must—of course—be very often, I
confess to feeling a most trying insignificance in the presence of the splendid Mercury who ushers me in. Why
is this ? Neither physically, mentally, by position, education, nor genius, am I his inferior, and yet I shrink before
him. On the other hand, if it is a butler in plain clothes
who admits me, like Bob Acres, I feel all my courage
ooze back again. I gave my nights, long and sleepless, to
the consideration of this problem, and have now arrived
at a satisfactory explanation. It is not the tall figure and
magnificent whiskers ; it is not the gold lace and rich red
plush ; it is not the majestically indifferent air of John
Thomas that appals me ; it is the consciousness that my
legs—my, as a man, most important and distinctive limbs
—are in an inferior position to his. As an artist, I cannot but recognize the superior beauty of his figure. And
for this disgrace, this ignominy I suffer, I have to thank

the Celts with their *braccæ*, and the bad taste of some calfless monarch or leader of fashion—probably a German, for all Germans have bad taste and bad legs—who revived this odious, long obsolete instrument of personal torture. It is nothing less, believe me. Independent of a loss of personal beauty, there is the unhealthiness of a tight garment clinging to the very portion which we exercise most, and which most demands a free circulation. It is true, that the old-fashioned breeches, if too tightly fastened round the knee, produced the same effect, and Maria Macklin, a celebrated actress of male characters, almost lost her leg by vanity in the matter of " Honi soit qui mal y pense;" but, after all, what is not a cool stocking to a hot bag of thick stuff round the leg; how far preferable the freedom of trunk-hose, to the hardly fought liberty of the " peg-top" trousers. But it is not all trousers that I rebel against. If I might wear linen appendices in summer, and fur continuations in winter, I would not groan, but it is the evening dress that inflicts on the man who likes society the necessity of wearing the same trying cloth all the year round, so that under Boreas he catches colds, and under the dog-star he melts. They manage these things better abroad. In America a man may go to a ball in white ducks. In France he has the option of light grey. But in England we are doomed for ever to buckskin. This unmentionable, but most necessary disguise of the "human form divine," is one that never varies in this country, and therefore I must lay down the rule :—

For all evening wear—black cloth trousers.

But the tortures of evening dress do not end with our lower limbs. Of all the iniquities perpetrated under the

Reign of Terror, none has lasted so long as that of the straight-jacket, which was palmed off on the people as a " habit de compagnie." If it were necessary to sing a hymn of praise to Robespierre, Marat, and Co., I would rather take the guillotine as my subject to extol than the swallow tail. And yet we endure the stiffness, unsightliness, uncomfortableness, and want of grace of the latter, with more resignation than that with which Charlotte Corday put her beautiful neck into the " trou d'enfer" of the former. Fortunately modern republicanism has triumphed over ancient etiquette, and the tail-coat of to-day is looser and more easy than it was twenty years ago. I can only say, let us never strive to make it bearable, till we have abolished it. Let us abjure such vulgarities as silk collars, white silk linings, and so forth, which attempt to beautify this monstrosity, as a hangman might wreathe his gallows with roses. The plainer the manner in which you wear your misery, the better.

Then again the black waistcoat, stiff, tight, and comfortless. Fancy Falstaff in a ball-dress such as we now wear. No amount of Embroidery, gold-trimmings, or jewel-buttons, will render such an infliction grateful to the mass. The best plan is to wear thorough mourning for your wretchedness. In France and America, the cooler white waistcoat is admitted. We have scouted it, and left it to aldermen and shopkeepers. Would I were an alderman or a shopkeeper in the middle of July, when I am compelled to dance in a full attire of black cloth. However, as we have it, let us make the best of it, and not parade our misery by hideous ornamentation. The only evening waistcoat for all purposes for a man of taste is one of simple black cloth, with the simplest possible buttons

These three items never vary for dinner-party, muffin-worry, or ball.   The only distinction allowed is in the neck-tie.   For dinner, the opera, and balls, this must be white, and the smaller the better. It should be, too, of a washable texture, not silk, nor netted, nor hanging down, nor of any foppish production, but a simple white tie without embroidery.   The black tie is only admitted for evening parties, and should be equally simple.   The shirt-front which figures under the tie should be plain, with unpretending small plaits.   All the elaborations which the French have introduced among us in this particular, and the custom of wearing pink under the shirt, are an abomination to party-goers.   The glove must be white, not yellow.   Recently, indeed, a fashion has sprung up of wearing lavender gloves in the evening.   They are economical, and as all economy is an abomination, must be avoided.   Gloves should always be worn at a ball.   At a dinner-party in town they should be worn on entering the room, and drawn off for dinner.   While, on the one hand, we must avoid the awkwardness of a gallant sea-captain who, wearing no gloves at a dance, excused himself to his partner by saying, " Never mind, Miss, I can wash my hands when I've done dancing," we have no need in the present day to copy the Roman gentleman mentioned by Athenæus, who wore gloves at dinner that he might pick his meat from the hot dishes more rapidly than the bare-handed guests   As to gloves at tea-parties and so forth, we are generally safer with than without them.   If it is quite a small party, we may leave them in our pocket, and in the country they are scarcely ex-pected to be worn ; but " touch not a cat but with a glove ;" you are always safer with them.

Not so in the matter of the hat. In France and Germany the hat is brought into a ball-room and drawing-room under all circumstances, and great is the confusion arising therefrom, a man having every chance of finding his new hat exchanged for an old one under a seat. I once walked home from a German ball as bare-headed as a friar, some well-dressed robber having not only exchanged his hat with mine, but to prevent detection carried off his own too. I shall not easily forget the consternation in an English party to which I went soon after my return from the Continent, unconsciously carrying in my hat, and the host could not restrain some small facetious allusion to it, when I looked for it under the table before going away. A "Gibus" prevents all such difficulties; yet as a general rule in England the hat should be left outside.

I must not quit this subject without assuring myself that my reader knows more about it now than he did before. In fact I have taken one thing for granted, viz., that he knows what it is to be dressed, and what undressed. Of course I do not suppose him to be in the blissful state of ignorance on the subject once enjoyed by our first parents. I use the words "dressed" and "undressed" rather in the sense meant by a military tailor, or a cook with reference to a salad. You need not be shocked. I am one of those people who wear spectacles for fear of seeing anything with the naked eye. I am the soul of scrupulosity. But I am wondering whether everybody arranges his wardrobe as our ungrammatical nurses used to do ours, under the heads of "best, second-best, third-best," and so on, and knows what things ought to be placed under each. To be "undressed" is to be dressed

8

for work and ordinary occupations, to wear a coat which
you do not fear to spoil, and a neck-tie which your ink-
stand will not object to, but your acquaintance might.
To be "dressed," on the other hand, since by dress we
show our respect for society at large, or the persons with
whom we are to mingle, is to be clothed in the garments
which the said society pronounces as suitable to particular occasions; so that evening dress in the morning,
morning dress in the evening, and top boots and a red
coat for walking, may all be called "undress," if not
positively "bad dress." But there are shades of being
"dressed;" and a man is called "little dressed," "well
dressed," and "much dressed," not according to the quantity but the quality of his coverings. The diminutive
jockey, whom I meet in my walks a month before the
Derby, looking like a ball of clothes, and undergoing a
most uncomfortable process of liquefaction which he de-
nominates "training," is by no means "much dressed'
because he wears two great-coats, three thick waistcoats
and the same number of "comforters." To be "littl-
dressed" is to wear old things, of a make that is no lon
ger the fashion, having no pretension to elegance, artistic
beauty, or ornament. It is also to wear lounging clothes
on occasions which demand some amount of precision.
To be "much dressed" is to be in the extreme of the
fashion, with bran new clothes, jewelry, and ornaments,
with a touch of extravagance and gaiety in your colors.
Thus to wear patent leather boots and yellow gloves in a
quiet morning stroll is to be much dressed, and certainly
does not differ immensely from being badly dressed. To
be "well dressed" is the happy medium between these
two, which is not given to every one to hold, inasmuch as

good taste is rare, and is a *sine qu? non* thereof. Thus while you avoid ornament and all fastness, you must cultivate fashion, that is *good* fashion, in the make of your clothes. A man must not be made by his tailor, but should make him, educate him, give him his own good taste. To be well dressed is to be dressed precisely as the occasion, place, weather, your height, figure, position, age, and, remember it, your *means* require. It is to be clothed without peculiarity, pretension, or eccentricity; without violent colors, elaborate ornament, or senseless fashions. introduced often by tailors for their own profit. Good dressing is to wear as little jewelry as possible, to be scrupulously neat, clean, and fresh, and to.carry your clothes as if you did not give them a thought.

Then too there is a scale of honor among clothes, which must not be forgotten. Thus, a new coat is more honorable than an old one, a cut-away or shooting-coat than a dressing-gown, a frock-coat than a cut-away, a dark blue frock-coat than a black frock-coat, a tail-coat than a frock-coat. There is no honor at all in a blue tail-coat, however, except on a gentleman of eighty, accompanied with brass buttons and a buff waistcoat. There is more honor in an old hunting-coat than in a new one, in a uniform with a bullet-hole in it than one without, in a fustian jacket and smock-frock than in a frock-coat, because they are types of labor, which is far more honorable than lounging. Again, light clothes are generally placed above dark ones, because they cannot be so long worn, and are therefore proofs of expenditure, *alias* money, which in this world is a commodity more honored than every other: but on the other hand, tasteful dress is always more honorable than that which has only cost much.

Light gloves are more esteemed than dark ones, and the
prince of glove-colors is undeniably lavender.

"I should say Jones was a fast man," said a friend to
me one day, "for he wears a white hat." If this idea of
my companion's be right, fastness may be said to consist
mainly in peculiarity. There is certainly only one step
from the sublimity of fastness to the ridiculousness of snob-
berry, and it is not always easy to say where the one ends
and the other begins. A dandy, on the other hand, is the
clothes on a man, not a man in clothes, a living lay figure
who displays much dress, and is quite satisfied if you praise
it without taking heed of him. A bear is in the opposite
extreme; never dressed enough, and always very roughly;
but he is almost as bad as the other, for he sacrifices
everything to his ease and comfort. The off-hand style of
dress only suits an off-hand character. It was at one time
the fashion to affect a certain negligence, which was called
poetic, and supp sed to be the result of genius. An ill-
tied, if not positively untied cravat was a sure sign of an
unbridled imagination; and a waistcoat was held together
by one button only, as if the swelling soul in the wearer's
bosom had burst all the rest. If in addition to this the
hair was unbrushed and curly, you were certain of passing
for a "man of soul." I should not recommend any young
gentleman to adopt this style, unless indeed he can mouth
a great deal, and has a good stock of quotations from the
poets. It is of no use to show me the clouds, unless I can
positively see you in them, and no amount of negligence
in your dress and person will convince me you are a genius, unless you produce an octavo volume of poems published by yourself. I confess I am glad th t the *n!glig!*
style, so common in novels of ten years back, has been

succeeded by neatness. What we want is real ease in the clothes, and for my part I should rejoice to see the Knickerbocker style generally adopted.

Besides the ordinary occasions treated of before, there are several special occasions requiring a change of dress. Most of our sports, together with marriage (which some people include in the sports), and going to court, come under this head. Now with the exception of the last, the less change we make the better in the present day, particularly in sports, where, if we are dressed with scrupulous accuracy, we are liable to be subjected to a comparison between our clothes and our skill. A man who wears a red coat to hunt in, should be able to hunt, and not sneak through gates or dodge over gaps. Of wedding-dress and court-dress we shall speak in separate chapters under the heads of " Marriage" and " The Court." But a few remarks on dresses worn in different sports may be useful. Having laid down the rule that a strict accuracy of sporting costume is no longer in good taste, we can dismiss shooting and fishing at once, with the warning that we must not dress *well* for either. An old coat with large pockets, gaiters in one case, and, if necessary, large boots in the other, thick shoes at any rate, a wide-awake, and a well-filled bag or basket at the end of the day, make up a most respectable sportsman of the lesser kind. Then for cricket you want nothing more unusual than flannel trousers, which should be quite plain, unless your club has adopted some colored stripe thereon, a colored flannel shirt of no very violent hue, the same colored cap, shoes with spikes in them, and a great coat.

For hunting, lastly, you have to make more change, if only to insure your own comfort and safety. Thus cord-

breeches and some kind of boots are indispensable. So
are spurs, so a hunting-whip or crop; so too, if you do
not wear a hat, is the strong round cap that is to save
your valuable skull from cracking if you are thrown on
your head. Again, I should pity the man who would attempt to hunt in a frock-coat or a dress-coat; and a scarf
with a pin in it is much more convenient than a tie. But
beyond these you need nothing out of the common way,
but a pocketful of money. The red coat, for instance, is
only worn by regular members of a hunt. and boys from
Oxford who ride over the hounds and like to display their
"pinks." In any case you are better with an ordinary
riding-coat of dark color, though undoubtedly the red is
prettier in the field. If you *will* wear the latter, see that
it is cut square, for the swallow-tail is obsolete, and worn
only by the fine old boys who "hunted, sir, fifty years
ago, sir, when I was a boy of fifteen, sir. Those *were*
hunting days. sir; such runs and such leaps." Again,
your "cords" should be light in color and fine in quality;
your waistcoat, if with a red coat, quite light too; your
scarf of cashmere, of a buff color, and fastened with a
small simple gold pin; your hat should be old, and your
cap of dark green or black velvet, plated inside, and with
a small stiff peak, should be made to look old. Lastly,
for a choice of boots. The Hessians are more easily clean-
ed, and therefore less expensive to keep; the "tops" are
more natty. Brummell, who cared more for the hunting
dress than the hunting itself, introduced the fashion of
pipe-claying the tops of the latter, but the old origina.
"mahoganies," of which the upper leathers are simply
polished, seem to be coming into fashion again.

We shall now pass to a subject which, in every respect,

is a much larger and more delicate one; larger in the space it covers in the surface of the globe; larger in the number of items which go to make it up; larger in the expenditure it demands; and larger in the respect of the attention paid to it. If it takes nine tailors to make a man, it must surely require nine women to make a thorough milliner.

CHAPTER IV.

LADY'S DRESS.

FAR from being of the opinion expressed by Catharine of Arragon, that "dressing time is murdered time," the woman, we are apt to think, who has not some natural taste in dress, some love of novelty, some delight in the combination of colors, is deficient in a sense of the beautiful. As a work of art, a well dressed woman is a study.

That a love of dress is natural in woman, and that it has some great advantages, is so plain as to be scarcely worth recording. It does not follow that it should engross every other taste ; it is only the coquette's heart, which, as Addison describes it, is stuffed with "a flame-colored hood." From the days of Anne Boleyn, who varied her dress every day, and who wore a small kerchief over her round neck to conceal a mark thereon, and a falling sleeve to hide her doubly-tipped little finger, dress has had its place in the heart of Englishwomen. And it is as well that it should do so; for the dowdy, be she young or be she old, is sure to hear of her deficiencies from her husband, if she has not already done so from brothers and fancy cousins. Indifference and consequent inattention to dress often show pedantry, self-righteousness, or indolence ; and whilst extolled by the "unco gude" as a virtue, may be noted as a defect. Every woman should, habitually, make the best of herself. We dress out our receiving rooms with natural flowers ; are their inmates to look in-

(176)

consistent with the drawing room over which they preside? We make our tables gorgeous, or at all events seemly, with silver, glass and china; wherefore should our wives be less attractive than all around them? Amongst the rich and great, the love of dress promotes some degree of exertion and display of taste in themselves, and fosters ingenuity and industry in inferiors; in the middle classes it engenders contrivance, diligence, neatness of hand; among the humbler it has its good effects. But in thus giving a love of dress its due, the taste, the consistency, and the practicability of dress are kept in view; the de-votion to dress which forms, in France, a "Science apart," and which occupies, it must be allowed, many, too many an Englishwoman's head, is not only selfish, but contemptible. So long as dress merely interests, amuses, occupies only such time as we can reasonably allot to it, it is salutary. It prevents women from indulging in sentiment; it is a remedy for *maladies imaginaires;* it somewhat refines the tastes and the habits, and gives satisfaction and pleasure to others.

Besides, an attention to dress is almost requisite in the present state of society; a due influence in which cannot be attained without it. It is useful, too, as retaining, even in the minds of sensible men, that pride in a wife's appearance which is so agreeable to her, and which materially fades during the gradual decay of personal attractions. "No one looked better than my wife did to-night," is a sentence which one often rejoices to hear from the lips of an honest hearted English husband, after a party or a ball, how much soever we may doubt the soundness of his decision.

But whilst the advantages of a love of dress are ad-

mitted, how mournfully we approach a consideration of
its perils. A love of dress, uncontrolled, stimulated by
coquetry and personal vanity until it cancels every right
principle, becomes a temptation first and then a curse.
Not to expatiate upon the evils it produces in the way of
example, the envy an undue passion for and excess in dress
excites, the extortionate class of persons in the shape of
milleners and dressmakers it unduly enriches, and the
enormous expenses it is known to lead to when indulged
criminally, that is, to the detriment of better employments,
and beyond the compass of means, let us remember how
it implies selfishness and vanity, and causes remonstrances
and often reproaches from the person most likely to suffer
from his wife's indulgencies—her husband.

Analyze the bill of a fashionable milliner when the
dresses, of which it comprises a fabulous reckoning, are
even only half worn out. What gauzes, and odds and
ends of lace, and trimmings, useless after a night or two's
wear, and flouncings and furbelows and yards of *tulle illusion* it enumerates ! *Tulle illusion*, indeed ! all is illusion ! and yet for this a husband's income is charged,
often at an inconvenience, or a wife's allowance encumbered, or angry words engendered, or the family credit
impeached ; and, worse than all, charity and even justice
must be suppressed, on account of this claim from a milliner as remorseless as she is fashionable, for these two
points are generally in the same ratio. Then there is
another evil ; it has been found that the indulgence in
personal luxury in women has an injurious effect on the moral tone. It is in some natures the first symptom, if not
the cause, of a relaxation in virtue ; at all events, it is
often mistaken for such. A woman of simple habits, ac-

companied with nicety and good taste, rarely goes wrong; at any rate is rarely supposed to do so. Luxury in dress at first an indulgence, becomes a necessity : discontent, a sense of humiliation, and a yearning for what cannot be had, are the effects of that withdrawal of the power of extravagance which so often happens in this changing and commercial country.

We used to point to America as the country in which excessive dress was a reproach ; the rich silks, the foreign lace, the black satin shoes, and the *décollée* evening dress of the fair inhabitants of New York, even in Broadway, are themes of comment to us all. We used to wonder at the French *dame du monde*, who gives six hundred pounds for her set of winter sables. Instances are not wanting, either, in Vienna and Bavaria, of ladies who spend seven or eight hundred a year on dress, independent of jewelry. It is remarked in Paris, that habits of *luxe* in every shape, but especially in dress, have come in with the present *régime*. The old Legitimist families, though habitually and innately *studious* in dress, prided themselves on their elegant simplicity, as distinguishing them from *bourgeoisie*. The Court of Louis Philippe was remarkable for its homeliness; and the Queen and the Duchess of Orleans set an example of a noble superiority to the vanities of life. Few carriages were kept, comparatively ; and where ladies cannot have carriages, they must dress plainly in the streets. But with the marriage of Louis Napoleon, the Empress has, probably without intending it, been the originator of extreme richness and variety in dress ; and the contamination has spread to England. Never did women require so *much*. Every lady, and even every lady's maid, must now have her petticoats edged with work. The cost of pocket-handkerchiefs is something marvellous; the plain fine cambric, than which nothing is more appropriate or more agreeable, is only fit for our inferiors. Cuffs, collars, *jabots*, *chemisettes*, are a genus that half ruin a lady of moderate means. Until lately, flounces went into such extremes that it required twenty or two-and-twenty yards to make a dress for the wife of a hard working physician or lawyer; but, happily, the excess has cured itself. France, in returning good sense, now decrees that everything shall be plain. Trimmings, that snare to the unwary, out of which dressmakers made fortunes, and husbands lost them, are put down. How long this salutary change may continue no one can tell; but a woman of sense should be superior to all these variations. She should keep within the bounds of the fashion. She should not dress out that perishable piece of clay with money wrung from the hands of an anxious, laborious husband; or taken, if her husband be a man of fortune, from his means of charity.

The proportion of what amongst the great we call pin-money, and amongst their inferiors an allowance for dress, is a very difficult matter to decide. Consistency, in regard to station and fortune, is the first matter to be considered. A lady of rank, the mother of three beautiful, ill-fated daughters, is reported " to be able to do" with two thousand a year for dress ! A monstrous sum ; a monstrous sin so to spend it ! When we look into the details of a recent bankruptcy case, in which the items of the famous Miss Jane Clark's bills for the dresses of two fashionable, and we must add most blamable, women were exposed, the secret of these enormous sums for dress is revealed. It consists in reckless orders, and their results, fabulous prices. A lady once followed the late excellent Princess Augusta into the rooms of a Court milliner. Having waited until that illustrious lady had retired, it was time for the humbler customer to make her selection. She asked the price of a dress, apologizing therefor, for she was much impressed by the royal and dignified aspect which had preceded her. "Don't make any apology, ma'am," was the Court milliner's exclamation; "her Royal Highness never orders an article without asking the price; and I always like to receive ladies who ask prices; it shows that they intend to pay."

The cost therefore of dress depends so much on the prudence as well as on the discrimination of a lady, for she should know how to *choose* her dress, that it is difficult to lay down any rule of expenditure. For married women of rank, five hundred a year ought to be the maximum; a hundred a year the minimum (and there are many peers who cannot easily afford to give their wives even so much). The wives of ministers, and more especially of diplomatists, who require to appear frequently either in foreign courts, or in our own, may require five hundred, or even more, though I am persuaded very few of our ambassadorial ladies have so much to spend.

With regard to unmarried women, what a revolt amongst them there would be if old Lord Eldon were now alive to lay down, as he did, as a maxim, that forty pounds a year was enough for any girl not of age, even if she had large expectations; and that was all he allotted to a ward of Chancery, who was heiress to five thousand a year. It was, perhaps, too little. In a trial, in which a celebrated barrister, who had an extravagant wife, was sued for dressmakers' bills for his reckless spouse, the judge stated that

sixty pounds a year was an ample allowance for the wife
of a professional man, and beyond *that* bills could not be
recovered. *That* was essential : more was extravagance.

Certainly these legal authorities were moderate in their
views; especially as no women are so extravagant—none so
luxurious, generally, as the wives of successful barristers.

The *Times*, whose range and power seem to resemble
the elephant's.trunk that can pick up a pin or crush a man,
in a late sensible and amusing " leader," made a remark
which will comfort struggling professional men, and, generally, be thankfully received by all who need some authority to aid in keeping the milliner's bill within due
bounds. It was simply to the effect that a tasteful, careful lady, with the start of a moderately good *trousseau*,
ought (and many do) to make twenty pounds a year suffice
for the dress of herself and children during the first few
years of married life, and this without any compromise of
respectability.

Much, however, depends on management, much on the
care taken of dress. In these respects the French are infinitely our superiors. Even the *grandes dames* of Paris
are not intimidated by their maids into throwing away a
half-worn dress; on the contrary, everything is turned to
account. On entering the apartment of a *couturière* one
day, a lady was struck by the elegance of ribbon trimming
on a court-train. The *couturière* smiled, and pointed to
an old dress from which the still unsoiled ribbon had been
taken. This was to be the dress, and the lady saw it the
next night at the Tuileries. and knew it at once; in this
the sister of a Duc and Maréchal of France, herself a
Countess, appeared. We should find it impossible to get
any mantua-maker to perform such an act of virtuous econ-

omy in favor of an English customer. The due *care of dress* is also a great point towards a reasonable economy. In England, ladies think it becoming their dignity to be indifferent to the preservation of their dresses when on.

In France the reverse is carried to an excess. " I once followed," said a lady, " a French lady in her carriage, as we both went to the same party. Her dress was composed of an exquisite tulle, with puffings of the same light material. She stood up in her carriage the whole way, for fear of crushing it."

Whatever may be thought of this over-care of the dress in the higher classes, the habit of conservativeness is of vast importance to women in the middle class, and yet, strange to say, it is less common in them than among the great. Old families are mostly conservative of personalities; it is a remarkable feature in them, and to it we owe those relics of times long gone by, which, had they been new in the present day, would have been deemed scarcely worth the preservation.

But whilst too much cannot be said against extravagance and destructiveness, it must also be stated, under the head of the minor virtues, the wonderful art some people have of making a good appearance on small means. " A man's appearance," says the good, old-fashioned, sensible *Spectator*, " falls within the censure of every one that sees him ; his parts and learning very few are judges of." So, in regard to women. No stranger knows the heart that beats beneath an ill-made gown, or the qualities of head that lie hidden beneath a peculiar old-fashioned, or hideous cap. A woman may be an angel of goodness, a Minerva in wisdom, a Diana in morals, a Sappho in sentiment, yet if she wears a soiled dress where all around are in new and fresh dresses, or has an ill arranged bonnet or head-dress, esteem, even affection, will not resist a smile or a sigh ; and the mere acquaintance will have every right to jeer at what seems to imply an ignorance of the habits of good society.

Next in injury to her who practises extravagance of dress, is extravagance in fashion. From the middle ages the English ladies have been bad dressers. Witness Queen Mary when married to Philip II. of Spain, spoiling the effect of a superb wedding-dress, in the French style, by wearing a black scarf and scarlet shoes, which, it has been sarcastically observed, was worse than burning Protestants. During the last century head-dresses rose to a stupendous height, each lady carrying on her head a tower composed of a cushion, on which the hair was drawn back, and clubbed or rolled on the top of the neck. On this fabric were arranged feathers, flowers, pearls dangling in loops, ribbons, and old point lace. Sometimes a tiny mob-cap was stuck on one side ; the whole was so immense that even the huge family coaches were too small, and the ladies usually sat with their heads hanging out of the window of the carriage. Powder was a main ingredient, and hair-dressing was indeed a science. On great occasions the hair-dresser waited on our fair ancestresses betimes : belabored their tresses with the powder-puff, and, with what looked like the end of a candle, a pomatum-stick, until no trace of nature could peep out to mar the belle. Then he placed the cushion, sticking it on with long pins of wire ; next he struck here and there the bows, or feathers, or flowers. After an hour's torture, in which neither back must be bent, nor head moved, he left her, not to repose, but to sit as if in a vice until the patches or *mouches* were stuck on skilfully; the tight corsets drawn to an agony point; the pointed and heeled shoes put on over the well-pricked silk stocking; and the dress that could have stood alone, composed over a fortification of strong whale-bone that sprung out a great circumference, being a series of bands, regulated by a spring, and constituting that great feature of full dress—the hoop.

In Paris, there was a champion of low heads in the person of a Swiss, who, not being able to see over these turrets of heads at the *grande* opera, used to cut away, as one does at evergreens, right and left, in order to clear away the view. At last, the ladies, in dismay, and alarmed at his scissors, gave him up a front place; but, eventually, the ridicule thus cast on the mode banished it, or helped to do so, and a less absurd *coiffure* came into vogue.

The art of placing patches on the face and neck was of earlier origin, and came in during the reign of Charles II. It was of French origin; and Henrietta of Orleans, the sister of the King, was amongst the first to display mouches or patches at court. This time even Mrs. Pepys was permitted by her husband to wear them; and the vanity of the *ci-devant* tailor spoke forcibly in these words:—"The Princess Henrietta is very pretty; but my wife, standing near her, with two or three black patches on, and well-dressed, still seems to me much handsomer than she." Patches long held their reign; and went out only with rouge, having even survived the reign of powder.

At length a more natural taste dawned in England; but it was reserved for Mrs. Siddons first to appear on the stage without powder, and her own rich dark hair arranged in massive tresses on her fine head.

Towards the beginning of the present century came in

the extremes of tight dresses and short waists. The skirts of dresses were made as scanty as possible, and gored, that is, made much wider at the base than at the top. There was an inch of sleeve, and two inches of boddice. It was impossible not to be indelicate, unless you put on what was called a "modesty-piece," or tucker, formed of lace or worked muslin; even then the requisite propriety was almost unattainable. As to the hair, that was drawn up to the top of the head, and two or three curls worn in front, just above the eyebrows. Since hoops had been outrageous, and head-dresses had obstructed the view of Her Majesty's liege subjects, society thus revenged herself. Politics, too, at that time influenced fashion. Then came the Brutus crop, in which style many of our fair ancestresses are depicted; this was in compliment to the Roman heroism of the First Consul, Bonaparte, and was caught up in England. Small Leghorn hats, like men's hats, were all the vogue, and were in their turn displaced for high-crowned bonnets with an inch or two of poke, which yielded, in due course, to the cottage-bonnet, or *capite*.

The hair at this time was getting higher and higher, until, about twenty years ago, it reached the *giraffe*—a bow of hair, or two, or even three bows raised on triangular pins made on purpose, and fastened skillfully into the hair; over this rose the bow called—in compliment to the first appearance of two giraffes in this country—the giraffe bows. Their reign was short, and the hair sank down to the very extreme, and ringlets, which reached the very waist, and plaits low down in the neck behind, succeeded. There was a transient reign of the Oldenburg bonnet, introduced by the beautiful Duchess of Oldenburg, when she visited this country in 1818. This bonnet was nothing more nor less than a coal-scuttle in straw, and turned up round the rim; it was tremendously warm to wear; and caricatures were drawn at the time showing a gentleman's difficulty in making love to his inamorata, whose face was enclosed in the Oldenburg bonnet. The effect of a number of these bonnets collected in a small space was ludicrous. A very pretty simple cottage, after all the best style, succeeded the Oldenburg. About 1821 the gored skirts gave place to those slightly gathered, or plaited round the figure. There was a perfect revolt against this fashion; many elegant women heading the malcontents. Happily they were obliged to yield, and the loose and full flowing dresses came into fashion, and kept their place, after a disgraceful interregnum of very short petticoats, only *not* showing the knees; which extreme, it is believed, induced the adoption of full and long skirts.

With occasional deviations, the form of the dress has not very greatly varied since the grand revolution which discarded gores, until that counter-agitation which brought in crinolines. This innovation is well exemplified by merely recalling the degeneracy in costume of the Imperial arbitress of fashion who introduced it. At one of the Tuileries balls in 1852, a young Spanish lady was the theme of all tongues. She was dressed in white, with a beautiful circlet of black velvet on her head; on this circlet were stars of diamonds. The hair, *blond dorée ;* the brow, alabaster; the somewhat melancholy eyes, with their long lashes, the regular but rather rigid pupil, were justly admired. Mademoiselle de Montijo, as she then was, was sparkling with happiness; the Emperor, that general who has since well-nigh dethroned Austria, yet, spared Venice, had that night signified his intention of making Eugenie de Montijo Empress of France, by placing on her head a white flower; she was radiant with excitement.

Her figure, however, was the subject of all praise. It was slight, and perfectly well dressed. The dress was tight in the corsage, and full, moderately full, in the skirt. Since then, what a change! That small, but matchless form, far more remarkable for grace than for dignity comes forth encumbered, unnaturally enlarged, and indeed deformed with an excess of fulness which can only be supported by a device which in principle is the grandchild of the hoop. As she walks, the petticoats shake about, and the artifice underneath is revealed. The Empress is there; but the beautiful *tournure* of Eugenie de Montijo is lost in the mass of bouffons and flounces over the invisible though protruding crinoline. The infatuation has spread from the palace to the private house; thence even to the cottage. Your lady's maid must now needs have her crinoline, and it has even become an essential to factory girls. The smart young needlewoman has long thought that neither she, nor any one else, could appear without it.

That there are some advantages in this modern fashion, cannot be denied. On State occasions it gives importance, shows off a dress, and preserves it from trailing on the floor. For walking, it has the recommendation of keeping the dresses out of the dirt; which may to some extent compensate for the very unpleasant and visible effect of "carrying one's tails behind one," since the skirt often shakes about as if there was a balloon around the person. Otherwise, the crinoline is unnatural—as some wear it, indelicate—and cumbersome, and gives an appearance of width below that is perfectly frightful. Now, however, the excess, seems abating. As if to make the contrast greater, those who so expand below, do not hesitate, in many instances, to contract above, by tight lacing; but this also is a custom that has very much decreased of late years. Formerly, instances were frequently known of young ladies nearly perishing under the self-imposed torture of what may not be inaptly called the waist-screw. A physician at dinner one day with his family, was summoned by knocks and rings to a house in the same street, where there had been a dinner party. The ladies had just retired to the drawing-room, when, suddenly, the youngest and fairest of them fell fainting back into her chair. Restoratives were applied, but consciousness did not return. The physician came; he was an aged and practical man, well versed in every variety of female folly. He took out his penknife; the company around thought he was going to bleed the still unconscious patient. "Ha, this is tight lacing!" he suddenly said; and adding, "no time to be lost," he cut open the boddice of the dress; it opened, and, with a gush, gave the poor young lady breath; the heart had been compressed by tight lacing. and had nearly ceased to act. In another moment it would have been too late; the action of the heart would have ceased altogether.

It has been found, also, that the liver, the lungs, the powers of the stomach, have been brought into a diseased state by this most pernicious habit. Loss of bloom, fixed redness in the nose, eruptions on the skin, are among its sad effects. If prolonged, there is no knowing to what malady tight lacing may not tend; its most apparent effect is an injured digestion, and consequent loss of appetite. Of this, however, it is often difficult to convince the practised tight-lacer; for vanity is generally obstinate.

No girl should wear bones or steels until she has done

growing. Until then a boddice, close-fitting, but not tight, or even a mere flannel waistcoat, is all that should be allowed, if a mother wishes to avoid seeing her child with a curved spine. During the reign of tight lacing, and of stays so stiff, that when spread out they resembled a board in texture, seven women in ten were crooked. Whole families leaned on one side or the other. "You are no worse than your neighbors," was the common expression of any surgeon called in to attend in a case of curvature of the spine. That is not the case now, to nearly such an extent.

But looking at tight lacing without consideration of its effect on health, and merely as its tendency to improve or to injure the appearance, nothing can be more absurd than to believe that it is advantageous to the figure. A very small waist is rather a deformity than a beauty. To see the shoulders cramped and squeezed together. is anything but agreeable; the figure should be easy, well developed. supple: if Nature has not made the waist small, compression cannot mend her work. Dress may do much to lessen the awkward appearance of a thick waist by clever adaptations; by the use of stays both easy and well fitting; by a little extra trimming on the shoulders. which naturally makes the waist appear smaller. All this may be done without injury; no stays can answer the purpose so well as those made by a good French stay-maker, who has the art of taking a sort of model of the figure by the extreme exactness of her measurements. The stays are made single, and therefore fit better than double ones; they give with every movement. Those lately introduced, which fasten at once, are not so advantageous to the figure as the old fashioned plan of lacing behind, but are.

admirable in point of convenience and despatch. By their aid, elderly ladies who have not dressed themselves, but have been dressed by a maid for years, have become independent; a great benefit to health and despatch. The slight exertion of dressing one's-self, the gentle exercise it induces after repose, the excellent habit of order, and the necessity it imposes of throwing off the thoughts, that may perhaps too much have occupied the mind during the hours of a wakeful night, render the operation of dressing to those in fair health, a very salutary exertion.

It is often disputed how far ladies are justified in following the fashion of the day; how far they could be praised or blamed for conforming or for resisting the influences around them in that respect. To adopt the prevailing fashion, but not carry it to excess, seems the most rational line of conduct; none but a great beauty, or a person of any exalted rank, can deviate, and hope to escape ridicule, from what fashion has introduced. Even in the acknowledged beauty, there is a presumption in doing so. Yet there were during the last reign three lively sisters, all now ennobled by marriage, who, at Court, when all were crowned with plumes, then worn like a crest on the head, nine or twelve in number, went to the drawing-rooms with a small feather on either side, and without diamonds: it was a courageous feat, but the effect was good, and produced, some thought, the reduction of plumes at Court.

A reasonable and tasteful acquiescence in the rapid changes—if not too rapid—in the modes of dress, is sensible and convenient. No single individual can successfully oppose the stream of fashion. Everything that is peculiar in dress is, we are convinced, more or less objectionable. Dr. Johnson was praising a lady for being very

well dressed. "I am sure she was well dressed," he re-
iterated, "for I cannot remember what she had on.'
Now, had not the lady's dress been modern in the fashion,
he would have been struck with some anomaly, some peculiarity, in form or colors The general effect was admirable; what more could be wished? details are important to the dress-maker and to the tailor: it is effect that
tells on society. Too much importance cannot be assigned
to the harmony of colors. No nation in this respect offends
so greatly as the English: they mistake gaudiness for effect,
or dowdiness for elegance. When full colors are in fashion, a lady, however well dressed, will look ill if she ad-
heres to the delicate pinks and almost invisible blues which
prevailed some years since, lovely as those pure and soft
shades are. She will, however, require an artist's eye to
combine the more glowing shades skilfully, in order to escape being the parroquet of the company. A certain
duchess, noted for the magnificence in which her stately
person is arrayed—so stately is it, as to bear down even
royalty itself in queenly dignity—is so aware of the importance of combining colors well, that one of her *femmes de chambre* is a "combination maid," selected on account of her judgment in colors; thus, every *toilette* for
the day or night is submitted by her; the shawl is affront-
ed with the gown; the bonnet is made to suit with both
The wreath of flowers is to be in keeping with the rich
boddice, the boddice with the sweeping train; the rich
jewelry, taken from a casket almost unparalleled among
the subjects of any country, must not eclipse, but heighten
the tints of the dress: the whole is placed for inspection,
as an artist dresses up a lay figure; and the repute of the
combination-maid is staked on the result. White was that

gorgeous lady's favorite attire; white, scarce purer than the face, "O call it pale, not fair;" white, which "combines" with every hue, ornament, or flowers: but the loveliness may now have fled before the approach of time, and rich colors have been selected as the appropriate tints for that middle age which is so beautiful in English women, and in English women alone.

After these general remarks, let us come to particulars, and consider what, in modern days, are the different dresses appropriate to every different occasion in the higher and middle classes of life. It is true that the distinction between these is, in many respects, nullified; that the wife of the merchant dresses much in the same way on ordinary occasions as the peeress: still there are nevertheless distinctions.

The peeress, or the baronet's lady, or the wife of a minister, or of an opulent M. P., of a very wealthy commoner, should, when she appears dressed for the morning, be richly dressed. Silk, or, if in winter, some material trimmed with silk or velvet, should compose her dress. All that family of half-worsted and half-silk dresses, convenient for ladies who walk much, are unsuitable to matrons of rank and fortune. Let them leave them to their housekeepers (if their housekeepers will wear them). Rich dark silks, perfectly well fitting, ample in skirt and length, with a moderate *bastion* of crinoline underneath, suit the woman of rank. The basque, introduced by the Empress Eugenie, and now gone out of fashion, was peculiarly elegant in morning dress: is marked so completely the difference between the morning and evening costume; it is becoming to most figures; it is convenient for those who like to fasten their own dresses. It is, however, dis-

continued, and a far less elegant form of dress adopted.
The morning dress of the present day is worn close up
to the throat, and the sleeves are loose and large; so that
underneath them, sleeves, richly worked, or trimmed with
lace, may be seen hanging down, or fastened round the
wrist with a bracelet. The fashion of these morning
dresses varies continually; but, as a general principle,
they should be, for a person moderately *embonpoint*, made
to fit and show off the figure perfectly. The accompaniments of sleeves, collars, should be of the most delicate
and richest work; the lace choice; the lady of rank must
remember that imitations of lace are not suitable to those
who can encourage art and industry; a lady must also be
bien chaussée. If stockings are visible, they should be
of the finest silk or thread: the shoe well made, slight,
and somewhat trimmed; the fashion of wearing gloves in-
doors, or even mittens, has much died away lately. The
hand, if exposed, should be habitually well taken care of.
Nothing is so unlady-like as a hand that is either rough,
or has become sun-burnt, in which case gloves should be
used. Too many rings are vulgar. Those worn in the
morning should be of a solid kind, not pearls or diamonds,
which appertain to full dress; but enamel, plain gold. opal,
perhaps sapphire, carbuncle, may not be inconsistent with
morning dress, and the same observation may be applied
to the brooch.

There is another style of morning dress which is elegant, that of the *peignoir,* a loose robe, which admits of
great richness of texture; it may be of Cashmere or of
fine Merino ; it may be made out of a shawl; of anything
but silk, which is more appropriate to gowns : but this
dress is scarcely suitable to any but the early morning

hours, and ceases to be consistent in the gay afternoons of
a London life, when the drawing-room is filled with callers.

The morning coiffure, be it a cap, or be it the dressing
of the hair, should be simple, compact, neat. The hair,
when dressed, should be becomingly but somewhat mas-
sively disposed. When it is rich and full, a very slight
head-dress of Mechlin or Lisle lace, for married women,
at the back of the head, is becoming; when thin and weak,
a cap should be worn with ribbon coming down in front.
Nothing looks so bad as thin hair, underneath which the
head is discernible in the day-time. Every ornament on
the head is in bad taste in the morning; one views with
horror huge gold pins, or would-be gold, corresponding to
ear-rings of the same false description. The peril of being
induced to wear ornaments so meretricious, is, however,
more to be dreaded in that class of society below the peeress's
rank, with which it is particularly inconsistent. The
French ladies are models of dress when they hold their
morning receptions. Everything they wear is the best of
its kind. The few ornaments they permit themselves are
more elaborate and valuable than dazzling, everything announcing, as plainly as if it had been written on their
doors, that they are in *demie toilette.* The perfect agree-
ment of their dress with the hour and the occasion, is the
secret of its almost invariable success.

The same rules apply to walking dress, which should be
quiet in color, simple, substantial, and, above all, founded
on the science of combination. To see a bonnet adorned
with crimson flowers, worn with a bright lilac dress; green
with scarlet, blue with plum, are sad departures from the
rules of combination. In a town, even when, according
to the time of the day, or time of the year, a walking

dress should be simple, there should still be some degree of richness in the dress.

The very dowdy and common-looking style of dress should be avoided; there should always be visible, through every change, the lady. Some of our ladies of rank, it must be allowed, though maintaining well the characteristics of *grandes dames* in society, are negligent in their walking dress, and seem to consider that it is only necessary to put on their dignity when they dress for dinner.

For the country, the attire should be tasteful and solid and strong. The bonnet may still, though plain, and perhaps of straw or whalebone, be becoming. The hat, now so prevalently used, admits of some decoration, that gives both character and elegance. Worn almost universally on the Continent in summer, and now in England, it is the most sensible as well as the most picturesque covering for the head; long feathers, even in the most tranquil scenes, are not inappropriate. Cloaks, of a light material for summer, and stout in the winter, are more elegant and suitable than shawls, which belong rather to the carriage or visiting dress. One point of dress has been much amended lately, owing to the good sense of our Queen. It was formerly thought ungenteel to wear anything but thin Morocco shoes, or very slight boots in walking. Clogs and goloshes were necessarily resorted to. "The genteel disease," as Mackenzie calls it, has, however, yielded to the remedies of example. Victoria has assumed the Balmoral petticoat, than which, for health, comfort, warmth, and effect, no invention was ever better. She has courageously accompanied it with the Balmoral boot, and even with the mohair and colored stocking. With these, and the warm cloak, the looped dresses, the shady hat, and, to complete a country walking dress, soft gloves of the kind termed *gants de si'cle*, the high born lady may enjoy the privileges which her inferiors possess—she may take a good walk with pleasure and safety, and not shiver at the aspect of a muddy lane.

Next, in the description of a lady's dress, comes the carriage, or visiting dress. This should be exceedingly handsome; gayer in color, richer in texture than the morning dress at home. The bonnet may either be as simple as possible, or as rich; but it must not encroach upon that to be worn at a fête, a flower-show, or a morning concert. It must still be what the French call "*un chapeau de fatigue.*" A really good shawl, or a mantle trimmed with lace, are the concomitants of the carriage, or a visiting dress in winter. In summer all should be light, cool, agreeable to think of, pleasant to look at. Nothing can be in worse taste than to keep on, till it makes one feverish to look at it, the warm clothing of winter after winter and even spring have passed away. Then light scarfs, of which those worn in muslin are very elegant, delicate muslins, slight silks, and grenadines, are infinitely more suitable, although they are less expensive, to summer and its bright hours than the heavy artillery of cashmeres and velvets, be they ever so handsome.

The ordinary evening costume at home admits of great taste and becomingness. In some great houses it differs little from that assumed at large dinner-parties, except that ornaments are less worn. In France, the high dress is still worn at dinners, even those of full dress. In England, that custom, often introduced, never becomes general; there is no doubt but that a low dress is by far the most becoming, according to age, complexion, and the *style*

of the house—a point always to be taken into consideration. Yet I should restrict this to dinners by candle-light.
In summer a thin high dress, at any rate, is more convenient and more modest. Since there is something in
exposing the bare shoulders and arms to the glare of day,
that startles an observer, the *demie toilette* of the French
may here be well applied. The hair should now be fully
dressed, and with care; flowers may be worn by the
young; caps with flowers by the elder; ornaments, especially bracelets, are not inconsistent; the dress should be
of a texture that can bear inspection, not flimsy and inexpensive, but good, though not heavy. The same rules
may be applied to the ordinary costume in an evening at
home, except that the texture may be lighter. For all
these occasions a lady of rank and fortune should have
her separate dresses. She should not wear out her old
ball or dinner dresses by her fireside and in intimate circles. They always have a tawdry, miserable look. She
should furnish herself with a good provision for the *demie
toilette*. Nothing is so vulgar as finery out of place.

The full dinner-dress, in England, admits, and indeed,
in the present days of luxury, demands great splendor.
The dress may be blue, silver-grey, crimson, maize, lavender, or (but rare) very pale green: pink is suitable
alone to balls; it may be of any thick texture of silk in
vogue; but in the fashion it must be. The dinner dresses
that last for ever are detestable. Trimmings of Brussels
lace, or of Mechlin, or of Maltese, are preferable to blonde
or tulle, which are for balls and soirees. The dress should
be made in the newest fashion : therefore no rule can be
set down, except that for state dinners it should be long,
and fresh, and sweeping. At large dinners, diamonds

may be worn, but only in a brooch, or pendant from the
throat; a full suite of diamonds is suitable to very full
dress alone. The same rule applies to emeralds, but not
to pearls. Rows of pearls, confined by a diamond snap,
are beautiful in every dress. They suit either the *demie
toilette*, or the stately solemn dinner. If flowers be worn,
they should be of the very choicest; ladies have so much
time to examine and to criticise after dinner, that too
much care of minutiæ cannot be taken; if but a rose, it
should be from the very first hand. The fan, to be consistent, should also be first-rate; it may be old, and painted after the manner of the exquisite fans in France, for
which one pays as high as twenty pounds; or it may be
a mere invention of the day; but it must be perfect in
its way. Nothing is so inimical to appearance as an ill-
made or soiled glove. There is such a wonderful mixture
of economy and prodigality in the highest classes of English society, that it is not uncommon to see ladies, resplendent in jewelry, with dirty gloves: in France, to
which we have, in all ages, looked as to a model, such a
barbarism could never occur. Every trifle in a lady's
costume is perfect. She would rather go out in a shabby
gown than in a collar of false lace, or with dirty gloves,
or begrimed white satin shoes. It is not so in England;
ladies who spend pounds upon a cap or a scarf, will hesitate before they put on a clean pair of gloves. Dinner-
parties are so often the prelude only, in London, to the
festivities of the evening, that no strict rules as to dress
can be set down. Generally speaking, there is a great
difference between the dinner-dress and that of the ball.
A concert, on the other hand, or the opera, requires only
the head to be somewhat more adorned than at a dinner,

and yet there was a fashion, several years since, of appearing even at the Italian opera in the simple toilette of a small dinner party. The *sortie du bal*, or short evening cloak, is one of the best modern suggestions for the health, and even appearance, of those who attend public places or enter into gay society. It should be of white merino, not of scarlet, which spoils the effect of the wreath of flowers. All complicated trimmings are inconsistent; but the same rule of perfect freshness and cleanliness in respect to gloves is applicable to the *sortie du bal*. I am sorry to say it is violated every night: rows of ladies are to be seen with resplendent gems in their hair, waiting for their carriages, in *sorties du bal* that are almost gray from the effects of London smoke. The striking relief and the contrast produced by one or two clean and fresh cloaks of this description is quite singular, and proves the truth of the above recommendation. And here let us marvel against the wonderful misplaced economy that will not permit an English lady to indulge in a new *sortie du bal* " this season," whilst she is, at the same time, lavishing sums upon all the endless *et ceteras* which Englishwomen of the nineteenth century cannot do without.

At one of the most brilliant balls at the Hotel de Ville in Paris, an order was given for the company, who were to be numbered on that occasion by thousands, to wait in relays on the grand staircase leading to the reception-rooms, until a certain hour of the night or rather morning. This order was to prevent a rush to the carriages, and the danger incident to such a concourse wishing to leave at the same time. The ladies sat for an hour or more on that ample and matchless staircase, to the right of which was the artificial pool of water, surrounded by plants, and lighted by lamps, amid which the spray of a fountain cast up crystal drops, which fell dimpling into the water again. The light played upon the white cup of a large water-lily in the miniature pool, and the scene was at once remarkable and brilliant. As I looked around from the bottom of the stairs, and about, I could see many pale and weary faces, but not one dirty *sortie du bal:* all here as fresh, as clear, as snowy white as if new only that day; some lined with cherry color; others with blue; a few with amber; most with white. Even after all the festivities were over, a Frenchwoman, if she could not look well, was resolved to look clean.

Ball-dressing requires less art than the nice gradations of costume in the dinner costume, and small evening party dress. For a ball, everything even in married women may be light, somewhat fanciful and airy. What are called *good* dresses seldom look well. The heavy, richly-trimmed silk, is only appropriate to those who do not dance; even for such, as much effect should be given to those dresses as can be devised. Taste, ingenuity, *style*, are here most requisite. Since the fashions continually alter, there is no possibility of laying down specific rules; the dress, however, for the married, and for the unmarried lady of rank or of fortune, should be distinctly marked. For the married lady *moiré* dresses, either trimmed with lace, or tulle and flowers, or white silk—no other color in plain silk looks well—or thin dresses over white satin, an article which is happily coming into fashion again, are most suitable. Diamonds on the head, neck, arms, she may wear; but the decoration of the dress with them should be reserved for court-balls, and for court. Formerly when diamonds were worn, flowers were either considered unnecessary, or even inconsistent; now they are frequently intermingled. Small feathers are even worn at balls; and, for the married, produce perhaps more effect than any other *coiffure;* but they are wholly out of fashion on a young lady's head. The unmarried, indeed, so long as they continue young, will best consult their own good looks by as much simplicity as is consistent with fashion. In Paris no ornaments, with the exception, perhaps, of a single bracelet, are allowed to the *jeune fille;* her dress must be white; the flowers in her hair white also. To these general rules there are exceptions, but the appearance of a French ball is that of spotless white; far different to the full colors often worn in England.

White tulle over white silk (or white lace), and bouquets of flowers, corresponding to the *guirlande* or cachepenie on the head, are the favorite dress of the young lady. A *parure* of flowers, consisting of two flowers mingled, is elegant; for instance, the rose and heliotrope, the *parure* forming the wreath which extends down the skirt; or, of white flowers, the acacia,—of blue, the myosotis,—of green, the maidenhair fern; these are all exquisite ornaments. Even the large white lily forms a beautiful *parure.* The French always make use of the flowers in season, but we English are less scrupulous. A young lady will wear a wreath of lilies of the valley mixed with roses, in the depth of the winter; holly and berries in June; scarlet geraniums in spring. Large daisies are also liable to suggest ludicrous ideas. "That lady's dress wants mowing." said a wag. looking at a beautiful tulle dress, covered with white daisies with flaring yellow centres.

Nothing, however, forms a more beautiful head-dress than natural flowers, carefully mounted. The French have a great art of mounting flowers on wire, and many of their ladies'-maids learn it; some of the ladies excel in it themselves. For country balls and *fêtes*, the effect is lovely; and the perpetual variety obtained a source of that surprise and novelty which add so much to the effect produced by dress. The flowers should be neatly and firmly stuck upon wires. Variegated geraniums, and all the white varieties only, answer well; white camellias (the red are too heavy), parti-colored carnations, the rose Devoniensis, large white lilies, are all suitable to hairs of various shades. A *parure* of ivy is elegant—but it has become common; in spring, the scarlet ranunculus has a rich effect; in winter, the hellebore or Christmas rose is very appropriate. There is one of the carnival balls at Munich, in which the custom of wearing natural flowers is almost *des rigueurs ;* it is on Shrove-Tuesday. Since in that severe climate it is difficult to obtain natural flowers in perfection, the wreaths are ordered in Paris, and are articles of great expense. On seeing them beside even the most exquisite artificial wreaths, the effect is striking; every tint in the latter has a want of that transparency which, in the natural flowers, is owing to the minute and almost invisible globules of water in the petals beneath the cuticle. The richest hues pall before the inimitable coloring of nature. Amongst the garnitures on one occasion, that of the Queen of Bavaria was pre-eminently beautiful. She wore on her head a wreath of natural roses; in the centre of each rose hung a diamond dew-drop. Her dress was white, trimmed down on either side with single roses, encircled with a single row of diamonds each, as if the dew hung round the petals; in the centre was the diamond-dew drop. This beloved and beautiful princess, now, by marriage, the first cousin of the Princess Royal of England, always superintends the arrangements of her own ball dresses, her taste is exquisite, and the ingenuity with which she varies her costumes is remarkable.

As ladies advance in life, the ball-room seems scarcely to be their province; but since many of them are obliged to be chaperons, the style of dress most becoming personally and also most consistent with that character, should be considered. Many persons think that it little matters what a middle-aged lady wears, so long as she looks neat and respectable, and displays a sufficient amount of expensive lace, diamonds, and so many ells of unexceptionable silk or satin. I am not of that opinion; as long as a face is a face fit to present itself to society, so long should good taste carefully preserve the fast-fading attractions, not by art and cosmetics, or false curls, or roses round a sallow brow, or the lilies of the field, which are appropriate to youth alone, but by an arrangement of cap or head-dress that is becoming to the poor old ruins; just as we like to see the mantling ivy clustering, and say how greatly it adds to the beauty of the old devastated fort or chapel.

Under the head of festive occasions, the court dress must not be admitted.

This costume consists, first, of an entire dress, generally made of some plain but costly silk.

The dress, therefore, forms one component part; next comes the petticoat, usually of some lighter material; and lastly, the train.

The dress is made, even for elderly ladies, low; and the boddice is trimmed in accordance with the petticoat and the train.

The petticoat is now usually formed of rich Brussels lace, or of Honiton lace, or tulle; and often looped up with flowers.

The train is of the richest material of the whole dress. Formerly it was often of satin ; now it is of moiré or glace silk, though satin is again beginning to be worn.

It fastens half round the waist, and is about seven yards in length, and wide in proportion. It is trimmed all round with lace, in festoons, or on the edge, with bunches of flowers at intervals, and is lined usually with white silk.

The petticoat is ornamented with the same lace as the train, sometimes in flounces, sometimes in puffings or *bouffons* of tulle, sometimes *en tablier*. that is, down either side.

The boddice and sleeves are all made in strict uniformity with the train and petticoat.

The head-dress consists of feathers, and comprises a lappet of lace, hanging from either side of the head down nearly to the tip of the boddice. Diamonds or pearls, or any other jewelry sufficiently handsome, may be worn in the hair, but the two former are most frequently adopted. The same ornaments should be worn on the boddice around the neck and arms.

The shoes should be of white satin, and trimmed according to fashion. The fan should be strictly a dress fan ; those spangled are the most suitable for a costume which requires everything to be as consistent as possible with the occasion.

Having thus treated of the dresses suited to the house, and to all festive occasions, there remains only the riding-dress to mention.

In this particular several changes have been made during the last two or three years. The round hat, of masculine appearance, is almost always exchanged for a slouched hat, sometimes of a round form, and turned up round the brim —sometimes turned up on either side, and coming with a point low down upon the forehead—and sometimes three-cornered : all these different forms have their votaries ; but it must be acknowledged that the more simple and modest the shape, the more becoming.

Formerly, the neat round hat, masculine in its form, was unembellished by even a bow ; but now, a long, sweeping feather on one, and sometimes on both sides, sets off the riding-hat. The color of the feather is varied. but is usually black or brown, like the hat. The feather, it may here be remarked, should be full, well-curled, long and firm, not thin and weak, as if taken from an ostrich in a moulting condition. In winter, the hat should be of felt of a soft kind, pliable and durable ; in summer, of a fine straw. It is not wise to get a hat made by an inferior hand. The style constitutes the grace, and renders it either a most becoming or a most tawdry feature in the riding-dress. And here let us remark on the great benefit of these slouching hats to the complexions which have so materially suffered of late years from small bonnets and round hats. Health, with delicacy, is the true charm of feminine *physique*, and, as far as a riding costume is concerned, nothing secures the freshness of the face better than the slouched hat. It is cool, and permits the free circulation of air around the face, while it protects the eyes, the forehead, and almost the chin, from scorching heat or withering blasts.

Finally, as far as regards hats, let a hint be thrown out

repressing the eccentricities of a fantastic taste : The art
of riding is in itself conspicuous enough. A lady decked
out in that position approaches the mountebank rider from
Astley's or Franconi's. Her costume may be elegant on
all occasions without being *outré*. The moment her taste
degenerates so as to produce a *striking* effect, she may be
sure she is making a mistake, and nowhere so fatally as on
horseback.

We must acknowledge that the change in riding-hats
has another good effect. The lady equestrian cannot now
be called masculine. " Bist ein Mann oder eine Mad-
schen ?" cried out a number of little Rhenish boys as a
young lady galloped through a village near D'isseldorf.
The *Spectator* has a sharp article on the ambiguous ap-
pearances of these Amazons, as he styles them ; and in
fact in the last century, when scarlet riding-habits were
often worn, it must have been difficult on the riding-field
to have distinguished a lady from a gentleman ; but now
there is something picturesque, stylish, and inconsistent in
the modern slouching hat, the sweeping feather, and beneath them the rich clusters of hair bagged, and so confined in a net of black *chenille*.

The habit has sustained some changes, and, as far as appearance is concerned, not for the better. It used to be
invariably tight, well-shaped, with close sleeves. It is now
often made loose, with deep cuffs, or, if worn tight, a loose
jacket, or *casaque*, can be put over it—an advantage in
cold weather, but certainly not to the figure, which is
never seen to more advantage, be it bad or good, than in
a tight body, such as the old riding-habit A plain white
collar of fine lawn should be worn with the habit, deep lawn
cuffs underneath the sleeves, while gauntlet gloves of thick

leather, and no ornaments, save perhaps a delicately-twined whip, need be displayed. Compactness and utility are the requisites for the riding-dress ; and, whilst touching on this point, let us impress strongly the danger arising from too long a skirt in the riding-habit: it is apt not only to alarm horses, but to entangle, in case of accidents, their fair riders.

There, as in other cases, the principle of all that relates to dress should be consistency and suitableness. If these are once lost sight of—if fifty apes fifteen—if the countess dresses worse than her own housekeeper, or the maid vies with her mistress—if modest middle rank puts on the garb of fashion—if good taste and good sense cease to be the foundation of the important whole, then all special directions will be unavailing.

CHAPTER V.

LORD BYRON in one of his letters tells us that he might have been a beau, if he had chosen to drink deep and gamble fast enough. In Ben Johnson's time the main points of a "compleat gentleman" were to swear a new oath in every sentence, "By the foot of Pharaoh," "As I am a gentleman and a soldier," and so forth; to take tobacco, and swear over its virtues; to be able to run friend or foe through the heart with a bodkin; and to write a copy of silly verses to a by no means inaccessible mistress. Beau Brummell had only three pet points: the way he took snuff, opening the box with one hand, the ease with which he cut an old acquaintance, and the grace with which he bowed to a new one. Lord Chesterfield seems to think that if a man can ride, fence, and dance well, he is skilled enough for good society. The three requirements are worth noticing. The first was essential, if you would have male friends, in days when knighthood was not quite a shadow; the second allowed you to make good enemies, and kill or keep them; the third fitted you for the society of women.

The accomplishments of to-day, though they differ in many respects, have the same general bearing. In a man they are the arts required to keep a friend, to make an enemy, and to charm a woman; in a woman, to surpass a rival and to captivate a man of more taste than heart. For both, however, they have a far higher object, that

(209)

namely, of giving pleasure to our-fellow-creatures in some
form or other, and of increasing the general harmony of
society.   They are in fact those corollaries to the problem
of education, by which a person is fitted not only to "pass,"
but to "take honors" in the social examination.   While
it is impossible to deny that a man may be a perfect gentleman, a woman a well-bred lady, and both of them
agreeable in society, without a single accomplishment, we
all of us feel that such a person must either possess no
usual wit, like Dr. Johnson, who had not one accomplishment to add to his sound sense and learning, or be one
who, content to fill a quiet corner in life, does not care to
emerge from it even for the benefit of others.

Accomplishments have a heavy run against them in the
present day, and are decidedly at a discount. " Give me,"
cries Paterfamilias, bringing his fist with a heavy thump
down on the table, " give me good sterling practical knowledge, and none of your pishty-wishty humbugging accomplishments."   Paterfamilias, you err. like many a British
father, and in your love of the practical. you are blind to
the immense advantage of cultivating the beautiful in
every young soul.   Paterfamilias, to take the most serious
ground with you, it is the practical which shall lead you
to money bags and account books, but the beautiful which
shall guide you towards heaven.   These same accomplishments at which you sneer have a much deeper meaning and
value for your children than merely to shine in society.
They constitute the whole amateurship of art, and in the
present day to be thoroughly accomplished is to be half
an artist; yet the better half. You may not be able to
give a concert in Hanover Square Rooms, but you have
cultivated the music that lies within your soul.   And there

is music in every soul, and music is the most beautiful expression of peace and harmony; and harmony is the most
beautiful law of nature, of creation, the first rule of
God. You may not be able to exhibit a picture in the
Royal Academy, but you have learned to copy God's
work, and learning to copy you have learned to observe
and to know; and to know God's work, is to know God in
His work. Believe me, Paterfamilias, the study of art
rightly undertaken is the study of God, and it is by cultivating the beautiful that you approach heaven.

I do not say that every man can be a Crichton, but I
do say that every man should aim at that character in
some way, both for his own sake and that of those around
him. How much more so a woman, whose very mission is
to make life less burdensome to man, to soothe and comfort
him, to raise him from his petty cares to happier thoughts,
to purer imaginings, towards heaven itself.

At first sight accomplishments seem to belong to women
more than to men, but if we look more closely into the
subject we shall find that a man has a double necessity
upon him; he must be fit, on the one hand, for the society
of men, on the other for that of women, and this involves
a double list of acquirements; while those of women,
which make them charming to men, fit them also for the
company of their own sex.

Thus we must refuse in this case the *place aux dames*,
and take the men first. To mix comfortably with the
society of his own sex must be the first object to a man,
properly so called, and to do this he requires to know a
certain number of arts which are common among his
own.

Foremost of these is the art of self-defence, which is one which society constantly calls into requisition. Fortunately the duel is gone out of fashion, and a man need not now, as in the days of good Queen Bess, come to town to learn how to pick and take a quarrel, and how to get well out of it when made. Fencing in England is now nothing more than an exercise, no longer qualifying a man to take his place as a gentleman among his betters; but that which has succeeded to it is not without its importance, and the "compleat gentleman" should be able to use his fists. Low as this art is, and contemptible as are those who make a profession of it, it is nevertheless of importance to a man of every class, for a good blow often solves a difficulty as readily as Alexander's sword cut the Gordian knot. There are men whom nothing but a physical punishment will bring to reason, and with these we shall have to deal at some time of our lives. A lady is insulted or annoyed by an unwieldly bargee, or an importunate and dishonest cabman. One well-dealt blow settles the whole matter. It is true that it is brutal, and certainly should be a last resource; but to last resources we are often driven, and a show of determination brings impudence to an armistice. I would say, then, know how to use your fists, but never use them as long as any other argument will prevail, but, when all others fail, have recourse to that natural and certainly most convincing logic. A man, therefore, whether he aspires to be a gentleman or not, should learn to box. It is a knowledge easily gained. There are but few rules for it, and those are suggested by common sense. Strike out, strike straight, strike suddenly; keep one arm to guard, and punish with the other.

Two gentlemen never fight; the art of boxing is only brought into use in punishing a stronger and more impudent man of a class beneath your own.

There is good in everything, and there is a view to take of the pugilistic art which compensates in some measure for its brutal character in this country. The fist *has* expelled the sword and pistol. The former indeed went out about the beginning of last century, and Beau Nash, though by no means a coward, did his best to put down the wearing of a weapon which was a perpetual temptation to commit polite murder and disturb the harmony essential to good society. There could be no comfort and no freedom in conversation when, instead of politely differing with you, a man's hand moved to his sword-hilt. It is no argument against me that the rapier is still worn at court, for I feel convinced that nine-tenths of those ornamental but utterly useless appendages would never be induced to quit their scabbards, and, even if drawn, would be of no more value than a stick in the hands of at least nine-tenths of their courtly owners.

But it was another kind of biped who put down duelling, and a cock-pheasant of Wimbledon-Common, jealous, no doubt, at seeing the powder which ought to have been used for him, thrown away upon a human being, or perhaps anxious to try whether a bullet tasted better than shot, who had the honor of making these encounters so superbly ridiculous, that to call a man out in the present day is equivalent to calling him a fool and confessing yourself idiotic. There are those, however, who regret the palmy days of twelve paces and coffee for four, and tell us that the fear of a hole in the waistcoat kept many an impudent man in his place and restrained unwarrantable

familiarity. With all submission I would suggest that the
fear of being knocked down on the spot, and having his
beauty spoiled, is likely to be much more persuasive to a
man who can offend in this manner. But will you kindly
look across the water either way, and tell me if the silly
custom, kept up both in Europe and America, has there
the effect of awing men into even decent politeness? In
the latter country, especially, where a "difficulty" almost
always ends fatally, it is by no means uncommon for a
complete stranger to put his hands into his pockets, cock
his eye at you, and inform you by way of introduction,
"Wall, I guess you're a tarnation loggerhead, yecou
aire," proceeding to pass comments on your nationality,
your personal appearance, and your general mental capacities, according to the "guess," "reckoning," or "cal-
cyoo-lation" of the speaker. If you were to meet these
with astonishment, indignation, anger, or, in short, in any
way but by the retort personal and direct of the *tu quoque*
description, you would be looked on as a disagreeable,
testy, and pugnacious Britisher, and the rest of the company would probably request you to "shut up." In fact
so universal is insolence in America, that even in what is
here called good society—the "up town" sets—you are
liable to be assailed with the grossest epithets, and it is
only after being bespattered with essence of Billingsgate,
that you would be allowed to remark, "Wall. that's *some*,
that is; I reckon my dander's ris a bit after that." Of
course these remarks do not apply to New York, which,
in civilisation, is as far in advance of the States generally,
as London is of the Hebrides.

It is no longer necessary, therefore, to give the *etiquette*
of duelling, which may be gathered, as a curiosity, from

almost every novel written twenty years ago. It would be as sensible to give the *etiquette of murder*. As to its immorality, it has been discussed again and again, and the custom has been finally condemned on that score.

Of course to knock a man down is never good manners, but there is a way of doing it gracefully, and one rule should be observed, viz., whether you can command your temper or not, never show it, except by the blow. Never assail an offender with words, nor when you strike him, use such expressions as, "Take that," &c. There are cases in society when it is quite incumbent on you to knock an offender down, if you *can*, whether you feel angry or not, so that, if to do so is not precisely good manners, to omit it is sometimes very bad manners ; and to box, and that well, is therefore an important accomplishment, particularly for little men.

It is decidedly a relief to quit that subject, and I am not ambitious of emulating those gentlemen of the sword of Queen Elizabeth's day, who, for a small gratuity, would decide for you whether your honor was hurt or not—a question they usually contrived to answer in the negative, to the great relief and satisfaction of the applicant.

Our field sports have been so often and justly lauded, that I shall not now speak of them in a constitutional point of view, but their effect on society is a matter of no small interest, and it is extremely agreeable to Englishmen to be reminded of points of their superiority over their neighbors. I am inclined to think that our love of sports, if it spoils the London season, and makes dancing a torment, does none the less assist our women to be virtuous, and our men to be noble. The effect of a want of good, healthy out-door amusements is to make of a man either a carpet-knight, or a hanger about cafés. The life of cities tends to demoralize, and anything which takes a man away from a town for a time has its value. Thus hunting, shooting, riding, driving, cricket, and so forth, are as important elements of social life as dancing and music, and to be ignorant of their art will not only exclude one from much charming society we might sometimes enjoy, but will often cause us to put others to great inconvenience, if it does not equally annoy ourselves. Often in the country there is no other conveyance but a horse and saddle to be had. What are we to do if we cannot ride? Still oftener the whole arrangement of some party of pleasure depends on our being able to leave the coachman behind, and it is to us, the only gentleman perhaps, that the ladies apply to take his place. How, then, if we cannot handle a whip? Then, too, in the country, riding and driving are such common accomplishments, that besides the inconvenience, our ignorance of them subjects us even to ridicule. What more laughable than a man jolted up and down on his horse, till his hat slips to the back of his head, his hair flies about, his trousers creep up to his knees, and his face expresses either pitiable misery, or ludicrous discomfort? On the other hand, to hunt, shoot, handle a bat, or a billiard-cue, though by no means expected of every man, are often the only amusements in the country, and we may, if ignorant of them, not only be shut out from them ourselves, but even oblige our host to give them up on our account. In fact, the more of such accomplishments you know, the less tedious will your life be to yourself and your company to others, and though wit and conversation are worth all the amusements which a toy-maker could dream of, you must not forget that the

world is mainly peopled with fools, and that to appreciate
your sallies, and join in your mirth, requires an amount
of sense which is not to be found in every country bump-
kin. Should the weird sisters, in a fit of bad temper,
send you by express to sojourn for a month with a gentleman farmer or small hunting squire, what can you do
but shoot, ride, or drive with him? Will your heavy-
headed host, who dreams of patridges, and vacillates between long-horns and turnips in his waking thoughts, care
for your choice club-gossip, understand your fine-edged
wit, or thank you for your political news and Parliamen-
tary prospects? No, no; you must relate, slowly and
surely, how on such a day in such a year you " met" at
such a village, " drew ' such a cover, threw off in ' such
a direction, " cast" at such a spot, ran for so many minutes, and made so many wonderful, probably also apocry-
phal, leaps during that period. Relate how many birds
you bagged, what score you made at any insignificant
cricket-match, and how you swam from Barnes to Brent-
ford against tide and stream. Then, indeed, is your man
your friend, and he will privately impart to his wife that
evening that he thinks you " an amazingly fine fellow,"
which would have sounded very like '· horrid bore," if
you had not been able to come out on these subjects.

I have no intention to trespass on Mr. Rarey's province, and I am further of opinion that equitation cannot,
like grammar, be learned from a book, but there are a
few useful hints about the etiquette of riding, which may
well be introduced here. The first thing, then, is to
dress suitably. Boots and cords were once the *sine quâ
non* of a horseman, but though they are very comfortable, and may still be worn in the country, when you are

10

not going to ride with ladies, they have been interdicted
in town, and would mark you out as a riding-master. On
the other hand, you must avoid too fine a dress, such as
patent leather boots, and should wear a cut-away in preference to a frock-coat. Above all, let the stick or whip
be simple, with no gold head, no flummery about it. For
the country, you may have what is commonly called a
" crop," with a bone handle at the end; for town, you
may take either an ordinary walking-stick, or a gentleman's riding-whip, mounted simply with silver. In all
other respects, your dress should be that in which you
walk. The lady's dress has been described in the last
chapter.

A man who rides without ladies requires no groom to
follow him, and a young man particularly should never
take one, even though he intends to make calls. A lady,
on the other hand, should never ride alone, except in
quiet parts of the country. In London she would be
taken for a *demoiselle du cirque*, and in the country she
would be liable to accidents, with no one to assist her. A
young lady should not ride out without a gentleman, as
well as a groom, and, under most circumstances, mamma
would decidedly object to that gentleman being young
and single, unless he were a very intimate friend.

Having thus arranged your dress and your party, you
go down and mount—no, you do not mount yourself, but
assist the ladies. There never was so lame a legend as
that of a certain lady of Coventry, whom Tennyson and
Thomas the Inquisitive have rendered celebrated. Of
course it is very pretty, and we who honor women as we
should (though we burnt *la Pucelle d'Orléans*), and
have had a range of noble ones from Boadicea to Florence

Nightingale, can well believe that Godiva was as modest as she was merciful; but have we ever asked—*who assisted her?* Perhaps you will tell me that till a very recent period, no stable-yard was without a flight of three stone-steps standing by themselves, and that women always mounted from these. I know it, and have seen hundreds of them in the western counties; but before I admit your argument, you must show me that these steps existed in the days of the fair equestrian who wore no garb but modesty; you must prove that those people are wrong who describe the ladies of the olden time as mounting from the shoulder of a serving-man or a gallant.

However this may be, neither steps nor shoulders are so good as a steady hand, which is the means patronized by modern horsewomen. The lady having gathered up her skirt, and holding it in her left hand, must place herself as close as possible to the horse, with her face towards the animal's head, and her right hand on the pummel. The gentleman, whose part and privilege it is to assist her, having first obtained her consent to do so, then places himself at the horse's shoulder with his face towards the lady, and, stooping a little, places his right hand horizontally at a convenient elevation from the ground. On the palm of this hand the damsel sets her sweet little left foot, and it is then the gentleman's duty to lift it with a gentle motion as she herself springs upwards. But beware that you do not jerk it up too suddenly, lest she lose her balance and be thrown back over the saddle. I have seen a lady nearly killed by awkward mounting.

A man should be able to mount on either side of the horse, and ladies who ride much and wish to keep their figures straight, change the side from time to time. When

the lady is in the saddle you should offer to put her foot
in the stirrup and to pull down the skirt, and you then
give her the reins, and proceed to mount yourself.   Mr.
Rarey teaches us to do so without stirrups, and a man
who would be graceful should practise this on either side.
A horse, like most other animals, has two sides.   The one
which is to our left when we are in the saddle is called
the *near*, the other the *off* side, and it is on the former
that we generally mount.   We place our left foot in the
stirrup, our left hand on the saddle, and swing ourselves
up, throwing the right leg over the creature's back.   Nothing is more graceless than to see a man climb with both
hands into his seat.

The seat itself is one of those things which must be
learned by practice.   The chief rules are : sit upright,
but not stiffly, and well back in the saddle ; stick the
knees into the sides thereof, and keep the feet parallel to
the horse's body. the toes turned in rather than out.   The
foot should be about half-way in the stirrup, which in
rough-riding may be allowed to slip down to the hollow
of the foot.   The greatest obstacle to good riding is want
of confidence, and this can scarcely be acquired, except
by beginning at an early age.   If you cannot ride decently, you had better not attempt it in company, if you
would not risk the fate of Geordie Campbell,—

> " Saddled, and bridled, and booted rode he,
> Hame cam his gude steed, but never cam he."

The rule of the road need not be observed in riding as in
driving, but you should always ride to the right of the
lady who is with you, lest you risk crushing her feet.
Your own, of course, you must not care about.   When
you meet people whom you know on horseback, you have

no right to turn and join them, unless invited to do so.
If you overtake them, on the other hand, you have a
right to ride with them; but if you are not wanted, you
will be careful about exercising the privilege.

About hunting I shall say little, because I know little,
which is a confession you will find it the wisest plan to
make in the country. I shall only advise you not to
hunt unless you have a good seat and a good horse, and
never accept the loan of a friend's horse, and still less
an enemy's, unless you can ride very well. A man may
forgive you for breaking his daughter's heart, but never
for breaking his hunter's neck. Another point is always
to be quiet at a meet, and never join a small meet unless
you know some one in the field. The first essential for
hunting is pluck; the second, skill; the third, a good
horse. Avoid talking of your achievements, enthusiastic
shouting when you break cover, and riding over the
hounds. Whatever you do, do not injure one of those
precious animals.

There is a grace in riding which no jockey, no professional huntsman ever acquires. When once you have
confidence, ease may soon follow; but without much practice, you will always be more or less stiff in your seat.
A lady should be careful to sit straight in the middle of
the saddle, with her face full towards the horse's head.
Whatever the motion of the animal, you should attempt
to cling as closely as possible to the saddle. The Austrian officers pride themselves on being able to trot for a
mile with a glass of wine in one hand, and not spill a
drop of it. In England we rise in trotting, as a relief to
ourselves and the horse, but this is never done in any
other country. The first rule is to rise, not from the

stirrup, but from the knees ; the second, to rise as little
as possible. The man who "shows daylight" between
himself and his saddle is a bad rider. A lady should
rise even less than a man, and neither of them should lean
over the horse's neck, nor hold the reins in both hands.
But I am not a riding-master, and I am trespassing on
his ground.

Driving, again, is an accomplishment of butcher's boys
and hansom cabmen as much as of "gentlemen," but there
is a vast difference in the style. One rule may be given
at once, and we may unhesitatingly affirm that Jehu the
son of Nimshi was "no gentleman," when we remind
you that to drive furiously, as well as to ride furiously, is
not only forbidden by law, but a low, cruel, ungentleman-
like habit.

"The beggar mounted rides his horse to death."

If you drive too fast, I am tempted to ask whether the animal is your own, and whether you know its value. I may
add, that if wise you will never drive other people's horses
unless asked to do so. The rule of the road in England
is a curious instance of our national distinctiveness. In
every other country that I know. the law is simple enough :
always keep to the right side of the road. In this land,
on the contrary, you must take the left when you meet,
and the right when you pass. The custom, I believe orig-
inated in that of shaking hands with every one you met,
which reminds me of a pretty one they once had, and even
now retain in some parts of France, that of a man and
lady riding hand in hand together. I have even ridden
arm in arm with a fair-haired blue-eyed Norman girl, and
if I did not snatch a kiss there and then, it was not for

fear of losing my balance. Well, our grandmothers used to ride on one horse with our grandfathers, tucking their fingers into the belts which the latter wore, and seated on the pillion much more comfortably than their granddaughters on the pummel; but what horses they must have had in those days!

But to return to driving. It is a simple art, requiring care rather than aught else, unless it be a knowledge of the dispositions of the horse or horses you undertake to drive. One horse or a pair can give but little embarrassment, and you will seldom be called upon to drive tandem, unicorn, or four in hand. But, perhaps, more accidents occur in turning corners than in anything else, and I should not do my duty, if I did not advise you, when the corner is on your right hand, to give it a wide berth; when on your left, to turn it gently and as slowly as possible.

The exercises which come rather under the head of games, such as cricket, rackets, tennis, bowls, skittles, and a dozen others, are by no means compulsory on any man to know, and I shall therefore leave their description to the many and various guide-books destined to introduce the young athlete to British Olympics. But I may remark that, while these games are purely republican in spirit, and my lord, if clumsy, ranks lower for the time than the skilful villager, it is no way difficult to distinguish the well-bred man, whether a good player or not. For while he yields entirely to the excitement of the game, he will refuse to join in the silly familiarities to which it sometimes leads. You will never hear him banter another on his bad play, nor, as too common in some games, will he vent oaths and strong epithets on some one who has made a gross error. When he does so himself, he will

confess himself wrong, and not clamorously defend him·
self; and, if he has to ask another player for anything,
he will call to him in an affable not an impatient com-
manding tone, and use some such phrase as : " may I trouble
you for that ball, sir?" not " Ball, you there," as one
sometimes hears it. In short, he will retain, under the
excitement of the game, the same good bearing which he
displays in society.

Similar observations apply to all kinds of out-door
amusements, such as shooting, boating, and so forth. A
gentleman will never attempt to monopolize the sport, and
however superior in skill to his companions, will not parade
his superiority, still less boast of it, but rather, that the
others may not feel their inferiority, he will keep considerably within his powers. If a guest or a stranger be of the
party, the best place and the best sport must be offered to
him, even though he may be a poor shot, a bad oar, and so
on; but, at the same time, if a guest knows his inferiority
in this respect, he will, for more reasons than one, prefer
an inferior position. So, too, when a certain amount of
exertion is required, as in boating, a well-bred man will
offer to take the greater share, and will never shirk his
work. In short, the whole rule of good manners on such
occasions is not to be selfish, and the most amiable man
will therefore be the best bred.

Talking of boating reminds one of old college days, and
the healthy happiness that exercise used to bring one. It
is certainly desirable that a " compleat gentleman" should
be able to handle an oar as well as a gun, both that when
he has the opportunity he may get health, and that he may
be able to take part in the charming excursions which are
made by water. In fact a man ought to be able to turn

his hand to almost everything, and, what is more, should
do himself whatever he can. It is a false and vulgar pride
which prevents a man from stooping to cord his own box,
carrying his own bag, weeding his own garden, cutting his
own hedges (for he must take care not to cut anybody
else's), shutting his own shutters, putting coal on his own
fire, or what not. To ring up a servant for these things,
shows either laziness or a vulgar attempt at grandeur.
Indeed, for my part, nothing seems to me so comfortless
as the constant entrance of servants ; it interrupts conversation, and destroys the feeling of ease and privacy. I
once met, at the house of a lady friend, the son of a man
who had begun life as a grocer, made his fortune by a successful speculation, and settled down in the full conviction
that he was therefore a "gentleman." My friend had
requested the young man to put some coal on the fire, and
as he was rather clumsy about it, he excused himself in
the following speech : "You see, aw—Mrs. B—, that I
am—aw—really not accustomed to do this kind of thing,
don't you see? Now at home, you see, the governor,
when he wants coals, rings the bell, and the butler comes
in ; 'Coal,' says the old gentleman, and the butler disappears to tell—aw—the upper-footman, who thinks it beneath his dignity, and therefore tells—aw—the under-
footman, who comes up and puts it on." I thought of the
Anglo-Indians, who, in this country, have often had no
more servants than a cook, a maid, and a "buttons," and
had to do everything for themselves, but who once in
India, find it impossible to tie their own shoe-strings, and
are obliged to keep a twenty-oneth or even thirty-oneth
servant for equally trivial offices.

But if a certain amount of skill in out-door amusements

10*

is essential to a man who wishes to be agreeable, how much
more so in those in-door amusements, which are the very
objects for which people commonly assemble, and are therefore the continual accompaniments of society? The art
of talking is, of course, the first of such accomplishments,
and as it is a subject of the highest importance and very
large range, it has been taken up in the preliminary chapter. But besides conversation, and sometimes as an aid to
it, parties and balls are given for the purposes of dancing,
music, games (especially cards), and eating and drinking.
Of the etiquette of these parties I shall speak elsewhere.
I now content myself with a few hints on the accomplishments themselves which are displayed in them.

"Thank you—aw—I do not dance," is now a very
common reply from a well-dressed handsome man, who is
leaning against the side of the door, to the anxious, heated
hostess, who feels it incumbent on her to find a partner
for poor Miss Wallflower. I say the reply is not only
common, but even regarded as rather a fine one to make.
In short, men of the present day don't, won't, or can't
dance; and you can't make them do it, except by threatening to give them no supper. I really cannot discover
the reason for this aversion to an innocent amusement, for
the apparent purpose of enjoying which they have spent
an hour and a half on their toilet, and half-a-crown on a
hansom cabman. There is something, indeed, in the heat
of a London ball-room in the middle of July, there is a
great deal in the ridiculous smallness of the closets into
which the ball-giver crowds two hundred people, with a
cruel indifference only equalled by that of the black-hole
of Calcutta, expecting them to enjoy themselves, when
the ladies' dresses are crushed and torn, and the gentle-

men, under the despotism of theirs, are melting away almost as rapidly as the ices with which an occasional waiter has the heartlessness to insult them. Then, again, it is a great nuisance to be introduced to a succession of plain, uninteresting young women, of whose tastes, mode of life, &c., you have not the slightest conception: who may look gay, yet have never a thought beyond the curate and the parish, or appear to be serious, while they understand nothing but the opera and Lady So-and-so's ball—in fact, to be in perpetual risk of either shocking their prejudices, or plaguing them with subjects in which they can have no possible interest; to take your chance whether they can dance at all, and to know that when you have lighted on a real charmer, perhaps the beauty of the room, she is only lent to you for that one dance, and when that is over, and you have salaamed away again, you and she must remain to one another as if you had never met; to feel, in short, that you must destroy either your present comfort or future happiness, is certainly sufficiently trying to keep a man close to the side-posts of the doorway. But these are reasons which might keep him altogether from a ball-room, and if he has these and other objections to dancing, he certainly cannot be justified in coming to a place set apart for that sole purpose.

But I suspect that there are other reasons, and that in most cases the individual can dance and does dance at times, but has now a vulgar desire to be distinguished from the rest of his sex present, and to appear indifferent to the pleasures of the evening. If this be his laudable desire, however, he might at least be consistent, and continue to cling to his door-post, like St. Sebastian to his tree, and reply throughout the evening: "Thank you, I

don't take refreshments :" " Thank you, I can't eat sup·
per :" " Thank you, I don't talk :" " Thank you, I don't
drink champagne."—for if a London ball-room be purgatory, what a demoniacal conflict does a London supper-
room present : if young ladies be bad for the heart, champagne is worse for the head.

No, it is the will, not the power to dance which is wanting, and to refuse to do so, unless for a really good reason,
is not the part of a well-bred man. To mar the pleasure
of others is obviously bad manners, and though at the
door-post you may not be in the way, you may be certain
that there are some young ladies longing to dance, and
expecting to be asked, and that the hostess is vexed and
annoyed by seeing them fixed, like pictures, to the wall.
It is therefore the duty of every man who has no scruples
about dancing, and purposes to appear at balls, to learn
how to dance.

In the present day the art is much simplified, and if
you can walk through a quadrille, and perform a polka,
waltz, or galop, you may often dance a whole evening
through. Of course. if you can add to these the Lancers,
Schottische, and Polka-Mazurka, you will have more variety, and can be more generally agreeable. But if your
master or mistress (a man learns better from the former)
has stuffed into your head some of the three hundred
dances which he tells you exist, the best thing you can
do is to forget them again. Whether right or wrong, the
number of usual dances is limited, and unusual ones
should be very sparingly introduced into a ball. for as few
people know them, their dancing. on the one hand, becomes
a mere display, and, on the other, interrupts the enjoyment of the majority.

The quadrille is pronounced to be essentially a conversational dance, but inasmuch as the figures are perpetually calling you away from your partner, the first necessity for dancing a quadrille is to be supplied with a fund of small talk, in which you can go from subject to subject like a bee from flower to flower. The next point is to carry yourself uprightly. Time was when—as in the days of the *menuet de la cour*—the carriage constituted the dance. This is still the case with the quadrille, in which even if ignorant of the figures, you may acquit yourself well by a calm graceful carriage. After all, the most important figure is the *smile*, and the feet may be left to their fate, if we know what to do with our hands; of which I may observe that they should never be pocketed.

The smile is essential. A dance is supposed to amuse, and nothing is more out of place in it than a gloomy scowl, unless it be an ill-tempered frown. The gaiety of a dance is more essential than the accuracy of its figures, and if you feel none yourself, you may at least look pleased by that of those around you. A defiant manner is equally obnoxious. An acquaintance of mine always gives me the impression, when he advances in *l'été*, that he is about to box the lady who comes to meet him. But the most objectionable of all is the supercilious manner. Dear me, if you really think you do your partner an honor in dancing with her, you should at least remember that your condescension is annulled by the manner in which you treat her.

A lady—beautiful word!—is a delicate creature, one who should be reverenced and delicately treated. It is therefore unpardonable to rush about in a quadrille, to catch hold of the lady's hand as if it were a door-handle, or to drag her furiously across the room, as if you were Bluebeard and she Fatima, with the mysterious closet opposite to you. This *brusque* violent style of dancing is unfortunately common, but immediately stamps a man. Though I would not have you wear a perpetual simper, you should certainly smile when you take a lady's hand, and the old custom of bowing in doing so, is one that we may regret; for does she not confer an honor on us by the action? To squeeze it, on the other hand, is a gross familiarity, for which you would deserve to be kicked out of the room.

"Steps," as the *chasser* of the quadrille is called, belong to a past age, and even ladies are now content to walk through a quadrille. To be graceful, however, a lady should hold her skirt out a little. In France this is done with one hand, which I am inclined to think is more graceful than holding it with both. It is, however, necessary to keep time with the music, the great object being the general harmony. To preserve this, it is also advisable, where the quadrille, as is now generally the case, is danced by two long lines of couples down the room, that in *l'été*, and other figures, in which a gentleman and lady advance alone to meet one another, none but gentlemen should advance from the one side, and therefore none but ladies from the other.

Dancing masters find it convenient to introduce new figures, and the fashion of *La Tr. nise* and the *Grande Ronde* is repeatedly changing. It is wise to know the last mode, but not to insist on dancing it. A quadrille cannot go on evenly if any confusion arises from the ignorance, obstinacy, or inattention of any one of the dancers. It is therefore useful to know every way in which a figure may be danced, and to take your cue from the others. It is amusing, however, to find how even such a trifle as a choice of figures in a quadrille can help to mark caste, and give a handle for supercilious sneers. Jones, the other day, was protesting that the Browns were " vulgar." " Why so? they are well bred." " Yes, so they are." " They are well-informed." " Certainly." " They are polite, speak good English, dress quietly and well, are graceful and even elegant." " I grant you all that." " Then what fault can you find with them." " My dear fellow, they are people who gallop round in the last figure of a quadrille," he replied triumphantly. But to a certain extent Jones is right. Where a choice is given, the man of taste will always select for a quadrille (as it is a conversational dance) the quieter mode of performing a figure, and so the Browns, if perfect in other respects, at least were wanting in taste. There is one alteration lately introduced from France, which I sincerely trust will be universally accepted. The farce of that degrading little performance called " setting"—where you dance before your partner somewhat like Man Friday before Robinson Crusoe, and then as if your feelings were overcome, seize her hands and whirl her round—has been finally abolished by a decree of Fashion, and thus more opportunity is given for conversation, and in a crowded room. you have no occasion to crush yourself and partner between the couples on each side of you.

I do not attempt to deny that the quadrille, as now walked, is ridiculous; the figures, which might be graceful if performed in a lively manner, have entirely lost their spirit, and are become a burlesque of dancing; but, at the same time, it is a most valuable dance. Old and

young, stout and thin, good dancers and bad, lazy and
active, stupid and clever, married and single, can all join
in it, and have not only an excuse and opportunity for
tête-à-tête conversation, which is decidedly the easiest,
but find encouragement in the music, and in some cases
convenient breaks in the necessity of dancing.   A person of few ideas has time to collect them while the partner is performing, and one of many can bring them out
with double effect.   Lastly, if you wish to be polite or
friendly to an acquaintance who dances atrociously, you
can select a quadrille for him or her, as the case may be.
Intense patriotism still induces some people to affirm that
the English country-dance is far preferable to this importation from France.   These good creatures should inquire
a little further.   I think they would find that the country-
dance (*contre-danse*) came from the same source at a
somewhat earlier date.   But, however this may be, a
dance which tears me so completely away from the partner I have selected, ought in nine cases out of ten to be
hateful to me.

Very different in object and principle are the so-called
round dances, and there are great limitations as to those
who should join in them.   Here the intention is to enjoy
a peculiar physical movement under peculiar conditions,
and the conversation during the intervals of rest is only
a secondary object.   These dances demand activity and
lightness, and should therefore be, as a rule, confined to
the young.   An old man sacrifices all his dignity in a
polka, and an old woman is ridiculous in a waltz.   Corpulency too, is generally a great impediment, though
some stout people prove to be the lightest dancers.

The morality of round dances scarcely comes within my

province. They certainly can be made very indelicate; so can any dance, and the French *cancan* proves that the quadrille is no safer in this respect than the waltz. But it is a gross insult to our daughters and sisters to suppose them capable of any but the most innocent and purest enjoyment in the dance, while of our young men I will say, that to the pure all things are pure. Those who see harm in it are those in whose mind evil thoughts must have arisen. *Honi soit qui mal y pense.* Those who rail against dancing are perhaps not aware that they do but follow in the steps of the Romish Church. In many parts of the Continent, bishops who have never danced in their lives, and perhaps never even seen a dance, have laid a ban of excommunication on waltzing. A story was me told in Normandy of the worthy Bishop of Bayeux, one of this number. A priest of his diocese petitioned him to put down round dances. "I know nothing about them," replied the prelate, "I have never even seen a waltz." Upon this the younger ecclesiastic attempted to explain what it was and wherein the danger lay, but the Bishop could not see it. "Will Monseigneur permit me to show him?" asked the priest. "Certainly. My chaplain here appears to understand the subject; let me see you two waltz." How the reverend gentleman came to know so much about it does not appear, but they certainly danced a polka, a gallop, and a *troistemps* waltz. "All these seem harmless enough." "Oh! but Monseigneur has not seen the worst;" and thereupon the two gentlemen proceeded to flounder through a *valse à deux-temps.* They must have murdered it terribly, for they were not half round the room when his Lordship cried out, "Enough, enough, that is atrocious, and deserves excommunication." Accordingly this waltz was forbidden, while the other dances were allowed. I was at a public ball at Caen soon after this occurrence, and was amused to find the *trois-temps* danced with a peculiar shuffle, by way of compromise between conscience and pleasure.

There are people in this country whose logic is as good as that of the Bishop of Bayeux, but I confess my inability to understand it. If there is impropriety in round dances, there is the same in all. But to the waltz, which poets have praised and preachers denounced. The French, with all their love of dancing, waltz atrociously, the English but little better; the Germans and Russians alone understand it. I could rave through three pages about the innocent enjoyment of a good waltz, its grace and beauty, but I will be practical instead, and give you a few hints on the subject.

The position is the most important point The lady and gentleman before starting should stand exactly opposite to one another, quite upright, and not, as is so common in England, painfully close to one another. If the man's hand be placed where it should be, at the centre of the lady's waist, and not all round it, he will have as firm a hold and not be obliged to stoop, or bend to his right. The lady's head should then be turned a little towards her left shoulder, and her partner's somewhat less towards his right, in order to preserve the proper balance. Nothing can be more atrocious than to see a lady lay her head on her partner's shoulder; but, on the other hand, she wil. not dance well, if she turns it in the opposite direction. The lady again should throw her head and shoulders a little back. and the man lean a very little forward.

The position having been gained, the step is the next

question. In Germany the rapidity of the waltz is very great, but it is rendered elegant by slackening the pace every now and then, and thus giving a *crescendo* and *decrescendo* time to the movement. The Russian men undertake to perform in waltzing the same feat as the Austrians in riding, and will dance round the room with a glass of champagne in the left hand without spilling a drop. This evenness in waltzing is certainly very graceful, but can only be attained by a long sliding step, which is little practised in England, where the rooms are small, and people, not understanding the real pleasure of dancing well, insist on dancing all at the same time. In Germany they are so alive to the necessity of ample space, that in large balls a rope is drawn across the room; its two ends are held by the masters of the ceremonies *pro tem.*, and as one couple stops and retires, another is allowed to pass under the rope and take its place. But then in Germany they dance for the dancing's sake. However this may be, an even motion is very desirable, and all the abominations which militate against it, such as hop-waltzes, the Schottische, and ridiculous *Varso-vienne*, are justly put down in good society. The pace, again, should not be sufficiently rapid to endanger other couples. It is the gentleman's duty to *steer*, and in crowded rooms nothing is more trying. He must keep his eyes open and turn them in every direction, if he would not risk a collision, and the chance of a fall, or what is as bad, the infliction of a wound on his partner's arm. I have seen a lady's arm cut open in such a collision by the bracelet on that of another lady; and the sight is by no means a pleasant one in a ball-room, to say nothing of a new dress covered in a moment with blood

The consequences of violent dancing may be really serious. Not only do delicate girls bring on thereby a violent palpitation of the heart, and their partners appear in a most disagreeable condition of solution, but dangerous falls ensue from it. I have known instances of a lady's head being laid open, and a gentleman's foot being broken in such a fall, resulting, poor fellow, in lameness for life. Nay, even death hovers among the giddy waltzers, and Victor Hugo has written a beautiful little poem on girls who have died of dancing, of which one verse as a moral:

> " Quels tristes lendemains laisse le bal folatre '
> Adieu, parure, danse et rires enfantins !
> Aux chansons succedait le toux opiniatre,
> Au plaisir rose et frais la fievre au teint bleuatre,
> Aux yeux brillants les yeux eteints."

Be careful of the waltz, be sparing, lest it prove, in this land of consumption, to too many the true dance of death. Let us not mingle cypress with our roses.

It is perhaps useless to recommend flat-foot waltzing in this country, where ladies allow themselves to be almost hugged by their partners, and where men think it necessary to lift a lady almost off the ground, but I am persuaded that if it were introduced. the outcry against the impropriety of waltzing would soon cease. Nothing can be more delicate than the way in which a German holds his partner. It is impossible to dance on the flat foot unless the lady and gentleman are quite free of one another. His hand therefore goes no further round her waist than to the hooks and eyes of her dress, hers, no higher than to his elbow. Thus danced the waltz is smooth, graceful, and delicate. and we could never in Germany complain of our daughter's languishing on a young man's shoulder. On the other hand, nothing is more graceless and absurd than to see a man waltzing on the tips of his toes, lifting his partner off the ground, or twirling round and round with her like the figures on a street organ The test of waltzing in time is to be able to stamp the time with the left foot. A good flat-foot waltzer can dance on one foot as well as on two, but I would not advise him to try it in public, lest like Mr. Rarey's horse on three legs, he should come to the ground in a luckless moment. The legs should be very little bent in dancing, the body still less so. I do not know whether it be worse to see a man *sit down* in a waltz, or to find him with his head poked forward over your young wife's shoulder, hot, red, wild, and in far too close proximity to the partner of your bosom, whom he makes literally the partner of his own.

King Polka has been deposed after a reign of nearly twenty years. I cannot refrain from throwing up my cap. True, his rule was easy, and he was popular on that account, indeed, he has still his partisans in certain classes, but not in the best. For what a graceless, jogging, hugging, sleepy old creature he was! Then, too, he was not even a legitimate sovereign. The good family of the Polkas in Hungary, Poland, &c., would not recognize this pretender of England and France, who is no more like them than that other pretender Mazurka, is like the original spirited, national fling of the same name. It is curious to see how our D'Egvilles have ransacked Europe for national dances to be adapted to the drawing-room, and, indeed, there spoiled. The waltz is of German origin, but where it is still danced in Germany in the original manner (as for instance, among the peasants of the Tyrol), it is a very different dance. It is there very slow and graceful; the feet are thrown out in a single long step, which Turveydrop, I presume, would call a *jeté*. After a few turns, the partners waltz alone in the same step, the man keeping the time by striking together his iron-shod heels, until with a shout and clapping of hands he again clasps his partner and continues in the same slow measure with her. The very names of the dances bespeak their origin. The Sclavonic nations must have given us the Polka, Mazurka, Redowa, Gorlitza, and Eletczka, whatever that may be. The Varsovienne and Cracovienne are all that remain of Polish nationality.

> " Ye have the Pyrrhic dance as yet,
>   Where is the Pyrrhic phalanx gone?"

says Byron bitterly to the Greeks, and some future Russian agent may perhaps sing to the wearers of the kilt in the same strain :—

> " Ye have the Highland reel as yet,
>   Where are your Highland chieftains gone?"

Then the Madrilaine has been imported from Spain, which retains the oriental Bolero, Fandango, and Cachucha. The last is of purely Eastern character, and might be danced by a Nāch girl before a Lucknow Prince. The Americans with more patriotism than ourselves have preserved the only national and English dances, the hornpipe and jig, and have about twenty varieties of the former including a sailor's, college, gipsy's, and even bricklayer's and lamplighter's hornpipe. These American dances have names no less eccentric than their drinks. We should scarcely care to join in the " Devil's Dream," for instance, and the dance called " Jordan is a hard road" can hardly be a favorite out of Hebrew circles. " Money Musk" was once an English dance. When there was a quarrel between the country people and the rich tradesmen at the Bath balls, Beau Nash had some trouble to reconcile them, but he appropriately sealed his success by ordering the band to strike up "Money Musk." The "Lancers" are a revival after many long years, and perhaps we may soon have a drawing-room adaptation of the Morris-dance.

The only advice therefore which it is necessary to give to those who wish to dance the polka may be summed up in two words, "don't." Not so with the galop. The remarks as to the position in waltzing apply to all round dances, and there is therefore little to add with regard to the galop, except that it is a great mistake to suppose it to be a rapid dance. It should be danced as slowly as possible. It will then be more graceful and less fatiguing. It is danced quite slowly in Germany and on the flat foot. The polka-mazurka is still much danced, and is certainly very graceful. The remarks on the quadrille apply equally to the lancers, which are great favorites, and threaten to take the place of the former. The schottische, hop-waltz, redowa, varsovienne, cellarius, and so forth, have had their day, and are no longer danced in good society. The only dance I regret is the German cotillon, which was introduced a few years ago, but not approved. English people made a romp of it, and English young ladies, an opportunity for marked flirtation; besides which English chaperons, not so patient as the same class on the Continent, would not sit through it. Well I remember the long hours through which we used to keep it up in Germany, while mammas and aunts were dozing behind their fans, and how vexed we were when its varied figures, invented often on the spot, came to an end, and carriages were called for.

The calm ease which marks the man of good taste, makes even the swiftest dances graceful and agreeable. Vehemence may be excused at an election, but not in a ball-room. I once asked a beautiful and very clever young lady how she, who seemed to pass her life with books, managed to dance so well. " I enjoy it," she replied; " and when I dance I give my *whole mind* to it." And she was quite right. Whatever is worth doing at all, is worth doing well; and if it is not beneath your dignity to dance, it is not unworthy of your mind to give itself for the time, wholly up to it. You will never enjoy dancing till you do it well; and if you do not enjoy it, it is folly to dance. But in reality dancing, if it be a mere trifle, is one to which great minds have not been ashamed to stoop. Locke, for instance, has written on its utility, and speaks of it as manly, which was certainly not Michal's opinion, when she looked out of the window and saw her lord and master dancing and playing. Plato recommended it, and Socrates learned the Athenian polka of the day, when quite an old gentleman, and liked it very much. Some one has even gone the length of calling it " the logic of the body;" and Addison defends himself for making it the subject of a disquisition. If I say much more I shall have to do the same as Addison, and will therefore pass to some other accomplishments useful, if not necessary, in society.

On the Continent almost every boy is taught to play the piano. A very false principle has, till lately, kept our men from all the softer portion of life ; manliness was identified with roughness, and every accomplishment which was suitable to a woman, was considered beneath the dignity of a man. In short, it is not fifty years ago since to hunt, shoot, and drink your bottle of port, formed the only accomplishments necessary for male society, and refinement did not extend beyond an elegance in bowing, in taking snuff, and in gallantry to the ladies. Left to themselves, men were ashamed to be anything better than bears. Fortunately it is now agreed that manliness and refinement are not opposed to one another.

I believe that there is a taste for music in every child born, and that if it disappears in after life, it is for want of cultivation. Was there ever yet a baby which could not be sung to sleep? However this may be, to play some one instrument is of more value to a man than at first sight appears. To the character it is a refiner. Music is the medicine of the soul; it soothes the wrinkles of a hard life of business, and lifts us from thoughts of money, intrigue, enterprises, anxieties, hatred, and what not, to a calmer, more heavenly frame of mind. To a man himself, therefore, the power to play is of use. He may not always have a sister, wife, or daughter, to sing and play to him; he may not always be within reach of the opera and concert rooms, and then, too, half the enjoyment of music is gone, when you cannot enjoy it as you list, and of what kind you need, gay or grave, as your fancy lies. It is an indulgence to a pure mind, and it is one of those few indulgences which are free from harm.

But besides this, a knowledge of music is valuable to a man in the society both of his own and the other sex. It is a great recommendation among women, and vibrates on a chord of sympathy between the sexes, when possibly

11

there is no other. Still more so where women are not,
and their want is felt. The man who can play an air is
a boon to the camp, the college, or the Inn of Court.
Well do I remember how popular Jones was for his piano,
and Smith for his cornet, at St. Boniface's. Yet Jones
and Smith were very dull men in themselves, and kept
very bad wine. What did we care? We did not want
to drink with our mouths when we could do so with our
ears. But if instrumental music recommend a man, still
more the cultivation of the natural musical instrument.
" He can tell a good story and sing a good song," is almost the best recommendation one bachelor can give of
another in a social point of view, and if you can sing a
good ballad, or take part in a duct, quartett, chorus, or
what not, you are invaluable in an evening party.

There are, however, a few points to be attended to in
connexion with playing or singing in public. In the first
place, as to a choice of instrument. The piano is always
acceptable, but however good a man's touch, it must be
remembered, it is not so agreeable in a room as a lady's.
Every other instrument should be accompanied by the
piano, so that unless you have some fair friend ready to
play for you, it will be useless to take your instrument.
But under the most fortunate circumstances, your choice
is limited. The instrument must not be too loud or too
harsh for the sensitive tympanum of your fair audience.
No one would volunteer a solo on the drum, perhaps; but
men who play but little, will sometimes inflict the *haut-
bois* or *cornet-à-pistons* on their unhappy listeners; these
two instruments, and indeed every species of horn, can
only be tolerated in a drawing-room if extremely well
played, and therefore modulated. On the other hand, if

you care for your appearance, you will scarcely introduce the violoncello. The fiddle is so common that people will not care for it unless played with execution, and the flageolet is scarcely worth listening to. There remains the flute, and the guitar, which is a good accompaniment to the voice, but should not be played by a stout or an elderly man. Concerts are so common now, and first-rate performers so easily heard, that more than common proficiency will be expected from you on any instrument except the piano, and you should therefore never take your instrument with you unless particularly requested to do so by the inviter, nor play more than once unless pressed to do so by the lady of the house.

If you have a tenor or alto voice, a good ear, and a knowledge of a few songs, you need never be afraid of singing in public. A barytone being commoner, requires more excellence to back it. and a base should be prohibited, *I* think, from solo exhibitions, unless very good. But be the voice what it may, if you cannot sing *in tune*, never attempt it. Others in the company will have better ears than yourself, and politely execrate you. *Time* is not so important. unless you join a duet, trio, or chorus. The choice of songs is quite as essential as the choice of an instrument. A man should not sing women's ditties, and should never yawl out the namby-pamby ballads beloved of young ladies. A really honest love-song, in which the words are as good as the music, becomes a tenor or barytone well—scarcely a basso. On the other hand, the too ferocious style should be avoided. Comic songs, as a general rule, are atrocious. Their want of wit is not atoned for by the presence of slang, vulgarity. or even coarseness. They are usually written by men of inferior mind, often for the stage or public entertainments, and are purposely broad, in order to be understood by a mixed audience. On the other hand, if you have essentially a comic face and manner, and can sing a parody, or a more refined comic song with character, you may attempt it in small parties. In men's society, of course, the comic song is the most popular.

A man singing before ladies must remember their nerves, and modulate his voice. He must also bear in mind, that however well he sings, a lady's voice is more suited to a drawing-room, and unless pressed to do so, will content himself with one or at most two songs. But a man should not allow himself to be pressed too much, nor affect diffidence like a young miss of seventeen. If he has not sung or played before, he should do so (if he can) without hesitation, and with an amiable willingness, being confident that the lady of the house desires to amuse her guests rather than to flatter him.

In general society, the card-table in the present day is happily reserved for elderly people, but a young man may be sometimes called upon to make up a rubber, and if so he would mar the pleasure of others if he were not able to take a hand. At the same time it is generally understood that ladies and young men should not be asked to do so, unless absolutely necessary, and if a hostess opens a card-table, she should be able beforehand to select a sufficient and suitable number of players. It is always trying to see ladies play. It has been observed that women have only two passions, love and avarice. The latter ill becomes them, and yet so strong is it, that they can rarely conceal it at the card-table.

Where a number of guests are willing to play, the selection is made by drawing cards, and the highest drawers are excluded from the game. At whist the two lower and two higher drawers become partners respectively; the lowest has the first deal. The trial of temper then ensues, and if card playing has no other virtue, it may be commended as a test of temper and good-breeding. Lose without a murmur, win without triumph. Never insist too sharply on fines, and be ready to pay on the spot. If unable to do this, you should pay the next morning at the latest. It is always allowable to man or lady to say, "I do not play," and the words are understood to mean, that though able, you prefer not to do so. If a bad player, you will do well to keep away from the table; you have a partner's interest to consult as well as your own. As a general rule in good society, it should be understood that one does not play *for* money, but *with* money. The skill rather than the result of the game must be the point of interest.

In round games, which are patronized by people who have not the accomplishments to supply their place, or the wit to do without them, the main fault to be avoided is eagerness. Of single games, you should know as many as possible. The finest of them is chess, which is worthy of any man, and a splendid mental exercise. Without aspiring to be a Morphy or a Staunton, you may by practice and thought become an excellent chess player; but the game is not a social one, and requires too much abstraction to be introduced in social gatherings.

Perhaps the most useful accomplishment to one's self is a knowledge of languages. Independent of the great superiority it gives you in travel, and the wide field of literature to which it introduces you, you are liable in

really good society, especially in high London circles, to
meet with foreigners having a very slight acquaintance
with English.   From them you may derive a vast amount
of information, turn the slow current of your associations,
and even be amused more than by any conversation with
your own countrymen.   The most patriotic John Bull
now admits that foreigners understand better than ourselves the art of conversation, and though we may accuse
them of frivolity among themselves, we must remember
that in English society their first desire is to make themselves really appreciated.   As a rule, too, they are more
interested than we are in current history, and whatever
their prejudices or their ignorance, you will rarely meet
with a Frenchman, Italian, or German, from whom you
may not gather much curious information which will serve
you elsewhere.   An untravelled man is always at some
disadvantage in *good* English society, where almost every
one but himself will have crossed the channel, but if he
has a good knowledge of continental language and literature, this disadvantage is materially diminished.

An accomplishment much overlooked as an accomplishment, but one indispensable to good society, is to be able
to talk on current literature and passing affairs.   Every
gentleman in the present day should subscribe to a circulating library, and take in a London newspaper.   Besides
taking in the latter, he should read it with judgment.   He
should be able to form and give an opinion independent of
party prejudice on any question of common interest.
Whatever his views, he should be able as a man of sense,
and in order to be agreeable, to look on them independently, to support them reasonably, or abandon them gracefully.   Politics, and even religion, can, I rejoice to say,

be discussed in the present day without inflammation and acerbity, and, though the latter subject is better avoided in mixed circles, a thorough gentleman will be able to bow to another's opinion, and to put forward his own delicately and sensibly.

There is one more accomplishment which is, fortunately, fast falling into disuse. The days are done when an awkward servant could anoint your head and best coat with a whole dishful of gravy, or an unskilled gentleman might be forced to bow to the lady on his right, with : "Madam, I'll trouble you for that goose in your lap." Bad *carving* used to spoil three good things on the part of the carver, good joints, good temper, and a good digestion. Even good carving marred conversation, and to short.men it was a positive infliction, for I need scarcely say, that under no circumstances whatever could a man be permitted to stand up to carve. But because the carving of joints, game, &c., at a side table, is a foreign custom lately introduced into this country, there are people still found patriotic enough to prefer carving at the dinner-table. "I like the good old English custom," says one; "I like to see a host dispensing his hospitality himself;" and in the country, where some hosts prefer meat to manners, it is still retained. But I may ask whether hospitality consists more in severing the wings from a chicken's body, than in setting all your guests at their ease, and at once leading off the conversation. Does it demand a distribution of good morsels rather than of good will? The advocates of the "good old custom" may be reminded again, that in former days it was the hostess, not the host, who dispensed the viands, her husband being occupied with a distribution of the wine, which is the reason why the lady sat at the head of the table; but what is the v..lue of an old custom universally disregarded, since no longer the hostess, but the guest who has the misfortune to take her in to dinner, is called upon to play the part of butcher? Can it be any more satisfactory to me to have my mutton sliced by a guest than by the butler in my host's service?

Another argument maliciously advanced, is contained in the sneer: "No, no, thank you, I like to see my dinner, and know what I am eating." But what a slur upon the hospitality of your host, to suppose he would give you a cat for a hare, or a puppy for a rabbit! We might as well insist that he should sup our port before we drink it lest there should be poison in the cup—a custom, by the way, still retained in Bavaria where the *kellnerinn*, or waitress, who brings you your quart of beer, invariably puts it to her mouth before she hands it to you. But there is a reason for that, since many a soldier in the Thirty Years' War was poisoned at a beer-garden.

Carving is, however, still common at small parties and family dinners, and it will be a happy time when it is abandoned even there. I have seen many an unfortunate young man put to confusion when deputed to carve, by the anxious looks of the host or hostess, and have even heard such atrociously rude remarks as, "Thomas, bring that fowl to me; Mr. Jones seems not to understand it;" nay, I have seen people lose their temper so completely at having their pet dishes hacked by the unskilful, as to produce an awkward silence through the whole company. Then too, in family circles, more quarrels are to be traced to a blunt knife or a difficult dish, than even to milliners' bills, and I stayed for a short time in one house, whose master at last got into a habit of losing his temper over the joint, which he carved very ill at all times, and where, in consequence, dinner was more dreaded than the pillory. Indeed, as great results may often be traced to the most trifling causes, I am convinced that half the domestic tyranny of the British paterfamilias, and much of the bickering and irritation which deprive home of its charms, may be traced to no greater cause than the cutting up of a joint. The larger the family the greater the misery of the carver, who has scarcely helped them all round, before the first receiver has done and is ready for a second helping. When at last the hungry father or elder brother can secure a mouthful, he must hurry over it, at the risk of dyspepsia, in order not to keep the others waiting.

But we are a nation of conservatives, and a custom which descended from the days when a knight would stick his dagger into a leg of mutton, which he held by the knucklebone (hence the frill of white paper still stuck round it, to slop in the gravy and look disgusting before the joint is removed), and carve him a good thick slice without more ceremony, will not soon be got rid of, however great a nuisance. It is therefore necessary, if you would avoid irritation, black looks, and even rude speeches, to know how to carve at a friend's table, whatever you may do at your own. When thus situated, the following hints will be found useful.

HINTS ON CARVING AND HELPING.

1. *Soup* is helped with a ladle. Take care that the servant holds the plate close to the tureen, and distribute one ladleful to each person.

2. *Fish* is cut with a large flat silver knife or fish-slice, never with a common one. Of small fish, you send

one to each person.   All the larger flat fish, such as turbot, John Dorey, brills, &c., must be first cut from head
to tail down the middle, and then in portions from this cut
to the fin, which being considered the best part, is helped
with the rest.   Fried soles, on the other hand, are simply
cut across, dividing the bone.   The shoulder is the best
part, and should be first helped.   Salmon, being laid on
the side, is cut down the middle of the upper side, and then
across from the back to the belly.   A boiled mackerel
serves for four people.   The fish-knife is passed from tail
to head under the upper side, which is then divided into two.
Cod is always crossways, and a small piece of the sound
sent with each helping.

3. *Joints* are helped with a steel fork, of which, if
you value your fingers, you will take care that the guard
is raised, and a carving knife, which for the sake of your
neighbor's teeth, if you do not care for your own, you
will never yourself sharpen.   Let us premise that the
butcher and cook must assist the carver. and that an ill-
cut or ill-jointed joint augments terribly the torture of
the dispenser.   It must also be premised that there are
more ways than one of cutting the same joint, that sometimes one, sometimes another is preferred, and that one
way will often be the more economical, another the more
elegant.   Happy age when the butler shall have the re-
sponsibility of pleasing both the master and mistress of
the house, who invariably differ when there is an alternative !

The *roast beef* of Old England, on which our glory is
said to fatten and our pluck to thrive, appears on well-
kept tables in two forms only.   The sirloin has an upper
and under cut, about which tastes differ.   It is therefore

usual to begin with the upper or thicker side. The joint must lie with its chine bone towards the left, and its flap to the right of the carver. It must be held steady by inserting the fork near the flat-bone. (It may here be remarked, that in all carving the fork should never be left sticking in the meat, but withdrawn with the knife; nor should it ever be stuck in perpendicularly and grasped with the whole hand.) One long deep cut must then be made *across* the joint close to the chine-bone. The outside is next sliced off from the chine-bone to the flap, and you then proceed to cut the meat in very thin slices in the same direction. A slice of the fat on the flap must be given with each helping. If the under cut is asked for, you must carefully turn the joint so as not to splash the gravy—another of the fearful responsibilities of carving—and then cut the meat across in thick slices. A round of beef is easily carved till you come to the skewers, and then agony commences; and what with the impossibility of drawing them out with the hand, the difficulty of doing so with the fork, and the quivering looseness of the joint when the arrow is at last extracted from its wretched flesh, a round with a round of beef is a more trying combat, than successive rounds with the cook who skewered, the butler who served, and the host who compelled you to carve it. However let us hope for the best; there is good in all, even skewers; and let us, inserting our fork firmly into the enemy's side, cut his brown top off with a horizontal slice of our long sharp steel, the longer and sharper the better for this joint, and proceed to torture him by making a succession of very thin slices, of which one is enough for any guest, except an alderman.

Boiled beef is more favored at dining-houses in the

City than at company dinners at the West End. The side is cut in very thin slices, which should be as broad and as long as the joint itself, if you can cut them so.

Mutton appears generally in three forms. The saddle is the best joint, and is best cut in very thin slices close to the back-bone; or you may slice it horizontally from the tail to the other end; or again slanting from the back-bone towards the fat, so that each slice shall carry its own end of fat. A shoulder of mutton must lie with the knuckle towards your right, and the blade-bone towards your left. In the middle of the edge of the part farthest from you place the fork, and there give one sharp dexterous cut from the edge to the bone. The meat then flies open, and you proceed to cut rather thick slices on each side of the opening till you can cut no more. You may then cut three or four slices from the centre-bone to the end, and if there are more mouths to be filled, of which your own, of course, will be one, you must turn the joint over and slice the under side. The same shoulder of mutton is a disgrace to a sheep, for do what you will, you can never get enough off it. Much more satisfactory is the animal's leg. In the bosom of your own family, when funds are low and butcher's bills high, the best plan is to begin at the knuckle, cutting across in thick slices, and so on to the top. But if your wife puts up with a knuckle slice, your guests will not, and in company you must therefore begin in the middle. The knuckle should point towards your left. You then cut from the side farther from you towards yourself, thus opening the joint in the middle, and proceed to take thin slices on the right, which some people prefer, and thick slices towards the knuckle. The little tuft of fat near the thick end is a delicacy, and must be distributed as such.

The *lamb*, disturbed in its gambols, furnishes our ruth-
less appetites with two quarters (a fore and a hind), a
saddle, which is carved like a saddle of its elder relative,
mutton, and a loin which must be divided into chops.
The fore quarter consists of a shoulder, a breast, and the
ribs, which are served without separation, and the carver
has therefore the pleasure of turning butcher for the time.
This he does by placing the knife under the shoulder,
drawing it horizontally, and so removing the shoulder altogether. This limb is generally placed on a separate
dish, and carved like a shoulder of mutton. You have
then to cut off the breast, and finally separate the ribs.
The hind quarter consists of a leg and a loin, the former
being cut across, the latter lengthways.

Veal gives us a head, breast, and fillet. If the first of
these appears in its normal form, not having been boned
and rolled, you must cut it down the centre in rather
thin slices on each side. The meat round the eye, a delicacy, may be scooped out. A small piece of the palate
and the accompanying sweetbread must be sent on each
plate. A fillet of veal is simply cut in slices, which must
not be too thin; and the stuffing in the centre should be
helped with a spoon. In a breast of veal the ribs should
be first separated from the brisket, after which either or
both may be sent round.

Roast pork is not often seen on good tables. When it
appears it is as easy to carve as a leg of mutton, but the
slices should be thicker and not so large. Two very small
slices are enough for an epicure; let those who like it eat
more. The best part of roast pork is the crackling, if it
has been roasted with buttered paper over it. Boiled
pork, like boiled mutton, is only to be tolerated for the

sake of its proper accompaniments, but the taste for pease-pudding, unlike that for caper sauce, can only be acquired by a long residence in this country. Both these joints are carved like a roasted leg of mutton. The waiter at a hotel, who, when a Hebrew gentleman ordered " pork-chops," considerately and delicately returned with poach-ed eggs, was a man of taste as well as of breeding, and knew that it takes much to make pork palatable. Not so, however, with *ham* and *bacon*, which are meats to warm the cockles of the heart, even of a Pharisee of the Phari-sees, and while to enjoy the former one would always be rich, one could be content to be poor for the sake of the latter. Alas ! because bacon is a poor man's luxury, the rich, or their vulgar cooks, will never admit it, or very rarely. It must be cut as thin as a lady's vail, and in delicate long strips rather than slices. A *ham* may be cut in thred ways, by beginning either at the knuckle, which must be turned towards your left, and slicing in a slanting direction ; or at the thick end, which is then turned to your left ; or, in the commonest manner, like a leg of mutton, across the centre. In any case it must be cut in very thin, delicate slices, such as the waiters of now defunct Vauxhall won their fame for, and such as, to this day, few people but the owner of a London cook-shop can achieve. One small slice is enough as an ac-companiment to a helping of fowl or veal.

Last of the joints comes their best, the haunch of *Veni-son.* To carve this the knuckle should be turned towards your right hand, and above it a rapid cross cut made. A cut lengthways from the other end to the cross cut, should divide the meat about the middle, and slices of moderate thickness are then to be taken on each side of the long

cut; those on the left are the best, having the most fat
about them.

You are now wishing that edible animals grew like pil-
lows, to be sliced up like roly-poly puddings, and would
dispense for ever with the inconvenience of limbs, legs,
shoulders, saddles, haunches, loins, sirloins, breasts, ribs,
fore-quarters and hind-quarters. But you cannot have
everything. If meat grew on trees it would not be worth
eating; it is the exercise of the animal which makes it
tender and savory; while, on the other hand, the best
meat is generally t¹ . nearest to the bone. The only
riddle which Sir Edward Lytton was ever guilty of per-
petrating was this: " Why is a cat's taste better than a
dog's? Because the dog's is *bon* (bone), but the cat's is
mieux (mew)." With all deference to Sir Edward, I
must give my opinion that the dog has the best taste of
all animals, which he displays in his preference for bones,
well knowing that the meat nearest to them is always the
most savory.

However this may be, you have not done yet; indeed,
you have the worst to come, and there is fresh torture
for the carver in—

4. *Animals served whole.* You may perhaps master
a *Rabbit*, because he may be treated like Damien, who
was broken on the wheel, by removing the legs and shoulders with a sharp-pointed knife, and then breaking his
back in three or four pieces by pressing the knife across
it and pushing the body up against it with the fork but
when you come to that long, thin, dark, and scraggy animal, which with its crisp delicate ears sticking up, and
the large sockets where its eyes once were, looks like
roasted bottle-imp, rather than roasted *Hare*, what are

you to do, unless the cook has been skilful enough to
bone it for you? You must first take care that your
knife has a sharp strong point to it, and therewith, having the head of the hare towards your left, you will cut
off the legs,—to wit, the hind legs, for carving and natural history differ in this matter, the latter asserting that
the hare is a quadruped, the former that it has only two
legs, and two "wings." You will then cut two long
thin slices off each side of the back; then take off the
"wings" or shoulders; then *break* the back into four
pieces with the aid of the fork; then cut off the ears, and
lastly, turning the head towards you with the under side
uppermost, insert the point of the knife exactly in the
centre of the palate, and drawing it to the nose, thus divide it into two parts. If you do all this without splash-
ing the gravy, you may take your degree in carving. But
to help a hare is more diplomatic still than to carve it.
The difficulty is to find enough for everybody who wants
it. The best parts are the slices from the back, the head
and ears. Never, however, send head or ears to a lady.
There is a good reason for this, which I won't tell you.
But if there is a minister in office at table, and you
want to ask him for a place, or there is a father whose
daughter's hand you aspire to, or an uncle who may possibly leave you a legacy, it is for him that you reserve
half the face, and one if not both ears. If he be at all a
gourmet, you will get his ear by sending him puss's, and
the delicate brain of the animal will fully compensate for
a want of it in your own head.

A *fowl*, if not in its *premi`re jeunesse*, is more irri-
tating still than a hare, because you feel that when you
have done your best, the flesh is not worth eating, except

at supper. There are two ways of beginning. Either take the leg, wing, and part of breast off with one cut, after having laid the bird on its side; or, allowing it to remain on its back, with the breast and wings towards you, and the legs away from you, insert the knife in the side of the breast above the leg, and bring it down to the joint of the wing, which is thus removed with a slice of the breast. The liver wing, which lies to your right, is the best, and should be taken off first. This done, insert the knife just at the turn of the breast, bring it down, and you have the merry-thought. The meat of the breast is then easily sliced off, the legs having been turned back with the fork. The side-bones come off next, in a moment, if you insert the knife or fork in the right place, viz., under the angular joint, and turn them out. The back is then broken by lifting it with the fork against the pressure of the knife, and lastly, the sides are removed. The wing, breast, and merry-thought are the best pieces; the legs and sides are insulting. The great point in carving a fowl is to do it quickly, and with the *fork* as much, if not more than, the knife.

A *partridge* is carved like a fowl, but the legs being joined, are simply turned back with the knife before the operation commences. A *pheasant* is carved like a fowl. *Pigeons* are not carved at all, but cut in two down the middle; the eater kindly saving the carver any further trouble. *Snipe* is treated in the same way, and smaller birds are always sent round one to each person.

Of a *goose* or a *turkey* we are told it is "vulgar" to cut more than the breast, but there can be no vulgarity in making a good dinner, and in the family circle you will be obliged to apply to the wings and legs. However,

for company, slices of the breast suffice. The same
thing is said of the wild-duck, that best of birds; but we
did not think so at Oxford, where we never left anything
more than their carcasses. The most productive bird is
the Scotch and Swedish capercailzie. I have known one
satisfy fourteen large appetites one day, three heavy
eaters the second, and what with hashing, grilling, devil-
ling, and picking, last the original purchaser a whole
week for breakfast afterwards. It might perhaps be
"vulgar" to carve such a bird as that; little less so
than offering a lady a leg of ostrich.

CHAPTER VI.

FEMININE ACCOMPLISHMENTS.

An English lady without her piano, or her pencil, or her fancy work, or her favorite French authors and German poets, is an object of wonder, and perhaps of pity. Music, the cultivation of which was, at one time, severely censured as being carried to excess, has now become a national want. Painting, and even modelling, are not only pursued in the quiet of home, they furnish subjects for an amateur exhibition. No woman can be wholly fitted as a member of society, unless she can dance well; and to work neatly and skilfully at fancy work, is one of the attributes of good female society.

We are not, we English, a nation of talkers; naturally, our talent is for silence. The few who distinguished themselves in conversational powers have died out among us, and their places will never, we have every reason to believe, be filled up.

> " The seat is vacant—whereon Conversation
> Sharpe gave forth such studied *bon mots*,"

or culled from the treasures of his vast memory the titbits of old authors. Lady Morgan who, as she " circulated" through a party, to use her own expression, delighted both wise and simple, by her ever ready flow of words, and richness of anecdote and repartee, is gone, and *her* throne is vacant.

The *salon*, which she collected around her, was, in its capacity of passing hours in talking, more French than English; she its centre. We shall never see the like again; the world is too large, and we are too rich. Eloquence, even, went out with metal buttons and white waistcoats: the House of Commons is only *bored* by it now; the Lords are proud and thankful to say they never encouraged it. Eloquence, which is to conversation what the garden flower is to the wild flower, the hot-house grape to the poor sour thing that grows on the cottage walls—eloquence, which is but condensed conversation, with all the *essence* of many minds in one, is regarded in these practical days only as an interruption.

It therefore becomes more and more essential that there should be some talent to supply the want of good conversation. And, for that end, there is nothing like music.

Music is, I repeat, the substitute, and the only one, for conversational powers. It has its merits in that light. Conversation sometimes aggravates temper: music soothes it. Conversation challenges reply: music gives no answer. Conversation is the rock of peril to the impudent: they can scarcely, in playing or singing, commit an indiscretion. In talking, again, one may lose a friend, or even make an enemy. Music is, therefore, an excellent source of amusement for many occasions, and is become almost indispensable to those who have frequently parties to receive. A lively waltz, or a soft movement, carefully played, even without that great execution which *compels* listening, are often aids to conversation: it flows the more easily from that slight and agreeable interruption. It has indeed, still greater advantages : this world of ours has its work and its troubles; a parent or husband may leave home from either or from both, to find a solace in music, which changes the current of his ideas. A brother may be almost made domestic by the cheerful notes, which he finds pass the evening almost as rapidly as the club, or Jullien's, or the theatre. Few persons are wholly devoid of a capacity for enjoying music, and even, if not gifted with any great natural taste, a love of the art may almost be engrafted on the nature by early associations. And those associations, too, have their value. The air that brings back home-born thoughts, brings back in some degree the absent, the kind, the forbearing, the loving, the honored.

The piano still keeps its pre-eminence as the instrument best fitted for society. The harp, it is to be regretted, has for some years ceased to be fashionable; perhaps the greater attention, in modern times, to physical education has banished the harp from the school-room. There is every risk of the practising on this instrument producing curvature of the spine; whereas the piano, from exercising both hands at a time, and from the straight posture it requires, is useful to those disposed to such curvatures. Duets on the harp and piano are, nevertheless, very delightful; and they used to produce a good effect in a large room, when two sisters, or a professional lady and her young pupil, a daughter of the house, opened the evening's amusement with one of those exquisite Italian airs, set by Bochsa or Chatterton. Simple melodies, sung to the harp, are still very effective in society from their variety. A harp requires a large room; it should be played with feeling and grace, or it becomes very unpleasant, like the jingling of a hired band. It requires stout nerves, cer tainly, for the display necessary to execute an air on the harp, perched on a high stool, and forming a pleasing object, as well as being the vehicle of sweet sounds to the whole company.

The guitar makes a graceful variety; but is more appropriate to a man's than to a woman's playing. It is monotonous, and soon fatigues the attention; but, being easily portable, is often a resource in places and on occasions where a piano cannot be had.

The same may be said of the zitter, one of the sweetest and most touching of string instruments; but still, except for the occasional playing of Tyrolean minstrels, unknown in this country. It is of Bavarian origin, and is the oldest instrument known. Its plaintive and appealing sounds are heard in Alpine chalets, or by the forester's fireside, as well as in the country revels of the inhabitants of Vienna, Innspruck, and Munich. It is exquisite as an accompaniment of the voice; it is cheap and portable. A good zitter may be obtained for thirty shillings or two pounds. It is flat, and takes up little room, and should be placed horizontally on a table, without a cover. It requires, however, time and much practice to bring out those thrilling tones, at once so touching and so peculiar. The most eminent professors in Germany speak highly of the powers of this small instrument, and say that it produces notes nearer to those of the human voice than any other. Yet it is not calculated for large concerts: we English must have noise and show. The zitter is an instrument for the *boudoir*, for lovers in a bower, for the poet in his turret, for

the devotee to all that is soft, romantic, and unsophisti-
cated.

It seems scarcely needful to point to the violin and
violoncello as instruments unsuitable to young ladies; yet
there have been women who have successfully cultivated
both, to the great credit of their perseverance, and the
great detriment of their feminine attractions. The concertina is, however, a beautiful and not inappropriate instrument, though I confess the inelegance of the attitude
required much lessens the sentiment inspired by the beautiful tones of the concertina.

Nothing requires greater judgment, if not some experience of society, than the selection of pieces to play in
company. "Oh! how my head ached last night!" cries
an old lady; "we had a piece six pages long!" Some
ladies sit down (as it seems) with an intention of "giving
it rein" for their hearers. Through passage after passage, volleys of black notes are made to speak, and, as
page after page is turned over by a zealous friend, the
young musician labors at it, and does herself justice, and
her hearers a wrong: for a long piece is as bad as a long
story, and neither are fitted for society. A short, perhaps
brilliant, thoroughly well-learned air or movement by
some good master, is the best response to the often put
question, "Will you play something?" The loud, thump-
ing style should be avoided: if possible, the piece should
not be quite common and hackneyed; not what "every
one" plays. It should not be too mournful, nor too rapid.
On sitting down to the piano, it is very offensive to hear
a young lady find fault with the instrument, or complain
that it is out of tune—a proof either that her temper is

out of tune, or that she wishes to impress on you the superiority of her ear, which detects the defect to yours,
which has stupidly overlooked it. All self-assertion, be it
about music, or singing, or dancing, or anything, is unpleasant, and always seen through. There is a certain
art too, in sitting at the piano : all movements of the body
should be avoided : well-bred people play without them,
and they are unpleasant to those sitting behind. Be ready
also to quit the instrument after finishing : in some cases, ·
when once seated, ladies seem to be glued to the piano,
and however fascinating may be their efforts, it is bad
policy to wear your audience out. Then another hint to
the amateur musician : be lenient, at all events, and encouraging, if you can, to others. There is no need to
flatter ; but great reason, especially to those who play well,
to be amiable on this, as on other points. A little kindliness, a polite attention to the feelings of others, wins many
a friend ; for we are governed by the trifles of life.

Almost every well-educated lady can play a little ; but
that is not the case in respect to vocal music. Whether
it be owing to English climate or English constitution,
there is no saying ; but there is nothing more rare than a
good voice. It may, however, provided the ear be good,
be almost acquired ; but then the best instruction must b ?
obtained ; a dozen good lessons, taken not too soon, but
whenever the voice is formed, and the young lady plays
well are far more beneficial than a long course of inferior
teaching. It is important that a young lady should not
begin to sing in society too soon ; it is objectionable to
hear a learner, whose performance speaks of the school-
room ; it is far worse, however, to be condemned to listen
to a voice that is *passed*, of which the best notes are

cracked or feeble; and there is something absurd in hearing
a stout matron—

> "A mother with her daughters or her nieces,
> Looking like a guinea, with her seven shilling pieces."

as Byron impertinently has it—singing with bygone ém-
phasis about love; or a thin spinster, of forty or more,
holding forth in such songs as "I'll watch for thee," or,
"Don't forget me." Instrumental music is appropriate
to any age, but after forty the voice loses the delicious
freshness of youth, the style is no longer that of the day,
and even the finest amateur vocal performers have lost
something, we scarcely know what, but something we miss
painfully.

When asked to sing, if you do not intend to do so, refuse so decidedly that you cannot be compelled; but the
more decided the refusal, the gentler should the manner
be. There is a style of saying "No," that never offends.
You are asked as a compliment; as a compliment receive
the entreaty. If you intend to sing, accept at once; do
not hurry up to the piano, as if glad of an opportunity
of showing off, but go gently; if by request you have
brought your music, and it should never be brought to
those who know that you sing without request, leave it
down stairs; it can be sent for; but, since all pauses in
society are to be avoided, if you can sing without notes it
is as well; at the same time, never attempt to do so unless
sure of yourself. A half-forgotten or imperfect song is
irritating. Something light and brilliant is best for a
commencement, or a little air not too well known—German, perhaps. For the sake of all the Muses, do not
attempt a long Italian bravura of Verdi or Donizetti, that,

perhaps, half the company have heard Garcia or Piccolomini sing the week before, you *must* murder it to ears so artistic as theirs. Or if you are singing to a homely audience, the simplest song will please them better. The difference between a professional and an amateur singer should always be kept in view. The one is constrained by interest to astonish ; the other has no other inducement than to charm. The one is purchased, the other is a voluntary effort to pass away time, and to do justice to the composition of some of the popular masters of the day.

The form and movements of the body must be habitually controlled in singing. In nine cases out of ten they spoil the effect of the voice. Some ladies bend from side to side, cast up their eyes, or fix them, with a rapt expression, on the wax lights above them. Others make alarming faces, protrude the under jaw, or what is worse assume an affected smile. A good master suffers none of these defects to creep in. He regulates the mouth, which should be as little drawn as possible; open it must be, but should appear to have an inclination to smile, without the absolute smile. A great deal depends on the right mode of bringing out the voice. I confess it is a great sacrifice to see one's friends look frightful, even when giving out the most delicious sounds ; nor is it essential. In the choice of songs, variety is to be adopted. German music pleases, generally : but, let no one not conversant with the right pronunciation of any foreign language, sing in it ; there is nothing so unpleasant as to hear broad French, mincing German, or lisping Italian. Even in English, a good accent is the most essential thing possible ; and, also, a good articulation. A simple song. sung without great powers of voice, but well articulated, delights, because it touches the understanding to which it appeals, and gratifies the ear which approves the modest and careful effort of art. Witness the extreme pleasure, amounting to enthusiasm, afforded by the singing of the poet Moore. He had no compass of voice; what he had was musical, but not eminently so; but his singing captivated from the clearness with which every word was uttered; the way in which every word *told*; the easy, natural manner of the poet at the piano. On one occasion, Mrs. Billington being in one room, and Moore in another, of some great London house, crowds flocked around the poet, whose touching tones even drew them from the florid singing of the nightingale of her day. The same effect was produced by the singing of the late Mrs. Lockhart, the daughter of Sir Walter Scott, to the harp. She generally sang her father's poetry, set to music. Her taste, her feeling, and truth of expression, riveted the attention, though her voice had little power. The French excel in this species of intellectual singing, if one may use such a word, but theirs is chiefly professional. Who can ever forget Madame Jenny Denner's "Ma Tante," or Levassor's "Vie de campagne"? Yet neither had the average amount of vocal powers of a village chorister.

After finishing one song, a lady should rise from the piano, even if she be brought back again and again. Some ladies are so aware what great injustice they do themselves by being induced to sing too much, that they make a rule of only singing two songs at a party; but all set rules in society are bad. Nothing, however, can be worse than to go on from song to song, till admiration, and even patience are exhausted, and politeness is driven to her wit's end to be civil. Of course, it is almost needless to say that sacred songs should be avoided in parties. I doubt whether any of the deeper feelings should be paraded on light occasions, and if songs truly mournful are not better reserved for small reunions of the real lovers of deep pathos in music.

All accomplishments have the one great merit of giving a lady something to do ; something to preserve her from *ennui ;* to console her in seclusion ; to arouse her in grief ; to compose her to occupation in joy. And none answers this purpose much better than fancy work, or even plain work. The former can often be brought advantageously into the rear of other pursuits—as a reserve. The latter cannot well be carried into society, except as a charity. The Germans do this gracefully. At some of their courts the great set the example. During Lent, at Munich, they have working parties. The queen made a baby's shirt, one evening, when one of these réunions was held in the apartments of her *grande ma tresse.* The king, meantime, was pulling lint for the hospitals. Every lady of the court had some useful article before her ; warm shawls made with the crotchet-needle ; stockings knitted ; dresses, chiefly for children, from their being small. Such are the labors that employ on certain evenings the court and nobility of a nation whose aristocracy is among the most ancient and still the richest in Europe. And conversation went round cheerfully. Little tables were set about, and the assemblage was broken up into parties, each table holding a lady or two, with a gentleman near her. A terrible waste of time in small parties would, indeed, be avoided, if some sort of work could be introduced ; and, if young ladies were not condemned to be idle for several hours, they would look better, and be happier, more amiable. and less fatigued than they often are at what is facetiously termed a "friendly party." Not that it is recommended to take into a party your husband's stockings to mend, or dear Charles's shirts, over which he was naturally so irritable at the absence of buttons, or Louisa's pinafores to run strings into; let the work have the characteristics of recreation combined with utility, and the most scrupulous cannot be offended. Such is indeed the spirit of the day; for we are a more sensible people than our grandsires were.

Sketching and archery stand first among out-door amusements. They are healthy, elegant, and appropriate to the feminine character; while—first thought of mammas!—they assemble rather than exclude the younger members of the other sex.

CHAPTER VII.

MANNER, CARRIAGE, AND HABITS.

TRUE politeness comes from the heart, and this being good, the rest will soon follow. But, as Chesterfield says, "good sense and good nature suggest civility in general; but in good breeding there are a thousand little delicacies, which are established only by custom." That which militates most against good breeding is an indifference to or want of consideration for the feelings of others; and what does this amount to but a bad heart? A courtier may hate me with civility, and a brigand rob me politely. Is there not some good in the heart of both these men? Have they not a great consideration for my feelings? They cannot, they would tell me, help what they do; I stand in this one's way, and he must and does hate me; I have a purse and the other is a robber, he must and will take it; but both of them, compelled to treat me so ill, do it with a grace that removes half the annoyance of it. The courtier conceals his hatred, and what therefore do I care for it? I do not even know of its existence, and a passion which we never discover cannot affect us. Then, too, if the highwayman politely and delicately "invites" me to give up those few paltry bank-notes, assuring me it is his "profession," that he laments the necessity, and that if I show no fight, no vio-

ience will be used, I have at least the comfort of being
saved from a fright, of being allowed free speech, of being given the option to fight or yield, so that when I
come to think how much an agreeable manner may do to
console and conciliate, I don't know whether I could accuse my worst enemy of a want of heart, if he behaved
like a gentleman to me. However, I am convinced that
if a man had not a good only, but a perfect heart, if all
his attention were directed to the comfort of others, and
he was willing perpetually to make the sacrifice necessary
to insure it, he would need little or no instruction in manners more than a little experience. He would soon discover how this act or that gave offence or caused embarrassment to his neighbor; and while he saw nothing
wrong in it himself, would, for his neighbor's sake, avoid
it for the future. He himself might see no harm in
using a tooth-pick at dinner, but he would soon see the
obnoxiousness of it reflected in opposite faces, and down
would go the tooth-pick. Give such a man, ill-bred, even
unbred naturally, the time and the opportunity, and he
would turn out a gentleman. But first, where do you
find this perfect consideration for others, this brotherly
love, for it is nothing else, which descends to the minutest
details, and feels within itself the vibration of every
chord too rudely struck in other hearts? Alas, where?
Or, given the heart, how are you to insure the experience? Meanwhile, in waiting for hearts and experiences,
society grows depraved. It is for this reason that we set
up laws of etiquette, as it is called—but laws of Christian action we might call them—to insist upon the show
of that which ought to come spontaneously from the
heart. In doing so, we merely copy lawgivers of another

kind. Honesty is not honesty, for instance, if it come
not from within. The most respectable man *might* be
dishonest if he had the chance, and no fear of the law.
Nevertheless the law undertakes to make men appear
honest, because it knows that it is in vain to wait for
honesty in heart. The law tells the young thief he must
rob no more, and it may cure him of thieving and make
him turn out a respectable man—in appearance; but it
cannot be sure, because he does not thieve, that he has no
internal desire to do so, and would not do so if the fear
of the law were gone. So too, in just the same way, the
laws of society give rules by which a man may be amiable and well-bred—to all appearance; but it cannot a
whit the more insure the good feeling which ought to suggest the good acts.

I say, then, that because Etiquette lays down rules by
which you are to *appear* to have a heart, she does nothing worse than the laws of the realm, which show how
you may *appear* honest, and leave your heart alone.
This preface is necessary, because when I say a man is to
smile at such a time, and show dignity at such another,
the world might tell me I was teaching hypocrisy. I am
doing nothing of the kind. I am merely providing for
acts which are necessary to the wellbeing of society, because I know that if every one acted according to his
heart, the world would soon be turned upside-down.

So then I can manfully say that a good manner is a
good gift. We know all about oily serpents, we have
read enough of them in romantic novels, but I am bound
to say I prefer an oily serpent, by way of society, to an
unlicked bear. The serpent may not choose me to bite,
I may enjoy his society, I may never discover that he is

anything worse than a harmless blind-worm with no sting
in him ; but I cannot have been a minute with the bear,
before I am torn to pieces. When I hear of the serpent's
biting anybody, I can avoid him for the future, but in
the meantime he is an agreeable companion, and I have no
right to judge my neighbor. I say then that a man
should curb his heart first, but if he cannot do or has not
done this, he has no right to come bellowing with irritation into the society of quiet people, merely because he
will not take the trouble to be mannerly.

Manner, then, I am bound to confess, is the cloak of
character, but if to bare the character be indecent, it is
better it should wear a cloak than go about naked. Until we are all perfect, until there is a millennium on
earth, it will always be indecent to wear our feelings in
Adamite costume, and so long will a garment, like that
of Manner, be necessary.

A good carriage involves two things, a respect for one's
self and a respect for others. It is very difficult to draw
the line between the two, and to show where the one
should yield to the other ; but as the world goes, the man
who respects himself is generally respected, and for a
very good reason, since without a due recognition of the
Divine spark within him, a recognition owed to his Maker,
no man can be really good. On the other side, comes
the Christian precept which bids us love our neighbor as
ourself, and at once defines where self-respect must end.
Wherever our dignity, our prejudices, our opinions begin
to annoy our neighbors, to cause them pain, embarrassment, or confusion, they must give way. How often do
we hear, " I think Mr. —— is a very excellent man, but
he has a most disagreeable manner;" the fact being that

12*

Mr. ——, meaning very well, has not sufficient consideration for others' feelings to temper his enthusiasm. And
then such a man wins his reward. His zeal devours
him, and he annihilates by want of consideration all the
good he might have done. We see this very often in excellent well-meaning maiden ladies, who undertake the
supervision of their poorer neighbors. Wherever they
see a fault, they attack it harshly, unflinchingly, unpity-
ingly. The result is, that the poor they visit begin to
loathe them and their visits, and instead of improving,
despise the improver. Then send to them some mild un-
taught girl, all love, all heart, all warmth, and bid her
win them back. She begins instinctively by attaching
them to herself, she is all interest, all kindness to them,
and when she has made their hearts her own, the least
expression of a wish will make them give up their dearest
vices. How well has it been put, " Smoothe the way to
the head through the heart," and we may be sure that
what is good here in morals is good in manners. Rudeness will never win the day; an amiable, kind manner
rides over the course.

The first rule, then, for Manner, is self-respect. Without this, a man is not only weak and bad, but unfit for
society. The want of it shows itself in two most disagreeable forms, adulation and awkwardness. I believe both to
have no evil intent in themselves. Hundreds and thousands of flatterers and hangers-on have never hoped to
gain a single benefit from their adulation. It is simple
weakness : simple absence of self-respect. But the world
will not always see it in so charitable a point of view, and
the flatterer is denounced as interested. In any case, adulation is bad, for it is dangerous not only to the servile,

but to those to whom it is addressed. Awkwardness may often arise from shyness, but more often is the fruit of a want of self-respect. Both are to be sedulously avoided.

On the other hand, self-respect is liable to err on the side of dignity, and self-respect is only one step removed from self-esteem. The one is a vice; the other a virtue. Self-respect is the acknowledgment of manhood, of the good soul God has given you to take care of, of the part He has given you to play in life. Self-esteem is an arrogance of superiority in these points. In the young it takes the form of conceit; in the older, of stateliness; in the woman, of vanity. We pardon it most readily in middle-aged men, and yet I think that the oppressive, damping dignity of some of these is destructive of all ease in society. When Paterfamilias asserts his rights, standing with his coat-tails spread before the fire, which he hides from everybody else, we cannot, dare not object openly, but we certainly feel chilled, inwardly by his solemn dignity, and outwardly by the deprivation of caloric. Scarcely less chilling is the arrogance of the younger man, who can scarcely condescend to converse with us; who brings his superior information down upon our humble opinions, like an avalanche on an Alpine village; who contradicts us flatly, and sneers us into insignificance. Conversation becomes impossible, and society is deadened, under such influences.

More innocent, but not less contemptible, is the affectation which arises from incipient, often from full-grown, vanity. In men it is simply contemptible, because effeminate; and the youth who purposely lisps or minces his words, or the silky young curate who has, by dint of practice, forced down his natural voice into a low, but as Anna

Maria asserts, most thrilling, whisper; or the dilettante in music, whose hair hangs in profuse curls, and who, as he runs fat, white, beringed fingers over the notes, sways his body to and fro, and casts his glances to either side in a kind of rapture; nay, even the unnaturally solemn man, who looks you through as if he were casting up your little account of sin for you, together with a thousand other kinds of men, are all too obviously affected to retain long the respect of sensible people. We know that nature has its many faults to be curbed, but we know that where nature is not at fault, it is most truthful to let her have her run. By the side of the affected man, even the bluntest looks noble, and for the very reason that affectation arises from a want of self-respect or excess of self-esteem, extremes which resemble one another.

But I would almost dare to say that there never was a woman who had not more or less affectation in speaking to men. I am not a St. Anthony, but I believe it to be natural to woman to alter their manner towards the other sex; so that I involve myself in a paradox; it is natural for them to be unnatural under these circumstances. I am not going into the logic of it, but really this is only an apparent paradox, and I may say with perfect truth that it is natural for women to be sometimes unnatural. If you doubt me, watch how Clara, the simplest, sweetest, least sophisticated of her sex, talks to you, a man. Then put on the invisible cap and follow her to the drawing-room, where she and her sisters will sit alone and talk. If you see no marked change of manner in Clara, I will admit that I am wrong.

But then there are grades in woman's affectation, and while Clara seems to be "all nature," as they say in modern novels, we can exclaim at first sight that Belinda "is a mass of tarlatane and affectation." My dear Belinda, take in good part the warning of an old bachelor. Believe me that men who are worth your arrows will not be smitten with tinsel shafts; believe me that the better they are, the more they love nature in women, artlessness, frankness, modesty. But then there is even an affectation of naturalness, and you, Clarissa, who are past five-and-twenty—O yes, I know it, for your little brother let it out!—feel that you never can be really natural again in society, and so you affect to be so, by becoming brusque and somewhat pert. Men, Clarissa, are not such fools as you imagine; they will see through this even more easily, and there is no hope for you, but to be with them what you are before your own looking-glass. But I am trespassing on the province of my colleague, and I must return, very loath, to the men.

Let me give a few samples of manner to be avoided. First there is Tibbs, s'ort enough and clever enough to be a great man, and such, I dare say, he will be one of these days. But Tibbs feels within him the spirit of governance, and has reverence for neither old nor young. He walks with a short, sharp step, his little nose rather elevated, his eyes glaring to detect some weakness on which to pounce. You put forward an opinion, the meekest you can give : "It will turn out fine." "Beg your pardon," answered Tibbs, with that sharp snap, which makes the words sound like "Don't be a fool!" "it will *not* be a fine day. I have good reason to know it, there." What can you do with Tibbs, but collapse? He treats his father and grandfather, and mother and sister, all in the same way, and they are cowed before him. Tibbs is never

downrightly rude. You cannot catch him up and call
him a bear; but his manner of speaking continually conveys the impression that Tibbs believes in his own acuteness only, and in nobody else's. He is the kind of man
who can open Shakspere, read a passage, and exclaim,
"Did you ever hear such nonsense?" giving you good
reasons forsooth, if poets and philosophers could be measured by the lowest standard of the dryest common sense.
Tibbs is all common sense, but by no means a pleasant
companion.

Very different is old Mr. Dawdles. He seems to be in
a state of chronic plethora. Say what you will on his
dearest themes, he has no reply for you but a yes or no
snivelled out. When he speaks himself, he appears to be
grumbling at you, however kind his words. You knew he
is good and means very well, and he would give you half
his fortune out of sheer kindness, but with a gesture and
tone of voice which would seem to say, "There, take it,
and don't make a fuss." He does hate a fuss, more than
all other abominations.

There is Slouch, again, whom I believe to be an incar-
nation of honor and uprightness, but who gives you the
idea of a sneak and a villain. He never looks you full in
the face. His shaggy brows hang over his lurking eyes,
and his words come cautiously and suspiciously wriggling
up to you.

But Pompous has the best of hearts. He has been
known to go out of his way for miles to leave a little something with a poor widow. And how the man wrongs himself! He is very tall, and has a fine figure. He draws
himself up to the greatest height, and looks down on you
as if you were a Lilliput, and all the while he loves you

but is ashamed to show it. He orders his wife and servants about with a calm imperiousness which makes them
dread him, and yet they all acknowledge they never knew
a kinder man, though I never yet saw a smile of pity or
sympathy on his face.

Far less admirable is that weak young Fitzwhiskers, who
holds his head so very high, and walks down the room with
a curled lip, which seems to say, "What scum you all are!"
Then there is Commodus, an agreeable man, if you can
keep him within bounds. He sits down quietly enough
and you are pleased, but in two minutes he is making the
freest possible remarks, with no harm, no intentional offence in them, but yet so intolerably familiar for a man
you have known but five minutes, that they quite upset
you. Only the other day I rashly introduced him to a
young lady, and she afterwards told me how he had begun :—"Were you at the opera last night?" this was
politely and quietly asked. "No." "How very fortunate for those who were there! Those eyes would have
singed a dozen hearts."

But Vivax is one of the worst. He talks atrociously
loud; hails you from the other end of the table. "Will
trouble you for that, ha, ha! and for this, ho, ho!" and
"Have you been dancing, Miss Smith? ha, ha! Then
of course you have, Miss Jones? he, he! and what do
you say to it, Mrs. Brown?" and he is round the whole
circle, from one to another, in two minutes, not waiting
for answers. Then he bustles about; he must always
have something on hand. He drags you here one minute,
and rushes away from you the next. He talks as rapidly
as an auctioneer, and rattles over a dozen subjects in as
many minutes. He is quick and clever, but when he has

jerked out his own thought, he clinches it with a ha, ha! or a he, he! and never waits for your answer.

Glumme is just the reverse. You must do all the talking for him; he will only drawl out a "No-o-o," or a "Ye-e-es," and wears a perpetual scowl.

Then there is Trippet, who seizes you by the button-hole, and grows hot over the merest trifle; Courte, who replies with a sharp sneer; Sterne, who has for ever a look of reproof, though he does not mean it; Fidgette, who can never be prevailed upon to be comfortable; Bluff, who terrifies you with his curt blunt manner; and Lack-adaye, who is so languid that he cannot take the trouble even to look at you. One genius whom I knew, never removed his eyes from the lamp on the table; another rushed up to you, seized both your hands, and gazed with apparent affection into your eyes; a third spoke deep truths in a low solemn tone, as he gazed at a spot on the carpet; a fourth moved his head to and fro, as if to avoid your gaze: and a fifth, the greatest of all, never spoke at all.

The manner, in short, which a man must aspire to, is one which will give ease, and not embarrassment, to others. He must preserve a certain dignity, but yet be pliant; he must be open, frank; look you honestly in the face, speak out confidently, yet calmly; modestly, yet firmly; not be bluff or blunt, but yet be free and simple. In fact, let a man be natural, let him be in society what he is anywhere; but if he find his natural manner too rough, too loud, too curt, or too brutal, let him learn to tame it and calm it down.

But manner has various functions for various circumstances. Towards our elders and superiors, we must show

an honest, not servile deference ; towards women, gentleness ; towards juniors, tenderness ; towards inferiors, a
simple dignity, without condescension. Aristotle, who was
perhaps a better philosopher than gentleman, recommends
a haughtiness to superiors, and graceful freedom to inferiors. The world is old enough to judge for itself. But
when a man finds that his lively badinage suits a band of
merry lissome girls, he must not be so wild as to rush at
Papa with the same kind of banter. Paterfam. may give
a smile to real wit and laugh at a good story, but the
same trifling which makes his daughters laugh so ring-
ingly, will only appear to him a familiarity when addressed to himself. Then, again, the gravity into which
you have fallen when discussing great measures with a
philanthropist, will afford no satisfaction to the airy mass
of tarlatane with whom you dance soon after. Solomon
has said it : there is a time to weep and a time to laugh.
In other words, be you as merry a jester as ever sat at a
king's table, you must not obtrude your unweary mirth
at a visit of condolence ; or be you the " most bereaved"
of widowers, you will not bring your tears and sighs to
damp the merriment of social gatherings.

What applies to manner may be transferred in most
respects to that bearing which distinguishes a man in society. But the times change much in this respect, and
the old courteous dignity with which the beaux of my
younger days behaved, has given way to a greater ease,
and sometimes, I fear, to too great freedom. I do not
know whether to regret or not, the strict courteousness
of those times. It often amounted to affectation ; it was
not natural to be ever bowing low, making set speeches,
raising a lady's hands to one's lips, or pressing one's own

upon the region of the heart, but at the same time I regret the lounging familiarity which we see too prevalent
among young men of the present day. There is not in
fact sufficient reverence for the fair and the old. Sometimes this, I regret to say, must be charged to the fault
of the former; and a young lady who talks slang, or is
always with " the men," must expect to find them sometimes abuse her good-nature. But abstracts are ineffec-
tive; let me come to some details as to the physical carriage of a man.

A certain dignity is the first requisite, but we must not
expect too much of it in the young, and we should not
emulate the solemnity of Charles the First, who never
laughed. It is a mistake, too, to suppose that height is
necessary for dignity. Chesterfield, the most polished
gentleman of his day, was only five feet seven in height,
and Wellington and Bonaparte. both short men, have
never been accused of want of dignity. But at the same
time the assumption of it is more liable to become ridiculous in a short than in a tall man. Dignity can never go
along with a slouching gait, and uprightness should be
acquired in childhood by gymnastics and ample exercise.
This uprightness, however, should not go to the extent of
curving the back inwards. The chest should be expanded,
but not so much as to make " a presence." The head
should be set well back on the shoulders, but not tosse l
up nor jerked on one side with that air of pertness you
see in some men. People of height are often foolish
enough to mar it by bending the head forward, whereas,
if carried well, a tall figure is never awkward, even among
Lilliputs. In standing, the legs ought to be straight, or
one of them bent a little, but not set wide apart. In

walking, they should be moved gently but firmly from the hips, so that the upper part of the body may remain in the same position. How often from my window have I been able to mark a man by his walk! One comes striding stoutly like a captain on quarter-deck ; another shambles his feet along the pavement; a third swings his arms violently ; a fourth carries them bowed out before him like a dancing-master of the old school; a fifth turns out his huge feet at an angle of forty-five ; another jerks forward his pointed toes like a soldier at drill ; another sways his body from side to side ; another looks almost hump-backed, as he moves heavily on ; one more saunters listlessly with his hands in his pockets; this one moves his arms back behind him, and that one carries them stiff and straight as iron bars, with his fists clenched like knobs at the end thereof. The feet must be turned outwards very little indeed ; the arms should be carried easily and very slightly bent at the sides, and in walking should be moved a little, without swinging them ; and the shoulders should never be shrugged up. Avoid stiffness on the one hand, lounging on the other. Be natural and perfectly at your ease, whether in walking or sitting, and aspire to calm confidence rather than loftiness.

There is, however, one good habit which must not be overlooked. You should never speak without a slight smile, or at least a beam of good will in your eyes, and that to all, whether your equals or inferiors. To the latter it is especially necessary, and often wins you more love than the most liberal benevolence. But this smile should not settle into a simper, nor, when you are launched in a conversation, should it interfere with the earnestness of your manner.   To a lady it should be more marked than to a man.

In listening, again, you should manifest a certain interest in what a person is saying ; and however little worthy of your attention, you should not show that you think it so by the toss of your head or the wandering of your eyes.   In speaking to any one you should look them in the face, for the eyes always aid the tongue, but you should not carry this to the extent of wriggling yourself forward in order to catch their eyes, if there happen to be another person between you.

It is painful to see the want of ease with which some men sit on the edge of a chair ; but at the same time the manner in which others throw themselves back and stretch forward their legs savors too much of familiarity.   You may cross your legs if you like, but not hug your knees nor your toes.   Straddling a chair, and tilting it up may be pardonable in a bachelor's rooms, but not in a lady's drawing-room.   Then, if you carry a walking-stick or umbrella in the street, you should avoid swinging them violently about, or tucking them under the arm.   Both are dangerous to your neighbors, for in the one case you may inadvertently strike a person and get into as great trouble as the individual who was brought up the other day for assaulting a woman with a cricket-bat, which he affirmed he was merely swinging about carelessly; in the other, the point of your stick may run into some unfortunate creature's eye.

Foreigners talk with their arms and hands as auxiliaries to the voice.   The custom is considered vulgar by us calm Englishmen, and a Parisian, who laughs at our ladies' dressing, will still admit that our men are "*distingu s, mais très distingu s.*" If the face follows the words, and you allow, without grimacing, your eyes and smile to express what you are saying, you have no need to act it with the hands, but, if you use them at all, it should be very slightly and gracefully, never bringing down a fist upon the table, nor slapping one hand upon another, nor poking your fingers at your interlocutor. Pointing, too, is a habit to be avoided, especially pointing with the thumb over the shoulder, which is an inelegant action. In short, while there is no occasion to be stolid or constrained, you should not be too lively in your actions, and even if led away by the enthusiasm of an argument, should never grow loud, rant, or declaim. No manner is more disagreeable than that of vehement affirmation or laying down the law.

With these remarks I may pass to consider certain habits which are more or less annoying to your neighbors. First, there is that odious habit of touching the nose and ears with the fingers, for which there is no excuse. Every part of the person should be properly tended in the dressing-room, never in the drawing-room, and for this reason picking the teeth, however fashionable it may once have been, scratching the head, the hands, or any part of the body, are to be avoided. Mr. Curzon tells us that at Erzeroum it is quite the fashion to scratch the bites of a little insect as common there as in certain London hotels, and it is even considered a delicate attention to catch the lively creatures as they perch on the dress or shoulders of your partner. Fortunately we are not tempted to perform such attentions in this country; but if you have the misfortune to be bitten or stung by any insect, you must

endure the pain without scratching the bite in company
These same little insects being of very disagreeable origin,
are not even spoken of with us. Biting the nails, again,
is not only a dirty habit, but one which soon disfigures
the fingers. So too in blowing your nose, you must not
make the noise of a trumpet, but do it gently and quietly; and, when you sneeze, use your handkerchief. I do
not go the length of saying that you must repress a
sneeze entirely. There is a pleasant custom, still universal in Germany and Italy, and retained among the peasantry in some parts of England, of blessing a person who
has sneezed, *benedicite, Gott segne sie,* and "bless you,"
being the terms used, probably in the hope that the prayer
may keep you from cold.

Sneezing brings me to snuffing, which is an obsolete
custom, retained only by a few old gentlemen, and as it
is a bad one, no young man should think of reviving it.

But what shall I say of the fragrant weed which Raleigh
taught our gallants to puff in capacious bowls; which a
royal pedant denounced in a famous "Counterblast:"
which his flattering laureate, Ben Jonson, ridiculed to
please his master: which our wives and sisters protest
gives rise to the dirtiest and most unsociable habit a man
can indulge in; of which some fair favorers declare that
they love the smell, and others that they will never marry
an indulger (which, by the way, they generally end in
doing); which has won a fame over more space and among
better men than Noah's grape has ever done; which doctors still dispute about, and boys still get sick over; but
which is the solace of the weary laborer; the support of
the ill-fed; the refresher of over-wrought brains; the
soother of angry fancies; the boast of the exquisite; the

excuse of the idle ; the companion of the philosopher ; and the tenth muse of the poet. I will go neither into the medical nor the moral question about the dreamy, calming cloud. I will content myself so far with saying what may be said for everything that can bless and curse mankind, that, in moderation, it is at least harmless; but what is moderate and what is not, must be determined in each individual case, according to the habits and constitution of the subject. If it cures asthma, it may destroy digestion ; if it soothes the nerves, it may, in excess, produce a chronic irritability.

But I will regard it in a social point of view ; and, first, as a narcotic, notice its effects on the individual character. I believe, then, that in moderation it diminishes the violence of the passions, and particularly that of the temper. Interested in the subject, I have taken care to seek instances of members of the same family having the same violent tempers by inheritance, of whom the one has been calmed down by smoking, and the other gone on in his passionate course. I believe that it induces a habit of calm reflectiveness, which causes us to take less prejudiced, perhaps less zealous views of life, and to be therefore less irritable in our converse with our fellow creatures. I am inclined to think that the clergy, the squirearchy, and the peasantry are the most prejudiced and most violent classes in this country ; there may be other reasons for this, but it is noteworthy that these are the classes which smoke least. On the other hand, I confess that it induces a certain lassitude, and a lounging, easy mode of life, which are fatal both to the precision of manners and the vivacity of conversation. The mind of a smoker is contemplative rather than active ; and if the

weed cures our irritability, it kills our wit. I believe that
it is a fallacy to suppose that it encourages drinking.
There is more drinking and less smoking in this than in
any other country of the civilized world. There was
more drinking among the gentry of last century, who
never smoked at all. Smoke and wine do not go well
together. Coffee or beer are its best accompaniments, and
the one cannot intoxicate, the other must be largely im-
bibed to do so. I have observed among young bachelors
that very little wine is drunk in their chambers, and that
beer is gradually taking its place. The cigar, too, is an
excuse for rising from the dinner-table where there are no
ladies to go to.

In another point of view, I am inclined to think that
smoking has conduced to make the society of men when
alone less riotous, less quarrelsome, and even less vicious
than it was. Where young men now blow a common
cloud, they were formerly driven to a fearful consumption
of wine, and this in their heads, they were ready and
roused to any iniquity. But the pipe is the bachelor's
wife. With it he can endure solitude longer, and is not
forced into low society in order to shun it. With it too
the idle can pass many an hour, which otherwise he would
have given, not to work, but to extravagant devilries.
With it he is no longer restless and impatient for excitement of any kind. We never hear now of young blades
issuing in bands from their wine to beat the watch or
disturb the slumbering citizens, as we did thirty or forty
years ago, when smoking was still a rarity: they are all
puffing harmlessly in their chambers now. But, on the
other hand, I foresee with dread a too tender allegiance to
the pipe, to the destruction of good society, and the aban-

donment of the ladies. No wonder they hate it, dear creatures; the pipe is the worst rival a woman can have: and it is one whose eyes she cannot scratch out; who improves with age, while she herself declines; who has an art which no woman possesses, that of never wearying her devotee; who is silent, yet a companion; costs little, yet gives much pleasure; who, lastly, never upbraids, and always yields the same joy. Ah! this is a powerful rival to wife or maid, and no wonder that at last the woman succumbs, consents, and rather than lose her lord or master, even supplies the hated herb with her own fair hands. And this is what women have come to do on the Continent; but in America they have gone further, and admitted the rival to their very drawing-rooms, where the unmanly husband stretches his legs on the sofa, smokes, and spits on the carpet. Far be it from our English women to permit such habits; and yet, as things are, a *little* concession is prudent. There was not so much drinking when withdrawing-rooms were the privilege of palaces, and matrons sat over the cups of their lords, and there will not be near so much smoking where ladies are present. I have no wish to see English girls light their own cigarettes or puff their own chibouks, like the houris of Seville and Bagdad; but I do think that, as smoking is now so much a habit of Englishmen, it would be wise if it were made possible, within certain well-guarded limitations, in the society of ladies.

As it is, there are rules enough to limit this indulgence. One must never smoke, nor even ask to smoke, in the company of the fair. If they know that in a few minutes you will be running off to your cigar, the fair will do well—say it is in a garden, or so—to allow you to bring it out and

13

smoke it there. One must never smoke, again, in the
streets ; that is, in daylight.   The deadly crime may
be committed, like burglary, after dark, but not before.
One must never smoke in a room inhabited at times by
the ladies; thus, a well-bred man who has a wife or sisters,
will not offer to smoke in the dining-room after dinner.
One must never smoke in a public place, where ladies are
or might be, for instance, a flower-show or promenade.
One may smoke in a railway-carriage in spite of by-laws,
if one has first obtained the consent of every one present ;
but if there be a lady there, though she give her consent,
smoke not.   In nine cases out of ten, she will give it from
good-nature.   One must never smoke in a close carriage ;
one may ask and obtain leave to smoke when returning
from a pic-nic or expedition in an open carriage.   One
must never smoke in a theatre, on a race-course, nor in
church.   This last is not, perhaps a needless caution.   In
the Belgian churches you see a placard announcing, " Ici
on ne mâche pas du tabac."   One must never smoke when
anybody shows an objection to it.   One must never smoke
a pipe in the streets ; one must never smoke at all in the
coffee-room of a hotel.   One must never smoke, without
consent, in the presence of a clergyman, and one must
never offer a cigar to any ecclesiastic over the rank of
curate.

But if you smoke, or if you are in the company of
smokers, and are to wear your clothes in the presence of
ladies afterwards, you must change them to smoke in.   A
host who asks you to smoke, will generally offer you an
old coat for the purpose.   You must also, after smoking,
rinse the mouth well out, and, if possible, brush the teeth.
You should never smoke in another person's house without

leave, and you should not ask leave to do so, if there are
ladies in the house. When you are going to smoke a cigar
yourself, you should offer one at the same time to anybody
present, if not a clergyman or a very old man. You
should always smoke a cigar given to you, whether good
or bad, and never make any remarks on its quality.

Smoking reminds me of spitting, but as this is at all
times a disgusting habit, I need say nothing more than—
never indulge in it. Besides being coarse and atrocious,
it is very bad for the health.   .

There are some other habits which are disagreeable
to your company. One is that of sniffling or breathing
hard through the nostrils, which is only excusable if you
have a cold, and even then very disagreeable. Another
is that of shaking the table with your leg, a nervous habit,
which you may not always be conscious of. Then again,
however consoling to sing and hum to yourself, you must
remember that it may annoy others, and though you may
whistle when alone, " for want of thought," you will
whistle in company only for want of consideration of others. Ladies particularly object to whistling, which is a
musical, but not very melodious habit.

We now come to habits at table, which are very important. However agreeable a man may be in society,
if he offends or disgusts by his table traits, he will soon
be scouted from it, and justly so. There are some broad
rules for behavior at table. Whenever there is a servant
to help you, never help yourself. Never put a knife
into your mouth, not even with cheese, which should be
eaten with a fork. Never use a spoon for anything but
liquids. Never touch anything edible with your fingers.

Forks were undoubtedly a later invention than fingers,

but as we are not cannibals, I am inclined to think they
were a good one. There are some few things which you
may take up with your fingers. Thus an epicure will eat
even macaroni with his fingers ; and as sucking asparagus
is more pleasant than chewing it, you may as an epicure,
take it up *au naturel*. But both these things are generally eaten with a fork. Bread is of course eaten with the
fingers, and it would be absurd to carve it with your
knife and fork. It must, on the contrary, always be
broken when not buttered, and you should never put a
slice of dry bread to your mouth to bite a piece off. Most
fresh fruit too is eaten with the natural prongs, but when
you have peeled an orange or apple, you should cut it
with the aid of the fork, unless you can succeed in breaking it. Apropos of which I may hint that no epicure
ever yet put knife to apple, and that an orange should be
peeled with a spoon. But the art of peeling an orange
so as to hold its own juice, and its own sugar too, is one
that can scarcely be taught in a book.

However, let us go to dinner, and I will soon tell you
whether you are a well-bred man or not; and here let me
premise that what is good manners for a small dinner is
good manners for a large one, and *vice versâ*. Now, the
first thing you do is to sit down. Stop, sir ! pray do not
cram yourself into the table in that way; no, nor sit a
yard from it, like that. How graceless, inconvenient, and
in the way of easy conversation ! Why, dear me, you
are positively putting your elbows on the table, and now
you have got your hands fumbling about with the spoons
and forks, and now you are nearly knocking my new hock
glasses over. Can't you take your hands down, sir?
Didn't you learn that in the nursery? Didn't your

mamma say to you, "Never put your hands above the table except to carve or eat!" Oh! but come, no nonsense, sit up if you please. I can't have your fine head of hair forming a side dish on my table; you must not bury your face in the plate, you came to show it, and it ought to be alive. Well, but there is no occasion to throw your head back like that, you look like an alderman, sir, *after* dinner. Pray, don't lounge in that sleepy way. You are here to eat, drink, and be merry. You can sleep when you get home.

Well, then, I suppose you can see your napkin. Got none, indeed! Very likely, in *my* house. You may be sure that I never sit down to a meal without napkins. I don't want to make my tablecloths unfit for use, and I don't want to make my trousers unwearable. Well now, we are all seated, you can unfold it on your knees : no, no ; don't tuck it into your waistcoat like an alderman ; and what! what on earth do you mean by wiping your forehead with it? Do you take it for a towel? Well, never mind, I am consoled that you did not go farther, and use it as a pocket-handkerchief. So talk away to the lady on your right, and wait till soup is handed to you. By the way, that waiting is a most important part of table manners, and as much as possible you should avoid asking for any thing or helping yourself from the table. Your soup you eat with a spoon—I don't know what else you *could* eat it with—but then it must be one of good size. Yes, that will do, but I beg you will not make that odious noise in drinking your soup. It is louder than a dog lapping water, and a cat would be quite genteel to it. Then you need not scrape up the plate in that way, nor even tilt it to get the last drop. I shall be happy to send you some

more; but I must just remark, that it is not the custom
to take two helpings of soup, and it is liable to keep other
people waiting, which, once for all, is a selfish and intoler-
able habit. But don't you hear the servant offering you
sherry? I wish you would attend, for my servants have
quite enough to do, and can't wait all the evening while
you finish that very mild story to Miss Goggles. Come,
leave that decanter alone. I had the wine put on the
table to fill up; the servant will hand it directly, or, as
we are a small party, I will tell you to help yourself, but,
pray, do not be so officious. (There, I have sent him some
turbot to keep him quiet. I declare he cannot make up
his mind.) You are keeping my servant again, sir. Will
you, or will you not. do turbot? Don't examine it in that
way; it is quite fresh, I assure you. take or decline it.
Ah, you take it, but that is no reason why you should
take up a knife too. Fish, I repeat, must never be touched
with a knife. Take a fork in the right, and a small piece
of bread in the left hand. Good, but—? Oh! that is
atrocious; of course you must not swallow the bones, but
you should rather do so than spit them out in that way.
Put up your napkin like this, and land the said bone on
your plate. Don't rub your bread in the sauce. my good
man, nor go progging about after the shrimps or oysters
therein. Oh! how horrid; I declare your mouth was
wide open and full of fish. Small pieces, I beseech you :
and once for all, whatever you eat, keep your mouth *shut*,
and never attempt to talk with it full.

So now you have got a pâté. Surely you are not taking
two on your plate. There is plenty of dinner to come,
and one is quite enough. Oh! dear me, you are incor-
rigible. What! a knife to cut that light, brittle pastry?

No, nor fingers, never. Nor a spoon—almost as bad. Take your fork, sir, your fork; and now you have eaten, oblige me by wiping your mouth and moustache with your napkin, for there is a bit of the pastry hanging to the latter, and looking very disagreeable. Well, you can refuse a dish if you like. There is no positive necessity for you to take venison if you don't want it. But, at any rate, do not be in that terrific hurry. You are not going off by the next train. Wait for the sauce and wait for vegetables ; but whether you eat them or not, do not begin before everybody else. Surely you must take my table for that of a railway refreshment-room, for you have finished before the person I helped first. Fast eating is bad for the digestion, my good sir, and not very good manners either. What ! are you trying to eat meat with a fork alone ? Oh ! it is sweetbread, I beg your pardon, you are quite right. Let me give you a rule,—Everything that can be cut without a knife, should be cut with a fork alone. Eat your vegetables therefore with a fork. No, there is no necessity to take a spoon for peas ; a fork in the right hand will do. What ! did I really see you put your knife into your mouth ? Then I must give you up. Once for all, and ever, the knife is to cut, not to help with. Pray, do not munch in that noisy manner ; chew your food well, but softly. *Eat slowly.* Have you not heard that Napoleon lost the battle of Leipsic by eating too fast ? It is a fact though. His haste caused indigestion, which made him incapable of attending to the details of the battle. You see you are the last person eating at table. Sir, I will not allow you to speak to my servants in that way. If they are so remiss as to oblige you to ask for anything, do it gently, and in a low tone, and thank a servant just as

much as you would his master. Ten to one he is as good
a man : and because he is your inferior in position, is the
very reason you should treat him courteously. Oh ! it is
of no use to ask me to take wine ; far from pacifying me,
it will only make me more angry, for I tell you the custom
is quite gone out, except in a few country villages, and at
a mess-table. Nor need you ask the lady to do so. However, there is this consolation, if you should ask any one
to take wine with you, he or she *cannot* refuse, so you
have your own way. Perhaps next you will be asking me
to hob and nob, or *trinquer* in the French fashion with
arms encircled. Ah ! you don't know, perhaps, that when
a lady *trinques* in that way with you, you have a right to
finish off with a kiss. Very likely indeed, in England !
But it *is* the custom in familiar circles in France, but then
we are not Frenchmen. *Will* you attend to your lady,
sir ? You did not come merely to eat, but to make yourself agreeable. Don't sit as glum as the Memnon at
Thebes; talk and be pleasant. Now, you have some
pudding. No knife—no, *no*. A spoon if you like, but
better still, a fork. Yes, ice requires a spoon; there is a
small one handed you, take that.

Say " no." That is the fourth time wine has been
handed to you, and I am sure you have had enough.
Decline this time if you please. Decline that dish too.
Are you going to eat of everything that is handed? I
pity you if you do. No, you must not ask for more cheese,
and you must eat it with your fork. Break the rusk with
your fingers. Good. You are drinking a glass of old
port. Do not quaff it down at a gulp in that way. Never
drink a whole glassful of anything at once.

Well, here is the wine and dessert. Take whichever

wine you like, but remember you must keep to that, and
not change about. Before you go up stairs I will allow
you a glass of sherry after your claret, but otherwise drink
of one wine only. You don't mean to say you are helping yourself to wine before the ladies. At least offer it
to the one next to you, and then pass it on, gently, not
with a push like that. Do not drink so fast; you will
hurry me in passing the decanters, if I see that your glass
is empty. You need not eat dessert till the ladies are
gone, but offer them whatever is nearest to you. And
now they are gone, draw your chair near mine, and I will
try and talk more pleasantly to you. You will come out
admirably at your next dinner with all my teaching.
What! you are excited, you are talking loud to the colonel. Nonsense. Come and talk easily to me or to your
nearest neighbor. There, don't drink any more wine, for
I see you are getting romantic. You oblige me to make
a move. You have had enough of those walnuts; you
are keeping me, my dear sir. So now to coffee (one cup)
and tea, which I beg you will not pour into your saucer
to cool. Well, the dinner has done you good, and me too.
Let us be amiable to the ladies, but not too much so.

CHAPTER VIII.

THE CARRIAGE OF LADIES.

"To be civil with ease," it has been well remarked, constitutes good breeding. The English, it is added, have not *les manières prévenantes ;* "when they want to be civil, they are ashamed to get it out." Since the manners are generally formed for good or for bad before thirty—although they may improve or deteriorate after that age—it is to the young that a few admonitions should be offered.

"To the young?" The young are perfect now-a-days! Ours is the age of self-assertion. "I shall be surprised at any one who can point out a single defect in my daughters," says a well-satisfied mamma. "Teach *us !*" respond the young ladies in a chorus, "what does the creature mean?" "My dears," murmurs a tremulous voice from the other end of the room, grandmamma's corner, "don't say *that ;* in my younger days it was the fashion for young ladies, if they were not really humble and timid, to appear so. I never came into a room as you. Arabella, do, as if I could walk over every one, and didn't mind ; nor crept in, Helen, like you, as if you had been doing something in the passage you were ashamed of ; nor plumped down into a chair like you, Sophia, nor ——." Here they all interrupt poor grandmamma with a loud, simultaneous laugh. for she is certainly quite out of date, and knows nothing of the matter.

(298)

She might have laid down immutable rules for good breeding; she might have said, with the great Lord Chatham, who probably was the best-bred man of his time, that "politeness is benevolence in trifles;" with Rochefoucault, "that it is the mind that forms the manners;" but who would have listened to her? Arabella would have called out, "Who cares for such old fogrums now?" and Helen have added, that she thought Lord Chesterfield and "all that humbug about manners quite a sell."

Yes, it is true; *nous avons changé tout cela.* Except in the very highest classes, where politeness and' a good carriage are taught from infancy—the higher classes being more retentive of old forms than any others; except there, where what is called the "old school" has not died out, it is now not only allowable, but even thought clever, to be loud, positive, and rapid; to come into the room like a whirlwind, carrying all before you; to look upon every one else as inferiors, with the idea that it enforces that conviction; to have your own set of opinions and ideas, without the least reference to what others think; and to express them in terms which would have been far better comprehended in the stable than by a company of ladies and gentlemen some twenty years ago. Even in the highest classes, these watering-place manners—so let us call them—are on the increase, but only amongst a certain set, who give the tone to a set, emulating their merits below them.

It is as well to suggest to the young, "to be early, what they will, in later life, wish they had always been." Unhappily those who compose society are prone to borrow their ideas from the class above them, and do not think for themselves. Melissa, the attorney's daughter,

catches up a few words of slang from the county member's daughter at the last races, and thinks it pretty to
use those phrases vigorously. Philippa, the good old rector's favorite child, hears Lady Elizabeth contradict her
mamma, and takes the same cue herself, as the certainty
of doing the right thing. Modesty and simplicity, the
offspring of reverence, dare not show their faces, and are
voted "slow."

Since language is the exponent of character, it is necessary to refer to its abuse, as if it does not in all cases
actually show a vulgar and pretentious mind, it is apt to
render it so.

An agreeable, modest, and dignified bearing is, in the
younger period of a woman's existence, almost like a portion to her. Whatever may be the transient tone and
fashion of the day, that which is amiable, graceful, and
true in taste, will always please the majority of the world.
A young lady, properly so called, should not require to
have allowances made for her. Well brought up, her address should be polite and gentle, and it will, soon after
her introduction to society, become easy " to be civil with
ease." Let us repeat the golden rule, it should be the
guidance to the minor's morals of society. On first being
introduced to any stranger, there is no insincerity in the
display of a certain pleasure. We are advised by Wilber-
force to give our good-will, at first, on leasehold. To the
elder, a deferential bend or curtsey, though curtsies are
now unfashionable, marks the well brought up girl. She
must not receive her new acquaintance with a hysteric
laugh, such as I have seen whole families prone to; neither must she look heavy, draw down her mouth, and appear as if she did not care for her new acquaintance; nor

must she look at once over the dress of her victim (in that case) as if taking an inventory of it; nor appear hurried, as if glad to get away on the first break in the conversation. She must give a due attention, or reasonable time to perfect the introduction, to a certain extent. Volubility is to be avoided; to overpower with a volley of words is more cruel than kind; the words should be gently spoken, not drawled, and the voice loud enough to be caught easily, but always in an undertone to the power of voice alloted by nature. Some persons appear to go to the very extent, and deafen you for all other' sounds; they may speak the words of wisdom, but you wish them dumb. Others mumble so that you are forced continually to express your total inability to follow the drift of their remarks; others drawl so that you feel that life is not long enough for such acquaintance. All these are habits to be conquered in youth.

Avoid, especially, affectation. It was once in fashion. Some ladies put it on with their dresses; others, by a long practice, were successful in making it habitual. It became what was called their manner. Sophia has a manner; it is not affectation, "it is her manner, only manner." Affectation has long ceased to be the fashion, and like many other bygone peculiarities, one sees it only in shops.

There is a way also of looking that must be regulated in the young. The audacious stare is odious; the sly, oblique, impenetrable look is unsatisfactory. Softly and kindly should the eyes be raised to those of the speaker, and only withdrawn when the speech, whatever it may be, is concluded. Immediate intimacy and a familiar manner are worse than the glum look with which some young

ladies have a habit of regarding their fellow-mortals.
There is also a certain dignity of manners necessary to
make even the most superior persons respected. This
dignity can hardly be assumed; it cannot be taught; it
must be the result of intrinsic qualities, aided by a knowledge very much overlooked in modern education—"the
knowledge how to behave." It is distinct from pretension, which is about the worst feature of bad manners, and
creates nothing but disgust. A lady should be equal to
every occasion. Her politeness, her equanimity, her presence of mind, should attend her to the court and to the
cottage.

Neither should private vexations be allowed to act
upon her manners, either in her own house or in those of
others. If unfit for society, let her refrain from entering
it. If she enters it, let her remember that every one
is expected to add something to the general stock of pleasure or improvement. The slight self-command required
by good society is often beneficial both to the temper and
spirits.

One great discredit to the present day is the "fast
young lady." She is the hoyden of the old comedies,
without the indelicacy of that character. An avowed
flirt, she does not scruple to talk of her conquests, real or
imaginary. You may know her by her phrases. She
talks of "the men," of such and such "a charmer."
She does not mind, but rather prefers sitting with "the
men" when they are smoking; she rides furiously, and
plays billiards. But it is in her marked antagonism to her
own sex that the fast young lady is perceptible. She
shuts up her moral perceptions, and sees neither beauty
nor talent in her own sex. With all this she is often

violently confident, and calls all idiots who differ from her in—I can scarcely say her *opinions*—but rather her prejudices.

By degrees, the assumption of assurance which has had its source in bad taste, becomes real ; a hard *blasé* look ; a free tongue ; and, above all, the latitude of manners shown to her by the other sex, and allowed by her, show that the inward characteristics have followed the outward, and that she is become insensible to all that she has lost of feminine charm, and gained in effrontery. For the instant a woman loses the true feminine type, she parts with half her influence. The " fast girl" is flattered, admired openly, but secretly condemned. Many a plain woman has gained and kept a heart by being merely womanly and gentle. In one respect, however, the fast young lady may console herself; her flirtations are as fearless as her expressions ; they do little harm to any but herself. Broken hearts have not to turn reproachfully to loud, high-spirited, overbearing women, "jolly girls," as they are styled ; " chaff" in which they delight as often offends as amuses. To gain an empire over the affections of others, there must be somewhat of sentiment or sympathy in the nature of woman. Your loud, boastful, positive young lady will never be remembered with a soft interest, unless there be, perchance, some soft touch in her that redeems her from hardness.

With regard to flirtation, it is difficult to draw a limit where the predilection of the moment becomes the more tender and serious feeling, and flirtation sobers into a more honorable form of devoted attention.

We all dread for our daughters imprudent and harassing attachments ; let it not, however, be supposed that

long practised flirtations are without their evil effects on
the character and manners. They excite and amuse, but
they also exhaust the spirit. They expose women to censure and to misconstruction ; that is their least evil ; they
destroy the charm of her manners and the simplicity of
her heart. Yet the fast young lady clings to flirtation as
the type of her class ; the privilege of that social freemasonry which enables one flirt to discover and unkennel
another. She glories in number. Where a rival has
slain her thousands, she has overthrown her tens of thousands. She forgets that, with every successive flirtation,
one charm after another disappears, like the petals from a
fading rose, until all the deliciousness of a fresh and pure
character is lost in the destructive sport. On all these
points a woman should take a high tone in the beginning
of her life. It is sure to be sufficiently lowered as time
goes on. She loses, too, that sort of tact which prevents
her from discerning when she has gone too far, and the
" fast young lady" becomes the hardened and practised
flirt, against whom all men are on their guard.

It is true that, in comparing the present day with former times, we must take into account, when we praise the
models of more chivalric days, that we know only the
best specimens ; the interior life of the middle classes is
veiled from us by the mist of ages. Yet it is to be de-
duced from biography, as well as from the testimony of
poets and dramatists, that there was, before the Restoration, a sort of halo around young women of delicacy and
good breeding. owing. perhaps, in part, to the more retired lives that they led, but more to the remnants of that
fast-departing sentiment of chivalrous respect which youth
and beauty inspired. Then came the upsetting demorali-

zation of the Restoration, when all prudent fathers kept
their daughters from court, and only the bold and "fast"
remained to furnish chronicles for De Grammont: we are
not, therefore, to judge of the young women of England
by his pictures. The character of English ladies rose
again to a height of moral elevation during the placid and
well-conducted rule of Anne, and continued, as far as re-
lated to single women, to be the pride and boast of the
country. Even now, when the reckless flirtation, loud
voices, unamusing jokes, which are comprised under the
odious term "chaff," and the masculine tastes of the present day are deprecated, events bring forth from time to
time such instances of devotion and virtue as must convince one that there is no degeneracy in our own country-
women on solid points. Few, indeed, are these instances,
among the class we have described. We must not look
for Florence Nightingales and Miss Marshes among that
company of the fast.

Contrasted with the fast young lady, comes forth the
prude, who sees harm in everything, and her friend the
blue-stocking. You may know the prude by her stolid
air of resistance to mankind in general, and by her pat-
ronizing manner to her own sex. Her style of manner is,
like the Austrian policy, repressive; her style of conversation, reprehensive. She has started in life with an immense conceit of her own mental powers and moral attributes, of which the world in general is scarcely worthy.
Her manner is indicative of this conviction; and becomes
accordingly, without her intending it, offensive, when she
believes herself to be polite.

The prude and the pedant are often firm friends, each
adoring the other. The fast young lady deals largely in

epithets: "Idiot, dolt, wretch, humbug," drop from her lips; but the prude and her friend the blue-stocking permit themselves to use conventional phrases only; their notion of conversation is that it be instructive, and, at the same time, mystifying. The young blue stocking has, nevertheless, large views of the regeneration of society, and emancipation of woman from her degrading inferiority of social position. She speaks in measured phrase; it is like listening to a book to hear her. She is wrapt up in Tennyson and Browning. There is, in all this, a great aim at display, with a self-righteousness that is very unpleasing. Avoid, therefore, either extreme, and be convinced that an artless gaiety, tempered by refinement, always pleases. Every attempt to obtrude on a company subjects either to which they are indifferent, or of which they are ignorant, is in bad taste.

> "Man should be taught as though you taught him not,
> And things unknown proposed as things forgot."

It was well said by a late eminent barrister, that literature in ladies should be what onions ought to be in cookery; you should perceive the flavor, but not detect the thing itself.

The bearing of married women should so far differ from that of the unmarried, that there should be greater quietness and dignity; a more close adherence to forms; and an obvious, as well as a real abandonment of the admiration which has been received before marriage. All flirtation, however it may be countenanced by the present custom of society, should be sternly and for ever put aside. There is no reason for conversation to be less lively, or society less agreeable; it is, indeed, likely to be

more so, if flattered vanity, which may be wounded at
any moment, interposes, not to mar but to enhance enjoyment. If a young married woman wishes to be respected, and therefore happy in life, there should be a quiet
propriety of manner, a dignity towards the male sex,
which cannot be mistaken in her for prudery, since it is
consistent with her position and her ties. She should
change her tone, if that has been "fast;" she should
not put herself on a level with young unmarried women
of her own age, but should influence and even lead her
youthful acquaintance into that style of behavior which
is doubtless much esteemed by men of good taste. She
should rather discountenance the fast, but has no need to
copy or to bring forward the prude and the blue-stocking.
And it behooves married women to be more especially
guarded and sensible in their conduct, when it is remembered how rapidly the demoralization introduced, perhaps,
by our contiguity with France, is extending in every
class. Formerly, among trades-people and professional
men, separations and divorces were almost unheard of;
the vices that lead to them were looked on with horror
by the middle classes. But now, the schoolmaster runs
away with the wife of his apothecary; the brewer does
the fashionable with the attorney's wife; the baker in-
trigues with the green-grocer's hitherto worthy helpmate.
Never, in any time, have the seeds of vice been so scat-
tered by the gale from one condition of social life to another; and the infection of this appalling wickedness has
been spreading, as the Divorce Court proves, silently, but
widely, for some years.

Every woman, however humble, even however poor, may
do one thing for society. She may set an example: but

we call loudly on those in the higher walks of life to do so, and to wipe away the reproach on Israel.

In being introduced to a new acquaintance, there should be more dignity and a little more distance in the manner of the married woman than that of the single lady.

When she visits in a morning call, let her neither hurry off, after a few moments of empty talk; nor stay too long, never considering the convenience of her who receives her. She should walk gently down stairs, not talking loud to any one as she goes. Never let her apologize for not having called sooner, unless positively necessary; such apologies are vastly like affronts.

In receiving guests the English lady has much to learn from the French hostess. Many a time has the visitor in England been met with symptoms of hurry and preoccupation, remarkably embarrassing to those who call; or the carriage is announced directly after her arrival, and the lady of the house looks as if she thought her friend ought to go. Some under-bred ladies, in country towns, look out of the window half of the time, or put tidy their work-boxes, making you feel that you are secondary. As an immutable law of hospitality and good-breeding. a guest should always be the first and sole object when alone with you.

It is one advantage of the French system of having a day on which to receive morning callers, that the lady of the house is ready, and willing to let so many idlers into her drawing-room. In no respect does the French lady shine so much as in her reception of those who, as she appears to think, "do her the honor" to enter her house. It is this that makes the difference. In England we seem to think we do people an honor in letting them cross our thresholds and come up our stairs. The French lady advances to meet the ladies, but waits to receive the gentlemen. She has a chair ready for every one, and the rooms of the fashionable are often full to crowding, yet no one is neglected. Something civil (and "civil with ease"), appropriate, well-turned, and often gracefully kind, is said to every one. The stranger or foreigner is not left out of the conversation previously going on; he or she is not made to feel "you are not one of us; the sooner you go the better." The conversation is soon general, though without introductions. Having said all you wish, and stayed the usual time, you rise, and the lady follows you to the door, where a servant is waiting to conduct you down stairs and call your carriage into the *cour*. This agreeable *accueil* forms a strong contrast to the *ennui* which a *mal-à-propos* visit often seems to produce in a London drawing-room, and the evident despatch with which a lady often rings the bell to let you out, often sitting down and resuming a conversation before you are half across the old and spacious apartment.

In regard to the physical carriage of women, the graces of an upright form, of elegant and gentle movements, and of the desirable medium between stiffness and lounging, are desirable both for married and single. The same rules and recommendations are applicable to both. Control over the countenance is a part of manners. As a lady enters a drawing-room, she should look for the mistress of the house, speaking first to her. Her face should wear a smile; she should not rush in head-foremost; a graceful bearing, a light step, an elegant bend to common acquaintance, a cordial pressure, *not shaking*, of the hand extended to her, are all requisite to a lady. Let her sink gently into a chair, and, on formal occasions, retain her upright position; neither lounge nor sit timorously on the edge of her seat. Her feet should scarcely be shown, and not crossed. She must avoid sitting stiffly, as if a ramrod were introduced within the dress behind, or stooping Excepting a very small and costly parasol, it is not now usual to bring those articles into a room. An elegantly worked handkerchief is carried in the hand, but not displayed so much as at dinner parties. A lady should conquer a habit of breathing hard, or coming in very hot, or even looking very blue and shivery. Anything that detracts from the pleasure of society is in bad taste.

In walking the feet should be moderately turned out, the steps should be equal, firm, and light. A lady may be known by her walk. The short, rapid steps, the shaking the body from side to side, or the *very* slow gait which many ladies consider genteel. are equally to be deprecated. Some persons are endowed with a natural grace that wants no teaching; where it is not the case, the greatest care should be taken to engraft it in childhood, to have a master, not for dancing alone, but for the even more important attributes of the lady's carriage. To bow with grace. or to curtsey when required, to move across a room well. are points which strike the attention almost unconsciously to ourselves, and the neglect of which often provokes comment even on those in other respects well qualified to adorn society.

PART II.

THE INDIVIDUAL IN INDIVIDUAL RELATIONS.

CHAPTER IX.

IN PUBLIC. THE PROMENADE, ETC.

So now, my dear Sir and my dear Madam, you are dressed, you have your accomplishments ready for use, you know how to carry yourself, what good habits to attend to, what bad ones to avoid ; you have made a full examination of yourself; you feel confident that you are " a complete gentleman," or "a charming woman ;" you have had lunch, you feel comfortable and happy, and you say to yourself, " Let me go out and put these good rules into practice."

So then, if you are a man, you consult nobody but your watch ; if you are a young lady, you consult mamma, and both having obtained the requisite assent, you, sir, issue forth with your watch, and you, mademoiselle, with your chaperon, and you go to meet your acquaintance in the walk. Where the said walk may be is little matter. In the days of the Stuarts, you would have repaired to the transepts of old St. Paul's, then the fashionable promenade. In a later reign you would have turned your steps to the " Mall," and met Beau Tibbs there in all his glory. Now,

if you live in London, you make for Rotten Row; if in
a watering-place, for the Promenade or the Parade, or
bref, whatever may be the spot chosen for the gay peacocks
to strut in.

You have not been there two minutes before you meet
somebody you know. But that is a very vague term;
for you may know people in almost a dozen different
ways. First, then, you know them slightly, and wish to
recognize them slightly. Your course is simple enough.
If you are a lady, you have the privilege of recognizing a
gentleman. You wish to do so, because there is no reason that you should not be polite to him. So when you
come quite near to him and see that he is looking at you,
you bow slightly, and pass on. There are one or two
things to be avoided even in this. You must not, however short-sighted, raise your glasses and stare at him
through them before you bow; but as it is very awkward
for a lady to bow by mistake to a gentleman she does not
know, you should look at him well before you come up to
him. If you are a man, on the other hand, and you meet
a lady whom you know slightly, you must wait till she
bows to you. You then lift your hat quite off your head
with the hand, whichever it may be, which is farther from
the person you meet. You lift it off your head, but that
is all; you have no need, as they do in France, to show
the world the inside thereof; so you immediately replace
it. In making this salute, you bend your body slightly.
If, which should rarely occur, you happen to be smoking,
you take your cigar from your mouth with the other
hand; so too, if you have your hands in your pockets,
which I hope you will not, you take them out before bow-

ing. To neglect these little observances would show a want of respect.

But suppose it is a person whom you know rather more than slightly, and to whom you may speak. Well, then, no man may stop to speak to a lady until she stops to speak to him. The lady, in short, has the right in all cases to be friendly or distant. Women have not many rights; let us gracefully concede the few that they possess. You raise your hat all the same, but you do not shake hands unless the lady puts out hers, which you may take as a sign of particular good-will. In this case you must not stop long, but the lady again has the right to prolong the interview at pleasure. It is she, not you, who must make the move onwards. If she does this in the middle of a conversation, it is a proof that she is willing that you should join her, and if you have no absolute call to go your way, you ought to do so. But if she does so with a slight inclination, it is to dismiss you, and you must then again bow and again raise your hat.

If, however, you are old acquaintance without any quarrel between, you should, whether gentleman or lady, at once stop and give the hand and enter into conversation. The length of this conversation must depend on the place where you meet. If in the streets, it should be very short; if in a regular promenade, it may be longer; but as a rule, old friends do better to turn round and join forces. On the other hand, if you are walking with a man whom your lady friend does not know, you must not stop; still less so, if she is walking with a lady or gentleman whom you do not know. If, however, a decided inclination is evinced by either to speak to the other, and you so stop, the stranger ought not to walk on, but to

14

stop also, and it then behooves you to introduce him or her. Such an introduction is merely formal, and goes no further.

Lastly, let us suppose that you want to "cut" your acquaintance. O fie! Who invented the cut? What demon put it into the head of man or woman to give this mute token of contempt or hatred? I do not know, but I do know that in modern civilized life, as it goes, the cut is a great institution. The finest specimen of it which we have on record is that of Beau Brummell and George IV. These two devoted friends had quarrelled, as devoted friends are wont to do, and when they met again, George, then Prince, was walking up St. James' Street on the arm of some companion, and Brummell, dressed to perfection, was coming down it on that of another. The two companions happened to know one another, and all four stopped. George the Prince was determined to ignore George the Beau's existence, and talked to his companion without appearing to see him. George the Beau expected this, but was still mortified. They all bowed and moved away; but before the Prince was out of hearing, Brummell said to his companion in a loud voice, " Who's your fat friend?" It is well known that the Regent grieved at that time most bitterly over his growing corpulency, and the Beau was avenged.

But my advice to anybody who wishes to cut an acquaintance is, most emphatically, Don't. In the first place, it is vulgar, and a custom which the vulgar affect. It is pretentious, and seems to say, " You are not good enough for me to know." All pretension is vulgar. In the next place, it does the cutter as much injury as the cuttee. The latter, if worthless, revenges himself by denouncing the former as stuck up, unpolite, ill-bred; if himself well-bred, he says nothing about it, but inwardly condemns and despises you. Now, in a world where love is at a premium, and even respect is not cheap, it is a pity to add, by foolish pride, to the number of those who dislike you; but, if there were no other consideration, it is extremely unchristian, to say the least of it. It is a giving of offence; and woe to him by whom offences come. It is the consequence either of pride or of judging your neighbor, both of which are bad faults. Lastly, it raises up for ever between two people a barrier which neither years nor regret can surmount. It is a silent but desperate quarrel, but, unlike other quarrels, it is never followed by a reconciliation. The Christian law used to be, "If you have aught against your brother, go and expostulate with him." The modern social law—not, however, the law of good society—makes an amendment: "Do not take the trouble to go to him—it will do no good—but cut him dead when you meet, and so get rid of him for ever." Yes, "Dead!" Dead, indeed; for all the love, all the forgiveness there might flow between you, he is as good as dead to   is more, *you* have killed him.

But the cut is often a silly measure, and far too promptly resorted to. At Bath you have known the Simpkinses, and even been intimate with them, but in Town you take it into your head they are "inferior;" you meet and cut them. Well, a fortnight later, you find that Lady So-and-so is particularly partial to the Simpkinses. "Do you know those charming girls?" she asks, and how foolish you then feel. Or again, Captain Mactavish is your best and most amusing friend; slander whispers in your ear "Mactavish was cashiered for fraudulent transactions."

You go out, happen to meet, and cut him dead. The next day the truth comes out. It is another Mactavish who was cashiered, and your friend is a model of honor. What can you do? You cannot tell him you made a mistake. It would then be his turn to take a high hand. "No, no!" says he, when you offer to renew the friendship, "if you could so soon believe evil of me, you are not the man for Mactavish. Besides, you cut me yesterday, and I can forgive everything but a cut." Or again, papa is alarmed at the attentions of young Montmorency. "A penniless boy making love to Matilda!" he cries indignantly, and orders the said Matilda and her mamma to cut him. Montmorency, in pique, runs off to Miss Smith, offers, and marries her. It is then discovered that Montmorency has a bachelor uncle whose whole fortune will come to him, and Matilda is miserable.

But there are some cases in which a cut becomes the sole means of ridding one's-self of annoyance, and with young ladies especially so. A girl has no other means of escaping from the familiarity of a pushing and thick-skinned man. She cannot always be certain that the people introduced to her are gentlemen; pleased with them at first, she gives them some encouragement, till some occasion or other lays bare the true character of her new acquaintance. What is she to do? He requires so little to encourage him, that even a recognition would be sufficient to bring him on. She has nothing left but to cut him dead. The cut, however, should be positively the last resource. There are many ways, less offensive and more dignified, of showing that you do not wish for intimacy; the stiff bow without a smile is enough to show a man of any preception that he need not make farther advances;

and as for cutting people of real or imaginary inferiority, it is the worst of vulgarity. We laugh at the silly pride of the small dressmaker who declines to go through the kitchen. " Not accustomed to associate with menials," she tells you, and knocks at the front door ; we smile at the costermonger who cannot lower himself to recognise the crossing-sweeper ; and how absurd to those of a higher class than our own must the Smiths, whose father was a physician, appear, when they cut the Simpkinses, whose progenitor is only a surgeon, and so on. But if you have once known people you should always know them, if they have not done anything to merit indignation. If you have once been familiar with the Simpkinses, you are not only inconsistent and vulgar, but you accuse yourself of former want of perception, if now you discover that they are too low for you to know.

But, if a cut must be made, let it be done with as little offensiveness as possible. Let the miserable culprit not be tortured to death, or broken in the social wheel, like a Damiens, however treasonable his offence. Never, on any account, allow him to speak to you, and then staring him in the face, exclaim, " Sir, I do not know you !" or, as some people, trying to make rudeness elegant, would say, " Sir, I have not the honor of your acquaintance ;" nor behead him with the fixed stare ; but rather let him see that you have noticed his approach, and then turn your head away. If he is thick-skinned or daring enough to come up to you after that, bow to him stiffly and pass on. In this way you avoid insolence, and cause less of that destroyer of good manners—confusion.

There are some definite rules for cutting. A gentle-man must never cut a lady under any circumstances. An

unmarried lady should never cut a married one. A servant of whatever class—for there are servants up to
royalty itself—should never cut his master ; near relations
should never cut one another at all ; and a clergyman
should never cut anybody, because it is at best an unchristian action. Perhaps it may be added that a superior
should never cut his inferior in rank ; he has many other
ways of annihilating him. Certainly it may be laid down ·
that people holding temporary official relations must waive
their private animosities, and that two doctors, for instance,
however much opposed to one another, should never introduce the cut over the bed of a patient.

I pass now to a much pleasanter theme, that of salutation. I know not when men first discovered that some
sign was necessary to show their good-will to one another.
Hatred, the ugliest of all the demons, (and they are not
renowned for beauty), took a reserved seat early in the
history of the world, and the children of Cain and Seth,
if they ever met, must have found it necessary to hold out
some human flag of truce. What this may have been we
have no records to prove, but it is certain that prostration, which made a man helpless for the moment, was a
very early form of salutation, and one that has not yet
gone out, for kneeling, which is only a simpler form of it,
it still preserved in our courts. But this was too awkward
a practice for everyday life, especially when men gathered
into cities and met their fellow-creatures daily in large
numbers. Fancy a member of Parliament bobbing down on
his "marrow-bones" whenever he met a constituent, or a
clergyman wearing the knees of his black "limb covers"
into shining patches as he walked the parish and met Tim
Miles and George Giles at every corner. The question then

arose how to show the same good-will without the same inconvenience, and which of the senses should be employed in it. We looked at the brute creation, which, in its gift of instinct, seemed to have as it were a direct revelation for such things, but found little counsel. Dogs wagged their tails, but their masters had none to wag, except indeed among the Niam-Niam, and even with them it is doubtful whether the necessary pliability exists. Horses know their friends by the smell, and Mr. Rarey tells us that we need never fear a horse which has sniffed us all over, for the simple reason that it will no longer fear us. But though it is said you may tell a Chinaman, as the ancients told an Iberian, *par son odeur*, and though you may certainly recognize a modern fop by his " smelling of musk and insolence," yet it does not appear that there is any perfume by which the human being can assure you of his good intentions. The prostration was probably therefore first followed by a deep inclination of the body, which we preserve faintly enough in our modern bow, and which was the recognized form of worship in several eastern countries. Another modification of prostration, which was preserved in this country between servants and masters till the end of the seventeenth century, was that of " making a knee," as Ben Jonson calls it, which was nothing more than slightly bending one leg and so lowering the body. But these forms were too much for some people and too little for others. The children of this world soon discovered that they were not all children alike, and made early a marked distinction of persons. The salute fit for a chieftain was much too good for a serf, and the serf himself was not going to make a knee to a brother serf, however much he liked him. In fact, it became necessary to distinguish between the amount of respect due to position (for character soon lost its due recognition), and the amount of cordiality due to friendship. Thus some form of inclination remained in use for the salute of respect, and thus the eye was the sense there employed. The principle of respect was brought variously into practice, but in no way so prominently as that of baring some part of the body, thereby putting the saluter to a temporary inconvenience, and laying him open to the attack of the saluted. In one country the shoes were taken off, in another the headgear, though St. Paul's philosophic, if not very gallant, distinction relative to the honor of a man laying in his head, and that of a woman elsewhere, would seem to make the Orientals more consistent in keeping their turbans on and taking off their slippers. In no country, however, do we hear of women taking their bonnets off, as a salute, though in some to unveil the face was a mark of great reverence. That, of course would depend on whether it was a pretty face or not; but however this may be, the forms of salutation which have been retained among European nations are much the same; the bow, namely, as a relic of prostration, and baring the head, among men; while among women the prostration was kept up to a much later date, and the curtsey, in which the knees were bowed, is not yet quite vanished from the modesty of our land. Maid-servants and country wives retain it still.

But when we come to cordiality we find another sense brought into action. Words were known to be concealers of thought, so that the sense of hearing was out of the question, while smelling and tasting were unanimously voted brutish; and those poets who talk about " tasting

the honey of her lips," are fitted to be laureates in the
cannibal islands rather than in the British kingdoms.
There remained then the sense of touch, which, if not
the most delicate, is one which the human race particularly depend on, as our blind children learn to know even
colors thereby. Besides, owing to the absence of fur in
our race, the sense of touch is more acute in us than
in any other animals.

Well, on the touch-and-know principle, some races immediately undertook to conduce to each other's comfort as
a token of cordiality. In the frost-bitten regions of Lap-
land, for instance, it is the fashion to run up to your
friend and rub his nose with yours. It is a mute expression of the wish that his proboscis may not drop off
some cold morning; and indeed this custom must assist in
preserving that graceful feature from the effects of frost,
so that the man with the largest acquaintance is also likely to have the largest nose. In Southern Africa again,
where the feet get terribly dry from the heat of the soil,
it is the custom to rub toes; and in some country or other,
the height of elegance is to moisten the hand in the most
natural manner, and smear your friend's face with it.

These customs, however, must have had a somewhat
local appreciation, and have not received general approbation. There are now two recognised modes of cordial
salutation—the kiss and the shake of the hand. Whether
kissing was known in Paradise, as Byron, who had some
experience of it (kissing, I mean, not Paradise), assures
us :

> " One remnant of Paradise still is on earth,
> And Eden revives in the first kiss of love ; "

we cannot stop to investigate, but that it was a very early

discovery, those who read their Bibles may find out. It is a beautiful custom, an angelic custom; I say it without blushing, because it was originally, and in many countries is—let us hope even in England—the most innocent thing in the world. Certainly, about the period of our own era, the "kiss of peace" was a mark of love between men, though in some cases it was made to serve the deadliest ends. It is still in use between men in France and Germany. The parent kisses his grown-up son on the forehead; friends press their lips to others' cheeks; brothers throw their arms round one another's necks and embrace like lovers. Alack and alas! for our stiff humanity. Here in England it is reserved for children and girls, and for Minnie to stop my lips with when I am going to scold her. Well, it is a beautiful old custom. all the same, and if we were not so wicked in this nineteenth century, we should have more of it. In the days of good Queen Bess it was the height of politeness to kiss your neighbor's wife, and our grandfathers tell us that on entering a room they kissed all the women present as a matter of course. This privilege is reserved now for Scotch cousins, who make a very free use of it. But. alas! this beautiful symbol of pure affection. which sent a thrill from warm lips through all the frame. is now become a matter of almost shame to us. It is a deed to be done behind the door, as Horace Smith hints.

> "Sydney Morgan was playing the organ,
> While behind the vestry door
> Horace Twiss was snatching a kiss
> From the lips of Hannah Moore."

Poor Hannah Moore! how the very thought must have shrivelled her up.

The kiss of mere respect was made on the hand, a good old custom still retained in Germany, and among a few old beaux at home. Whether it was pure respect which induced Leicester often to kiss the Virgin Queen on her lips, " which," we are told, " she took right heartily," I cannot say; but at all events in this day, the kissing of the lips is reserved for lovers, and should scarcely be performed in public. But the kiss of friendship and relationship on the cheeks or forehead is still kept up a little, and might be much more common. I like to see a young man kiss his mother on her wrinkled brow; it shows " there is no humbug about him." I like to see sisters kiss, and old friends when they meet again. But I may like what I like. The world is against me, and as it is a delicate subject I will say no more on it, save only this,— As a general rule, this act of affection is excluded from public eyes in this country, and there are people who are ashamed even to kiss a brother or father on board the steamer which is to take him away for some ten or twenty years. But then there are people in England who are ashamed of showing any feeling, however natural, however pure. This is a matter in which I would not have etiquette interfere. Let the world say it is rustic, or even vulgar, to kiss your friends on the platform of a railway, before they start or when they arrive. It is never vulgar to be loving, and love that is real love will show itself, though there were ten Acts of Parliament against it.

" A cold hand and a warm heart" is an old saw, which may be true for the temperature of the skin, but is certainly not so for the mode of pressing it. A warm heart, I am persuaded, gives a warm shake of the hand, and a man must be a hypocrite, who can shake yours heartily while he hates you. The hand is after all the most natural limb to salute with. Next to those of the lips, the nerves of touch are most highly developed in the fingers, which may be accounted for by the perpetual friction and irritation to which they are subjected, for we know that those portions of the skin are the most ticklish which undergo the most friction. However this may be, the hand is the most convenient member to salute with. The toe-rubbing process, for instance, must subject one to the risk of toppling over in any but a dignified manner; "making a knee" was liable to be followed by breaking a nose, if the balance were not carefully preserved, and as for the total prostration system, I feel convinced that it must have been given up by common consent after dinner, and by corpulent personages. But the charm of the hand, as a saluting member, lies in the fact of its grasping power, which enables the shaker to vary the salute at pleasure. The freemasons well know this, and though they begin the mysterious salute with signs for the eye, they are rarely satisfied till they have followed them up by the grasp, which varies for almost every grade, for apprentice, master, royal arch, knight templar, and all their other absurdities. My worthy masons, do not suppose that you possess a monopoly of this art. There is as cunning a freemasonry in all society, and the mode of taking, grasping, and shaking the hand, varies as much according to circumstances, and even more, than your knuckling system.

First, there is the case where two hands simply take hold of one another. This is the mode of very shy people, and of two lovers parting in tears: but then in the one case the hold is brief, in the other continued. Next, there is the case where one hand is laid clammily in the other, which slightly presses the fingers, not going down to the palm. This is a favorite mode with ladies, especially young ladies, towards slight acquaintance ; but when my heart flutters a little for Mariana's smile, I should be piqued indeed, nay, shocked, if there were nothing more than fingers laid in my hand, no responsive thumb to complete the manœuvre, and when Sybilla told me she could not love me, and when she would not listen, but hurried away up the terrace steps, and turned to give me the last—last shake of a 'hand, I have never touched again, I cannot tell you what of despair she saved me in the friendly warmth—I do not say affection—with which she wrung my hand that passionately clung round hers. Ah ! Sybilla, better have left that hand with me, have given it me for ever, than to the wealthy wig-wearing, rouged and powdered bear, to whom they sold you afterwards.

Next, there is the terribly genteel salute of the under-bred man, who with a smirk on his face, just touches the tips of your fingers, as if they were made of glass; there is the blunt honest shake of the rough, who lays out his hand with the palm open and the heart in the hollow of it, stretches it well out, and shakes and rattles the one you put into it; there is the pouncing style of him who affects but does not feel cordiality, who brings the angle between thumb and finger down upon you like gaping shears; there is the hailing style of the indifferent man who seems to say to your hand, " Come and be shaken;" there is the style of the man who gives your hand one toss, as if he were ringing the dinner-bell; and another bell-ringing style is that of milady, who shakes her own hand from the wrist with a neat fine little movement, and does not care whether yours shakes in it or not; there is genius who clasps your hands in both of his and beams into your face; and there is love who seizes it to press it tighter and more tightly, and sends his whole soul through the fingers.

But the styles are infinite; there is the mesmeric style where the shaker seems to make a pass down you before getting at your hand; there is papa's style, coming down with an open-handed smack, that you may hear half the length of Parliament Street; there is the solemn style, where the elbow is tucked into the side, like the wing of a trussed fowl, and the long fingers are extended with the thumb in close attendance; there is the hearty double-knock style of three rapid shakes; there is the melancholy style, where the hand is heaved up once or twice slowly and lowered despairingly; there is the adulatory style, where it is raised towards the bent head as if to be inspected; there is the hail-fellow style, where the arm is stretched out sideways, and the eyes say, "There's my hand, old boy!" Then of styles to be always avoided, there is the swinging style, where your arm is tossed from side to side; there is the wrenching style, by which your knuckles are made to ache for five minutes after; and there is the condescending style, where two fingers are held out to you as a great honor. But, the best style of all, *me judice*, is the hearty single clasp, full-handed, warm, momentary, just shaken enough to make the gentle grasp well felt but not painful.

The etiquette of hand-shaking is simple. A man has no right to take a lady's hand till it is offered. It were a

robbery which she would punish. He has even less right
to pinch or to retain it. Two ladies shake hands gently
and softly. A young lady gives her hand, but does not
shake a gentleman's, unless she is his friend. A lady
should always rise to give her hand; a gentleman, of
course, never dares do so seated. On introduction in a
room, a married lady generally offers her hand, a young
lady not; in a ball-room, where the introduction is to
dancing, not to friendship, you never shake hands; and
as a general rule, an introduction is not followed by shaking hands, only by a bow. It may perhaps be laid down,
that the more public the place of introduction, the less
hand-shaking takes place; but if the introduction be particular, if it be accompanied by personal recommendation,
such as, "I want you to know my friend Jones," or, if
Jones comes with a letter of presentation, then you give
Jones your hand, and warmly too. Lastly, it is the privilege of a superior to offer or withhold his or her hand,
so that an inferior should never put his forward first.

There are other modes of salutation, which, being too
familiar, are well avoided, such as clapping a man on the
shoulder, digging him in the ribs, and so forth. The
French rarely shake hands, and only with intimate friends.
They then give the left hand, because that is nearer the
heart, *la main du cœur*. The most cordial way of shaking hands is to give both at once, but this presupposes a
certain or uncertain amount of affection.

When you meet a friend in the street, it must depend
on the amount of familiarity whether you walk with him
or not, but with a lady you must not walk unless invited
either verbally or tacitly. A young and single man should

never walk with a young lady in public places, unless especially asked to do so. How Sybilla's words thrilled through me, when she said, " Mamma, I am going to walk home with Mr. ——, if you have no objection." I had not proposed it, it was her own doing. No wonder I am a bachelor still, and she the Amy in Locksley Hall! If you walk with a lady alone in a large town, particularly in London, you must offer her your arm; elsewhere it is unnecessary, and even marked.

In driving with ladies, a man must take the back seat of the carriage, and when it stops, jump out first and offer his hand to let them out. In your own carriage you always give the front seat to a visitor, if you are a man, but a lady leaves the back seat for a gentleman.

In railway travelling you should not open a conversation with a lady unknown to you, until she makes some advance towards it. On the other hand, it is polite to speak to a gentleman. If, however, his answers be curt, and he evinces a desire to be quiet, do not pursue the conversation. On your part, if addressed in a railway carriage, you should always reply politely. If you have a newspaper, and others have not, you should offer it to the person nearest to you. An acquaintance begun on a railway may sometimes go farther, but, as a general rule, it terminates when one of the parties leaves the carriage. A Frenchman always takes off his hat in a carriage where there are ladies, whether a private or public one. This is a politeness which really well-bred Englishmen imitate. If you go in an omnibus (and there is no reason why a *gentleman* should not do so), it is well to avoid conversation, but if you enter into it, beware of inflammatory subjects. An acquaintance of mine once talked politics to a radical in an omnibus. The two got heated, and more heated, and my acquaintance—for he was no friend, I assure you—ended by driving his opponent's head through the window of the vehicle. It was agreeable— very—·to see his name next day in the police reports.

CHAPTER X.

THERE are many great men who go unrewarded for the services they render to humanity.   Nay, even their names are lost, while we daily bless their inventions.   One of these is he, if it was not a lady, who introduced the use of visiting cards.   In days of yore a slate or a book was kept, and you wrote your name on it.   But then that could only be done when your acquaintance was "not at home."   To the French is due the practice of making the delivery of a card serve the purpose of the appearance of the individual, and with those who have a large acquaintance this custom is becoming very common in large towns.

The visit or call is, however, a much better institution than is generally supposed.   It has its drawbacks.   It wastes much time; it necessitates much small talk.   It obliges one to dress on the chance of finding a friend at home; but for all this it is almost the only means of making an acquaintance ripen into a friendship.   In the visit all the strain, which general society somehow necessitates, is thrown off.   A man receives you in his rooms cordially, and makes you welcome, not to a stiff dinner, but an easy-chair and conversation.   A lady, who in the ball-room or party has been compelled to limit her conversation, can here speak more freely.   The talk can descend from generalities to personal inquiries, and need I say that if

(330)

you wish to know a young lady truly, you must see her at home, and by daylight.

The main points to be observed about visits are the proper occasions and the proper hours. Now, between actual friends there is little need of etiquette in these respects. A friendly visit may be made at any time, on any occasion. True, you are more welcome when the business of the day is over, in the afternoon rather than the morning, and you must, even as a friend, avoid calling at meal-times. But, on the other hand, many people receive visits in the evening—another French custom—and certainly this is the best time to make them.

As however, during the season, you have but a slight chance of finding your friends at home in the evening, another custom has been imported from France into the best circles of English society, that, namely, of fixing a day in the week on which to receive evening visitors without the ceremony of a party. The visit may then last from one to two hours, and be made either in morning or evening dress, the latter being the better. However, this custom is not yet a common one, but I beg to recommend it to those who wish to have friends as well as mere acquaintance.

The principal class of visits, then, is those of ceremony. The occasions for these are—with letters of introduction, after certain parties, and to condole or congratulate.

In the first case, letters are rarely if ever given to persons in Town. The residence in town is presumed to be transitory, and letters of introduction are only addressed to permanent residents. On the other hand, they are necessary in the country, particularly when a family take up their residence in a district, and wish to enter the best society of the place. In this last case the inhabitants always call first on the new-comer, unless he brings a letter of introduction, when he is the first to call, but instead of going in, leaves it with a card or cards, and waits till this formal visit is returned. In returning a visit made with a letter it is necessary to go in if the family is at home. " A letter of introduction," says La Fontaine, "is a draft at sight, and you must cash it." In large towns there is no such custom. It would be impossible for the residents to call on every new comer, and half of the new arrivals might be people whose acquaintance they would not wish to improve. If however, you take a letter of introduction with any special object, whether of business or of a private or particular character, you are right to send in the letter with your card, and ask for admission. Such letters should only be given by actual friends of the persons addressed, and to actual friends of their own. Never, if you are wise, give a letter to a person whom you do not know, nor address one to one whom you know slightly. The letter of introduction, if actually given to its bearer, should be left open, that he may not incur the fate of the Persian messenger, who brought tablets of introduction recommending the new acquaintance to cut his head off. A letter of this kind must therefore be carefully worded stating in full the name of the person introduced, but with as few remarks about him as possible. It is generally sufficient to say that he is a friend of yours, whom you trust your other friend will receive with attention, &c. In travelling it is well to have as many letters as possible, but not to pin your faith on them. In foreign towns it is the custom for the new comer to call on the residents first just the reverse of ours.

Ceremonial visits must be made the day after a ball, when it will suffice to leave a card; within a day or two after a dinner party, when you ought to make the visit personally, unless the dinner was a semi-official one, such as the Lord Mayor's; and within a week of a small party, when the call should certainly be made in person. All these visits should be short, lasting from twenty minutes to half-an-hour at the most. There is one species of "bore" more detestable than any other—the man, namely, who comes and sits in your drawing-room for an hour or two, preventing you from going out to make your own calls, or interrupting the calls of others. It is proper when you have been some time at a visit, and another caller is announced, to rise and leave, not indeed immediately, as if you shunned the new arrival, but after a moment or two. In other cases, when you doubt when to take your leave, you must not look at your watch, but wait till there is a lull in the conversation.

Visits of condolence and congratulation must be made about a week after the event. If you are intimate with the person on whom you call, you may ask in the first case for admission; if not, it is better only to leave a card, and make your "kind inquiries" of the servant, who is generally primed in what manner to answer them. In visits of congratulation you should always go in, and be hearty in your congratulations. Visits of condolence are terrible inflictions to both receiver and giver, but they may be made less so by avoiding, as much as consistent. with sympathy, any allusion to the past. The receiver does well to abstain from tears. A lady of my acquaintance, who had lost her husband, was receiving such a visit in her best crape. She wept profusely for some time upon the best of broad-hemmed cambric handkerchiefs, and then turning to her visitor said : " I am sure you will be glad to hear that Mr. B—— has left me most comfortably provided for. "*Hinc illæ lacrymæ.* Perhaps they would have been more sincere if he had left her without a penny. At the same time, if you have not sympathy and heart enough to pump up a little condolence, you will do better to avoid it, but take care that your conversation is not too gay. Whatever you may feel, you must respect the sorrows of others.

On marriage, cards are sent round to such people as you wish to keep among your acquaintance, and it is then their part to call first on the young couple, when within distance.

I now come to a few hints about calling in general ; and first as to the time thereof. In London, the limits of calling hours are fixed, namely, from three to six, but in the country people are sometimes odious enough to call in the morning before lunch. This should not be done even by intimate friends. Everybody has, or ought to have, his or her proper occupation in the morning, and a caller will then sometimes find the lady of the house unprepared. It is necessary before calling to ascertain the hours at which your friends lunch and dine, and not to call at these. A ceremonial call from a slight acquaintance ought to be returned the next day, or at longest within three days, unless the distance be great. In the same way, if a stranger comes to stay at the house of a friend, in the country, or in small country towns, every resident ought to call on him or her, even if she be a young lady, as soon as possible after the arrival. These calls should be made in person, and returned the next day.

The card is the next point. It should be perfectly simple. A lady's card is larger than a gentleman's. The former may be glazed, the latter not. The name, with a simple "Mr." or "Mrs." before it is sufficient, except in the case of acknowledged rank, as "The Earl of Ducie," "Colonel Marjoribanks," "The Hon. Mrs. Petre," and so forth. All merely honorary titles or designations of position or office should be left out, except in cards destined for purely official visits. Thus our ambassador at Paris returns official visits with a card thus: "L'Ambassadeur de Sa Majesté Britannique," but those of acquaintance with "Lord Cowley" simply. The address may be put in the corner of the card. The engraving should be in simple Italian writing, not Gothic or Roman letters, very small and without any flourishes. Young men have adopted recently the foreign custom of having their Christian and surname printed without the "Mr." A young lady does not require a separate card as long as she is living with her mother; her name is then engraved under her mother's, as :—

Mrs. Jones Brownsmith.
Miss Jones Brownsmith.

Or if there be more than one daughter presented, thus :—

Mrs. Jones Brownsmith.
The Miss Jones Brownsmiths.

Which latter form can be defended as more idiomatic, if less grammatical, than "The Misses Jones Brownsmith;" but it is a matter of little importance. I cannot enter here on a grammatical discussion, and the one form is as common as the other.

You will find a small card-case neater and more conven-

ient than a pocket book; and in leaving cards you must
thus distribute them: one for the lady of the house and
her daughters—the latter are sometimes represented by
turning up the edge of the card—one for the master of
the house and if there be a grown up son or near male relation staying in the house, one for him. But though
cards are cheap, you must never leave more than three at
a time at the same house. As married men have, or are
supposed to have, too much to do to make ceremonial calls,
it is the custom for a wife to take her husband's cards with
her, and to leave one or two of them with her own. If,
on your inquiring for the lady of the house, the servant
replies, " Mrs. So-and-so is not at home, but Miss So-and-
so is," you should leave a card, because young ladies do
not receive calls from gentlemen, unless they are very intimate with them, or have passed the rubicon of thirty
summers. It must be remembered, too, that where there
is a lady of the house, your call is to her, not to her husband, except on business.

The Roman Assembly used to break up if thunder was
heard, and in days of yore a family assembly was often
broken up very hurriedly at the thunder of the knocker,
one or other of the daughters exclaiming, "I am not
dressed, mamma!" and darting from the room; but ladies
ought to be dressed sufficiently to receive visitors in the
afternoon. As nerves have grown more delicate of late
years, it is perhaps a blessing that knockers have been
superseded by bells. Where they remain, however, you
should not rattle them fiercely, as a powdered Mercury
does, nor should you pull a bell ferociously.

Having entered the house, you take up with you to the
drawing-room both hat and cane, but leave an umbrella in

the hall. In France it is usual to leave a great-coat down stairs also, but as calls are made in this country in morning dress, it is not necessary to do so.

It is not usual to introduce people at morning calls in large towns; in the country it is sometimes done, not always. The law of introductions is, in fact, to force no one into an acquaintance. You should therefore ascertain beforehand whether it is agreeable to both to be introduced; but if a lady or a superior expresses a wish to know a gentleman or an inferior, the latter two have no right to decline the honor. The introduction is of an inferior (which position a gentleman always holds to a lady) to the superior. You introduce Mr. Smith to Mrs. Jones, or Mr. A. to Lord B., not *vice versa*. In introducing two persons, it is not necessary to lead one of them up by the hand, but it is sufficient simply to precede them. Having thus brought the person to be introduced up to the one to whom he is to be presented, it is the custom, even when the consent has been previously obtained, to say, with a slight bow to the superior personage: "Will you allow me to introduce Mr.—?" The person addressed replies by bowing to the one introduced, who also bows at the same time, while the introducer repeats their names, and then retires, leaving them to converse. Thus, for instance, in presenting Mr. Jones to Mrs. Smith, you will say, "Mrs. Smith, allow me to introduce Mr. Jones," and while they are engaged in bowing, you will murmur, "Mrs. Smith—Mr. Jones," and escape. If you have to present three or four people to said Mrs. Smith, it will suffice to utter their respective names without repeating that of the lady.

A well-bred person always receives visitors at whatever time they may call, or whoever they may be; but if you

15

are occupied and cannot afford to be interrupted by a mere
ceremony, you should instruct the servant *beforehand* to
say that you are "not at home." This form has often
been denounced as a falsehood, but a lie is no lie unless
intended to deceive ; and since the words are universally
understood to mean that you are engaged, it can be no
harm to give such an order to a servant. But, on the
other hand, if the servant once admits a visitor within the
hall, you should receive him at any inconvenience to yourself. A lady should never keep a visitor waiting more
than a minute or two at the most, and if she cannot avoid
doing so, must apologize on entering the drawing-room.

In good society, a visitor, unless he is a complete stranger, does not wait to be invited to sit down, but takes a
seat at once easily. A gentleman should never take the
principal place in the room, nor, on the other hand, sit at
an inconvenient distance from the lady of the house. He
must hold his hat gracefully, not put it on a chair or table,
or, if he wants to use both hands, must place it on the
floor close to his chair. A well-bred lady, who is receiving two or three visitors at a time, pays equal attention to
all, and attempts, as much as possible, to generalize the
conversation, turning to all in succession. The last arrival
however, receives a little more attention at first than the
others, and the latter, to spare her embarrassment, should
leave as soon as convenient. People who out-sit two or three
parties of visitors, unless they have some particular motive
for doing so, come under the denomination of "bores." A
"bore" is a person who does not know when you have had
enough of his or her company. Lastly, a lady never calls
on a gentleman, unless professionally or officially. It is not
only ill-bred, but positively improper to do so. At the **same**

time; there is a certain privilege in age, which makes it possible for an old bachelor like myself to receive a visit from any married lady whom I know very intimately, but such a call would certainly not be one of ceremony, and always presupposes a desire to consult me on some point or other. I should be guilty of shameful treachery, however, if I told any one that I had received such a visit, while I should certainly expect that my fair caller would let her husband know of it.

A few words on visits to country houses before I quit this subject. Since an ·Englishman's house is his castle, no one, not even a near relation, has a right to invite himself to stay in it. It is not only taking a liberty to do so, but may prove to be very inconvenient. A general invitation, too, should never be acted on. It is often given without any intention of following it up ; but, if given, should be turned into a special one sooner or later. An invitation should specify the persons whom it includes. and the person invited should never presume to take with him any one not specified. If a gentleman cannot dispense with his valet, or a lady with her maid, they should write to ask leave to bring a servant; but the means of your inviter, and the size of the house, should be taken into consideration, and it is better taste to dispense with a servant altogether. Children and horses are still more troublesome, and should never be taken without special mention made of them. It is equally bad taste to arrive with a waggonful of luggage, as that is naturally taken as a hint that you intend to stay a long time. The length of a country visit is indeed a difficult matter to decide, but in the present day people who receive much generally specify the length in their invitation—a plan which saves a great deal of trouble and doubt. But a custom not so commendable has lately come in of limiting the visits of acquaintance to two or three days. This may be pardonable where the guest lives at no great distance, but it is preposterous to expect a person to travel from London to Aberdeen for a stay of three nights. If, however, the length be not specified, and cannot easily be discovered, a week is the limit for a country visit, except at the house of a near relation or very old friend. It will, however, save trouble to yourself, if, soon after your arrival, you state that you are come " for a few days," and, if your host wishes you to make a longer visit, he will at once press you to do so.

The main point in a country visit is to give as little trouble as possible, to conform to the habits of your entertainers, and never to be in the way. On this principle you will retire to your own occupations soon after breakfast, unless some arrangement has been made for passing the morning otherwise. If you have nothing to do, you may be sure that your host has something to attend to in the morning. Another point of good-breeding is to be punctual at meals, for a host and hostess never sit down without their guest, and dinner may be getting cold. If, however, a guest should fail in this particular, a well-bred entertainer will not only take no notice of it, but attempt to set the late comer as much at his ease as possible. A host should provide amusement for his guests, and give up his time as much as possible to them ; but if he should be a professional man or student—an author, for instance— the guest should, at the commencement of the visit, insist that he will not allow him to interrupt his occupations, and the latter will set his visitor more at his ease by accepting this arrangement. In fact, the rule on which a host should act is to make his visitors as much at home as possible; that on which a visitor should act, is to interfere as little as possible with the domestic routine of the house.

The worst part of a country visit is the necessity of giving gratuities to the servants, for a poor man may often find his visit cost him far more than if he had stayed at home. It is a custom which ought to be put down because a host who receives much should pay his own servants for the extra trouble given. Some people have made by-laws against it in their houses, but, like those about gratuities to railway-porters, they are seldom regarded. In a great house a man-servant expects gold, but a poor man should not be ashamed of offering him silver. It must depend on the length of the. visit. The ladies give to the female, the gentlemen to the male servants. Would that I might see my friends without paying them for their hospitality in this indirect manner.

PART III.

THE INDIVIDUAL IN COMPANY.

CHAPTER XI.

DINNERS, DINERS, AND DINNER-PARTIES.

" BOARD !" cried a friend of mine one morning after a heavy dinner-party ; " It ought to be spelt ' bored.' Never was a more solemn torture created for mankind than these odious dinner-parties. Call it society ! so you might call the Inquisition ; and I really have my doubts whether I should not be as happy between a couple of jailers, inserting another and another wedge into the terrible boot, as between that garrulous old woman, who never waited for an answer, and that nervous young lady who never gave one, with a huge *épergne* between me and the rest of my fellow-creatures, an occasional glimpse of an irritable, solemn host at one end, and a most anxious hostess at the other. Upon my word, two whole hours of this. with the most labored attempts at conversation all round. in a dark room with a servant perpetually thrusting something across my shoulder, exciting each time a fresh alarm of a shower of sauce or gravy ; stupidity worked up to silliness by bad

(342)

champagne and worse port, and, when every one is wearied
to death a white-mouse ditty from the shy young lady,
and another hour and a half of that frantically garrulous
old one—really is this society ?"

Perhaps not ; but that is no reason why a dinner-party,
properly selected and properly served, should not be as
pleasant a meeting as any other. Indeed in England it
ought to be pleasanter. The English are not famous for
conversation ; but it has been proved, that if you want
them to talk, you must put something substantial into their
mouths. One thing is certain, namely, that a dinner-party
is the main institution of society in this country, and one
which every class and every denomination recognizes and
permits. Many people denounce balls as wicked, and consider evening parties frivolous, but none see any harm in
being well fed, and made to drink a certain or uncertain
quantity of wine. It certainly has often surprised me,
that at the very time when we are appealing to men of
all positions and all fortunes for subscriptions to relieve
the destitute poor—when starving brethren are crawling
in their filthy rags along the crowded pavement—when the
homeless are crouching on our door-steps, and perishing of
hunger but a few streets off, the noble philanthropist who
presides at a meeting for their relief, and the bishop who
calls for charity for them from the pulpit, should see no
harm in encouraging, by their presence, the prodigality
and Sybarite luxury of professional dinner-givers (for
they make it almost a profession). It is certainly strange,
that while Scripture is ransacked for texts inculcating
almsgiving and the duty of feeding the hungry, those
words of Solomon, which denounce the man who gives to
the rich, should be so completely overlooked. It is re-

markable, that the man who can with difficulty be brought
to give a ten-pound note to keep a hundred souls alive,
should, of his own free-will, spend twice the sum once a
week in feasting with dainties some dozen of his fellow-
creatures, who can scarcely get up the requisite amount
of appetite to enjoy them. But, after all, it is not so
strange, for men are selfish, and the good-will of a few
rich is more highly prized than the gratitude of many
poor.

But let this pass, and let us console ourselves by the
reflection that common sense, if no higher feeling, will in
time simplify our social banquets; and that charity, some
fifty years hence, will see no *harm*, as it now would, in
calling in the blind, the halt, and the needy, to partake
of the dishes we now spread only for the rich, the fashionable, and the appetiteless. One rule, however, we may
gain at once from these considerations, that only the
wealthy should be dinner-givers, and the man who cannot
"afford" £5 for the starving, should on no account afford £20 for the well fed.

A dinner, like a pun, should never be made public unless it be very good, but at the same time modern improvements enable it to be that without being also very
expensive. The goodness of a dinner does not consist in
the rarity and costliness of the viands, but in the manner
in which they are cooked and served, in the various concomitants which contribute to give it brilliance and elegance, and yet more in the guests who eat it.

This last point is, in fact, the most important, so that
the invitation is only a second consideration to the dinner
itself. The rules for invitations, and some hints whom
to invite are given in the next chapter by my colleague

I need give but a few hints of my own. People who have a large acquaintance and give dinners, should keep a book in which to write the names of those who compose each party, which prevents the mistake of asking the same person twice, and of bringing precisely the same people together again when their turn comes round. There are indeed some privileged persons like myself, agreeable old bachelors, who, being free from encumbrance and full of talk, are always welcome and generally wanted. In fact, such men run a risk of being known as professional diners-out, like the *convivæ* of Rome, so that it is a greater charity not to invite them too often. And this reminds me that you should not ask a man without his wife, though you may leave his sons and daughters out of the calculation. Then, again, the very ancient had better be left to dine at home, unless, like Lady Morgan, they preserve their conversational powers. The invitation must be answered as soon as possible, and the answer addressed to the lady of the house.

But the question whom to invite, is one which cannot be so easily answered. First, there are some people whom you *must* invite sooner or later, namely, those at whose houses you have dined ; because you may neglect every Christian duty, and be less blamed than if you omit this social one. This is certainly absurd, and society becomes almost *low* when dinner-parties take the semblance of a tacit contract, in which the one party undertakes to feed the other to-day, if the other will feed him in return before the end of the season. Yet I have known people not at all ashamed to complain that they have not been asked to dinner, and not blush to say, "They *owe* us a dinner, you know." Somehow, then, you must manage

15*

to acquit yourself of these dinner debts before the season is over. Society condemns you severely if you do not pay your debts of hospitality. Of course this applies only to people who are known to be in the habit of giving dinners. Those who from one cause or another do not do so, are still invited, though not so often.

But when you have done your duty religiously in this respect, you have the world before you. Where to choose? Now, after taking into due consideration the congruities and sympathies of those you may select, the chief point is to invite men and women—an equal number of each of course—who can *talk*. By this I do not mean your rapid utterers of small-talk, who can coin more pretty nonsense in half an hour than a modern novelist in three months, but men, who having gone through the world, and tamed their Pegasus with the curb of experience, not being bound, Mazeppa-like, on the back of some wretched hobby, can gallop smoothly over the themes that life and the newspapers supply to wit; men who view life calmly from the height to which they have climbed, without prejudice and without awe; and women who are capable of understanding and answering such men as these. But you must carefully avoid the *eater*, by which I mean both the *gourmand* and the *gourmet*, both the alderman whose motto is quantity, and the epicure who cries for quality. Of what good is it to pander to the greediness of a vile being, whose soul lies in the stomach, as the Greeks affirmed that it always did, and whose mind and thoughts are much in the same region. If such men can talk at all, it is only of eating, and if you do not feed them with the especial dainties they look for, their gratitude shows itself in sneers at your hospitality when they next dine out. Wits, again, and men who think themselves to be so, should never be asked singly, for they will engross the conversation, and silence the rest. When asked in numbers, they keep one another within limits.

The number of the guests is a difficulty. People find that it is more economical to give large than small dinners, and will therefore continue to go on in solemn grandeur. But the best dinners are those at which all the guests can join in a common conversation, to which the host being within hearing of all his party can give the proper lead. Such dinners alone can be agreeable to all, because no one is dependent on the liveliness of his or her nearest neighbor for conversation. As it is, too many at dinner is nothing better than an eating quadrille, where each person has a partner and is at his mercy; only that the dance lasts not an eighth of the time which the leashed diner is compelled to pass in company with his partner. Brillat Savarin says, that no dinner should have more than twelve guests, and the old rule was, "neither less than the graces, nor more than the muses;" but London dinners oftener exceed these limits than the reverse, while country dinners mount up to twenty. Indeed, with some senseless people, the *éclat* of the dinner seems to consist in the number of the guests, and the more you can feed the more your glory. I am inclined to think that the old rule is the best; but as it was made for tables at which ladies never appeared, some alteration must be made in it, and we may say generally, that an even number is better than an odd one, and that it should be either six, eight, or ten. The first of course is reserved for your dinners of honor, when the men you admire and the

women you love—(two of each, for no man can find more
than that number in the world)—dine with you and your
wife; the second is your sociable dinner, at which all the
guests are more or less known to one another; and the
third is your company dinner. If you exceed these numbers, you may do what you will to make your dinner
perfect, your guests will spoil it all by falling into couples and eating in quadrille.

But there is another reason for limiting the number,
namely, that to give a good dinner, your means, your establishment, your dining-room, the capacities of the table,
and so forth, must all be taken into consideration. But
if the dinner is given to fourteen, sixteen, or even eighteen, as is now common in large towns, you must either
increase your establishment and your expense not a little,
or be content, as people are, to give them the regular
" feed," in which everybody knows beforehand what they
will have. One cook, for instance, cannot serve up *properly* for more than a dozen people: three men cannot
wait properly on more than ten; and a table which will
hold more than that number will be so large as to separate the opposite guests too far for easy and general conversation. Lastly, if your means enable you to dine a
hundred or a thousand every week, you would be a mad-
man to do so; you might as well give your dinner to two
only, for what of that essential harmony, that communion
of mind and spirit, " the feast of reason and the flow of
soul," can there possibly be between a hundred, nay, even
seventy people, some of them so far from one another that
they could scarcely be heard without a speaking-trumpet?

Having well selected your guests, you consider in what
room to dine them, for the regular dining-room is not

always the most comfortable. If the party be small—six or eight—a large dining-room will look very ghastly, and it should be borne in mind that dinner-givers of good taste study comfort more than grandeur, which latter is simply vulgar whether in the house of a duke or a haberdasher. The furniture of our dining rooms is certainly improving a little. Nothing could be more chilling to the mind and appetite alike than the stone-colored walls, displaying the usual magnificent oil-paintings of an unknown school, the bust of the master of the feast at one end looking almost less solemn than the original under it, the huge table with its cumbrous silver adornments, the stiff side-board and the stiffer chairs. Whether it was a Puritanical attempt at simplicity which insisted that if we *would* have a good dinner we should mortify the flesh with bad concomitants, or whether it was a foolish fancy that a dining-room should be cold, though the dinner were hot, I cannot say; but I feel that the man who makes dining a study—and he who gives dinners should in charity do so—must go farther in the improvements of the room than we yet have. Light and an air of comfort are the main essentials. The temperature must not, even in summer, be too low, for sitting at dinner produces a chill in itself. Thirteen to sixteen degrees of Réaumur are fixed for it by the author of the *Physiologie du goût ;* but whatever the exact temperature, it must be obtained before dinner by lighting the fire some hours previously, and allowing it to burn rather low until near the end of the meal, when it must be replenished. There are very few days in an English summer when a small fire *after* dinner is not acceptable. In very cold weather, when a large one is necessary, it is not easy to manage so that

one-half of the guests shall not have their backs roasted
and the other not be frozen, but there are two ways of
preventing it—the one by a large glass screen before the
fire, the other by a table in the shape of a horse-shoe
or of a segment of a circle, of which the chord will be
towards the fire.   A dinner-giver will then have his round
or oval table so made as to be divisible into two separate
ones.

The shape of the table is, in fact, a more essential point
than some people think.   In order that a dinner may be a
social meeting, not a mere collection of *t·tes- -t tes*,. as
it used to be till recently, and still is sometimes, the table
must be of a shape which will not make conversation difficult between any two or more of the guests: The old
parallelogram, with the stately host at the end and the
radiant but anxious lady at the other, was fatal to conversation.   It was too broad, too long, too stiff—the corners cut off the lord and lady of the feast from their honored guests. and necessitated leaning across ; while if
Monsieur wished to make a remark to Madame, he had,
independently of the joints, épergne, and candelabra. a
length of table to impede him which compelled him to
raise his voice most unmusically.   It caused a complete
divorce, in fact, and- Sir Cresswell Cresswell could not
more effectually sever man and wife than that ancient
" board"—for such it literally was in shape—used to do.
The modern table is oval.   Some people dine at round
tables, like Arthur and his knights, but these if large
enough for a party, will have a diameter every way too
long to allow any two opposite guests to converse.   The
horse-shoe table is suited only for a small party, and the
base should not be occupied.   As for the long "planks,"

which served us for tables at college, and still do so at public dinners, they have the advantage over the mahogany of the dinning-room, of allowing a guest five persons to talk to instead of one, but they make elegance almost impossible. A lozenge-shaped table, with the points rounded off, sounds Epicurean, but it leaves open the question—where are the host and hostess to sit? At the oval table I need scarcely say they sit in the middle of each side, opposite to one another.

The dining-room must be, of course, carpeted even in the heat of summer, to deaden the noise of the servants' feet. The chairs should be easy, with tall slanting backs, but without arms. As they should not be much higher than drawing-room chairs, the table must be lowered in proportion. Each person should be provided with a foot-stool.

Light is positively necessary to digestion, and no party can be cheerful without it. It is difficult to have too much light, but profusion is less desirable than arrangement, while a mere glare becomes painful. Gas and candles should both be avoided on that and other accounts, and the best media for lighting are carcelle, or moderator-lamps, covered with open pink muslin, or tarlatane, which, without diminishing, softens the light. The principal object is to throw as much of it as possible on the table, with sufficient on the faces of the guests. Lighting from the walls is apt to throw the latter into shade, and a chandelier in the middle must be hung very low to do justice to the former. Lamps on the table itself are simply unpardonable, and must on no account be admitted. The best plan is to have four chandeliers, containing each one large lamp, and hung over the places where the four corners of the table would come if it were a parallelogram instead of an oval. The rest of the room, however, must not be left in darkness, and lamps may be placed on the side-board and side-tables. The latter must be very neat, and both should be ornamented richly with flowers rather than with that pompous display of plate which is too commonly seen.

A few words about servants before we come to the table itself. Women wait more quietly and quite as actively as men, but a butler, who can carve well and rapidly, is indispensable. If, however, you have men-servants, they should not be too many. A party of ten can be perfectly well served by two men and a butler, and, if there are more than these, they only get in the way of one another, or stand pompously by staring while you eat. Your servants should be well trained and instructed, and should obey every order given by the butler. A master or mistress should never speak to them at dinner, and they must be themselves as silent as Sappists. They should wear light shoes that cannot creak, and if they have a napkin instead of gloves, you must see that their hands are perfectly clean. They should have their "beats" like policemen, one beginning at the guest on his master's right and ending with the lady of the house, the other with the guest on his mistress's right ending with the master.

The table, on which all eyes are turned, is the next point. Great changes have taken place in the last ten or fifteen years in its arrangements, and as the Russian plan is now adopted in the best houses, and is, at the same time, the most elegant, I shall not stop to speak of any other. The main point is to secure beauty without interfering with conversation. Given, therefore, a table-cover, and a white damask table-cloth over it, what are we to place thereon? First, nothing high enough to come between the heads of any two of the party, and therefore must épergnes, lamps, and so forth, be eschewed as nuisances. Next, that which is pleasant and agreeable to the eye, and something that it can dwell upon with pleasure. A common object for the centre is desirable, and this should be some work of art, of Parian or china, not too high nor too large, and on each side towards the thin ends of the oval should be bowls of biscuit-ware or china, filled with flowers; or, to be elegant, you may have two little table-fountains, provided their basins are low. The rest of the table must be covered with dessert. By this arrangement plate becomes a secondary matter, and indeed a display of massive silver is rather chilling, and always looks ostentatious. In addition to the flowers mentioned, the French often place a bouquet on the napkin of each lady, and the attention is certainly a pretty one. The place for each guest should be roomy, but not too far from his neighbors. The dinner-service of the present day may be reduced to plates alone, since everything else is served at the side-table. I am inclined to think that pure white china with a gilt edge, and the best of its kind, is the fittest service to dine off, but this is a matter of taste only. At any rate, the dessert-service should be handsome. Bachelors at dinner have a great advantage in having their light wine placed by their glasses in black bottles, but in other dinners the wine is handed. It will, however, be well on all occasions to have sufficient glasses for all the wines to be drunk placed on the right hand of each plate, and the same may be said of knives, spoons, and forks. The napkins may be folded according to fancy. Sometimes they are placed on the plate with a roll of bread inside, and sometimes arranged in a fan-shape in the champagne-glasses. For my own part, I prefer to think that no hands have been soiling mine before I use it, and perhaps the most elegant way is to lay them on the table or plate just as they come from the washerwoman's.

No dish but those of dessert is placed on the table. I have spoken of this, in the chapter on accomplishments, under the head of carving, and shall not again discuss the question. It suffices to say that where "l'on sait dîner" no dish is either carved or helped at table. But I am now going to recommend the revival of an ancient practice which is now gone out. It is that each plate should be filled with soup and put in its place at table, at the very moment that the guests are coming into the room. The object of this is to enable every one to begin dinner at the same moment. The hungry do not talk well, and the warm soup at once revives the spirits and slakes the appetite. It is hard on a man to expect him to begin conversation while the ladies are sipping their soup and he is waiting for it. Harmony and union are the essentials of dinner, and where it can be so simply obtained, it is foolish to neglect it. Yet I have little hope that this practice will be adopted, because English people seem to think more of the pomposity than the comfort of their dinner, and the butler and men are required to stand and look grand as the guests pass in. I may here observe that the object of soup being to "take the chill off" the appetite and prepare the inner man for the reception of solids, a light soup is better than a thick one, which clogs the appetite; turtle is only fit for an alderman, and your soup may therefore be inexpensive.

After the soup the wine. Modern Englishmen have so far improved upon their ancestors, that they no longer meet to drink but to dine, and the amount of the wine is therefore of far less importance than its quality. The order of the wines, reversing that of the solids, is from the lightest to the strongest. The author of the *Art of Dining* tells us, that "sherry, champagne, port, and claret" are indispensable to the dinner-table. I should be inclined to knock off two of these, champagne and port, and put in a light Rhenish in their place. Port has become almost an impossibility, for age is a *sine qui non* of this wine, and unless you have long had a good cellar, you have very little chance of obtaining it good. In fact, though still placed on the table, the use of it seem to be restricted to a few old gentlemen, who cannot give up their customary drink. George the Fourth declared for sherry, and I cannot help thinking he was right. At any rate, bad port is less drinkable than bad sherry, and as you will too often have only this choice of evils, I beg to hint how the alternative may be most prudently taken. Champagne, again, should be very good to be enjoyable, and it is also becoming more and more difficult to procure. Both port and champagne are doctored for every European market, and a friend of mine visiting a famous wine-grower at Epernay, tasted from the *same* cask no less than five different wines, all manufactured in a few hours out of the the same original juice. I suspect that even an English wine-merchant can produce as many different " vintages" from the same stuff, as M. Houdin does wines from the some bottle.

The mingling of water with wine is said to have been discovered by an accident. A party of old Greeks, not famous for sobriety, had been drinking on the sea-shore, when a storm arose, and in rapid haste they retreated to a cave to take shelter. Probably they were not in a fit condition for carrying their goblets with them steadily. At any rate they left them on the shore, and when the storm was over, found their wine converted by the rain into wine and water. The allegation that the mixture spoils two good things, as two good people are sometimes spoiled by marriage, is one which a tippler will support more zealously than an epicure. Mr. Walker, in the " Original," recommends even port and water; but however this may be, some Bordeaux wines gain, rather than lose, by the mixture, and you may thus have, to accompany your eating, a cooling drink which will not destroy your taste for the good wines to follow it. A sensible man avoids variety in drinking. One French wine during dinner, and sherry after it, or a German wine for the meal, and claret for dessert, will leave you much happier than mingling sherry, champagne, claret, and port. Great care should be used in decanting wine, so as not to shake or cork it. Claret appears in a glass jug, but rare French wines, particularly *Bourgogne* and the *Vins du Midi*, should be brought up and placed on the table in their baskets, as decanting spoils them. Although the guest should avoid variety, the host must provide it in order to meet the tastes of all, and his servants should be taught to pronounce properly the names of the different foreign wines, which are often so indistinct that we are led into taking a white one when we wanted red, or a French one when we expected Rhenish.

The bachelor has the great privilege of drinking beer at dinner if he likes it. I cannot conceive how so good and harmless an accompaniment of eating came to be excluded

from the well-served table, unless from a vulgar fancy that
what is not expensive should not be set before a guest,
however góod it may be.   How happy people with these
notions would be in Ceylon, where Bass costs nearly a shilling a glass.   This reminds me of a story of some vulgar
man whose name I have forgotten, and do not care to remember.   His host simply enough said to his guest, "This
wine cost me six shillings a bottle."   "Did it?" cried the
other, "then pass it round, and let's have another six-
penn'orth."   The connoisseur of beer rightly judges that
it is spoiled by bottling; draught beer is also the more
wholesome.   A glass of old port is generally substituted
for the beer with cheese, but the drink with the German
student, an ardent lover of it, tells you was discovered by

> " Gabrantius Konig von Brabant
>   Der zuerst das Bier erfand."

is its more natural accompaniment.

If there were no other advantage in the Russian system, as it is called, it would be worth adopting, only because it enables the dinner-giver to offer more variety,
instead of forcing him to sacrifice taste to the appearance
of his dishes.   Thus the turbot and the cod were once
becoming standing dishes at all English dinners, and
small fish were banished because they did not put in a
majestic appearance.   Yet there are many better fish
than cod and turbot, and there are many ways of dressing
fish which may not be so agreeable to the eye as to the
palate.   Then, again, how exquisite is the flavor of some
fresh-water fish, and of several kinds of shell-fish, which
we so seldom see at great dinners!   How much better the
variety of trout, perch in *souchet*, fried gudgeons, even

eels, mussels, and lampreys (both of which must be moderately indulged in, the one producing very often a rush on the face, which is cured by large quantities of fresh milk, and the other being notorious as a regicide, which those who read the commonest history of England will remember), than that perpetual turbot. In fact, no kind of eating can be more varied than that of fish ; yet, by sticking to antique traditions, we deprive ourselves of the enjoyment of all the wealth of sea and stream. There are scores of ways of dressing them all too, which you can learn in any good cookery-book, and almost any fish can be made not only eatable but delicious by clever cooking. But vulgarity has driven many a good but cheap eatable from the table of the rich ; and the Duke of Rutland was quite right to give Poodle Byng his *congé*, when one of these despised delicacies appeared at the Duke's table, and Poodle exclaimed, " Ah ! my old friend haddock ! I have not seen a haddock on a gentleman's table since I was a boy." Oysters, though eaten at dinner in France, are properly excluded from table in England, as being much too heating, and carp is very indigestible : but there are the Devonshire John Dory, a far better fish than turbot, red mullets, salmon-trout, whitings, smelt, mackerel, sturgeon, the favorite of the Emperor of China, and even sprats and herrings, to form a variety besides those mentioned before.

But our chief thanks to the new system are due for its ostracizing that unwieldy barbarism—the joint. Nothing can make a joint look elegant, while it hides the master of the house, and condemns him to the misery of carving. I was much amused at the observations of a writer on the subject of dinners, who objected to flowers on the table,

" because we don't eat flowers, and everything that is on the table ought to be eatable." At this rate the cook would have to dish up the épergnes and candelabra. But the truth is, that unless our appetites are very keen, the sight of much meat reeking in its gravy is sufficient to destroy them entirely, and a huge joint especially is calculated to disgust the epicure. If joints are eaten at all, they should be placed on the side-table, where they will be out of sight.

Vegetables should properly be served separately on a clean plate after the roast, but when served with it, a guest should be satisfied with at most two kinds at a time, nothing showing worse taste than to load your plate. Asparagus, pease, artichokes, haricots, vegetable marrows, and spinach ought, if not a component part of a made dish, to be served separately. There are many ways of dressing potatoes and carrots, which last are a vegetable much neglected at English tables, but when quite young, and dressed with butter in the French fashion, a delicious eatable, and a preventive of jaundice, which should recommend them strongly to professional diners-out.

But I am not a cook, and cannot go through every course with you. It must suffice to say, that the dishes should not be too many, and that good cooking and management make a better dinner than either profusion or expenditure, or delicacies out of season. The main points are originality and rarity, and to have the best of everything, or not have it at all. Perhaps the strangest dinner I ever ate was in *tête-à-tête* with a bachelor of small appetite. There were but two courses. To the first we stood up, opening our own oysters, and devouring them till we could eat no more. The second course, to which we sat down, consisted of a dozen marrow-bones, of which we each discussed six. They were as hot as they could be, and excellent. A variety of vegetables completed this light repast, and though I could have dined more largely, I was bound to confess that my friend had given me a dinner which I should scarcely have got elsewhere. Lest you should be tempted to offer a similar repast to a large party, I must warn you that the marrow-bone is not considered a presentable dish, and that the marrow must be extracted by a special kind of spoon, of which a clean one is required for every bone.

Brillat Savarin says, that the order of the solids should be from the heaviest to the lightest. This is not strictly observed either in France or England, and it may be useful to know what is the order generally adopted in this country. It is as follows :—

1. Soup.
2. Fish.
3. Patties (of oysters, lobsters, shrimps, or minced veal.)
4. Made dishes, or *entrées*, which include poultry.
5. The roast, or *pièce de résistance.*
6. Vegetables.
7. The game.
8. Pastry, puddings, omelettes.
9. The ice.
10. The dessert.

The salad ought to have, but seldom has a place in this list, namely, after the ice, and with cheese. When made as a *mayonnaise*, that is with chicken, cold fish, or shell-fish, it comes in as a made-dish. But a pure salad, well dressed is "a dish to set before a king," and that you

may be able to dress it yourself, and we may finish our
dinner with cheerfulness, I give you Sydney Smith's receipt to learn by heart,—

> " Two large potatoes, passed through kitchen sieve,
> Unwonted softness to the salad give.
> Of mordent mustard, add a single spoon ;
> Distrust the condiment which bites too soon :
> But deem it not, thou man of herbs, a fault
> To add a double quantity of salt.
> Three times the spoon with oil of Lucca crown,
> And once with vinegar procured from town ;
> True flavor needs it, and your poet begs
> The pounded yellow of two well-boil'd eggs.
> Let onion atoms lurk within the bowl,
> And, scarce suspected, animate the whole ;
> And lastly, on the favor'd compound toss
> A magic spoonful of anchovy sauce.
> Then, though green turtle fail, though venison's **tough,**
> And ham and turkey are not boil'd enough,
> Serenely full, the epicure may say—
> Fate cannot harm me—I have dined to-day ! ' "

Well, dinner is done, but not the diners. There remains on the table what is a whole dinner in Italy, and
what is dinner enough for a poet—fruit and wine. Talking of poets, though, reminds me that their chameleon
exsistence is only a poetic license. Byron, who dined off
potatoes and vinegar in public, generally rewarded himself in private with an unspiritual beef-steak, and " cut
from the joint ;" and the poets of " olden time," by which
I mean *the* days of eating in Athens and Rome, were
also the paraistes of the feast, and for a stave or two,
gladly accepted a steak or two, just as some later poets
have dined with my Lord to-day, on the tacit understanding that they should write him a dedication to-morrow.
In fact, *Grub* street was not inappropriately named, if

16

slang be English ; and most of our own poets,—Mooro and Rogers, *e. g.*,—have been careful diners. But, then, the legend which made Minerva spring from the *head* of Jupiter, has long been proved a good-natured mistake, destined to encourage "our minion lyricists," and there is now no doubt that the muse of song and literature had as large a corporation as any other of the nine. What else is the meaning of "writing for bread ?"

But stop, I had nearly forgotten Grace. Well, that is nothing very extraordinary, for the thanksgiving is positively the last thing thought of by the diner, and when it is remembered, it is too often reduced to a mere formality. What ridiculous mockeries are the long Latin graces through which we had to stand at college. and the chanted graces at public dinners! If a man be really thankful to God for what he gives him, a few thoughts, not words, best express it ; but if words be necessary, let them be short and solemn, that each one's heart may echo them. Dr. Johnson was well reproved in his formal religion, when his wife told him it was of no use to ask his Maker to make him truly thankful, when the next moment he would sit down and abuse every dish on the table ; and what was said to Johnson may be said to many a pampered diner-out, and to many a grumbling father of a family ; " Better a dry morsel where love is, than a stalled ox, and"— let me adapt it to the present day—"*grumbling* therewith." How often does a man say the words of his grace, and soon after find fault with the dinner, ungrateful alike to his host and his Maker. But, as far as etiquette goes, there is only this to be said,—that the audible grace is spoken by the master of the feast, or if a clergyman be present, by him. So in India, a Brah-

min was always invited to bless the banquet, and give it
the sanction of his presence.

The etiquettes of dinner are not very numerous. We
have already spoken in Chapter VII. of the manners proper at the dinner table. We have now to consider a few
duties of host and guest.

Punctuality may be the soul of business, but it is also
that of knife-and-fork play. Everybody must be punctual at the great event of the day. " Dinner," said a
French cook, " is the hope of the hungry, the occupation
of the idle, the rest of the weary, and the consolation of
the miserable !" Can any one be guilty of delaying such
a moment? The Romans complained that before the sun-
dial was discovered, one dined when hunger ordered, but
afterwards hunger had to wait for time. In our modern
dining rooms, we have little fear that hunger will annoy
any one, but sometimes a delay may occur which may
make hunger a very intimate acquaintance. Thus, Cam-
bacèr s, one of the best dinner-givers of his day, once
kept his guests waiting three hours, while he was engaged
on state business ; and Walpole relates how he once had
to wait nearly four hours for dinner at Northumberland
House, because the Lords were reading the Poor Bill.
The guests sat down at last without the Peers, but had
not done when the legislators tumbled in and had the
whole dinner served up again. This dinner had been
fixed for the then fashionable hour of five, and did not
finish till eleven. However, this was more excusable than
the case of a late nobleman, who was seen mounting his
horse for his afternoon ride, just as his guests assembled
in the drawing-room.

Next to the host and hostess, the cook ought to be punctual. But the guest's arrival is more important still; and the guest has no excuse, because from the merest selfishness, or want of consideration, he may put a whole party to inconvenience. The invited having arrived, the lady receives them in the drawing-room, and the conversation is necessarily more or less formal, for everybody is waiting for *the* event. At last a servant announces that dinner is ready. It is then the part of the host to pair off the guests. He himself takes down the lady of the highest rank, or the greatest stranger. Distinctions of rank are going out in *good* society, although precedence exists just as a herald's office does; but it may generally be said that age has the real precedence, and a lady of advanced years should not be put behind any one of rank under royal blood. The most intimate with the family take the lowest, the least so, the highest place. At dinner, the gentleman sits to the right of the lady, so that the arrangment is easily made. In France there is no procession of this kind, and the awkwardness of precedence is thus avoided. There, all the guests enter pell-mell, and find their names written on papers placed on their napkins. Besides these papers a bill of fare is placed on each plate, when the dinner is really good, and the dinner-giver an epicure.

It is the duty of the host to lead the conversation as much as possible, and it is still more his duty to make it general. As, however, this art is little understood by Englishmen, a man will generally have to talk more or less to the lady on his left. He must take care not to neglect her for the one on his right, however charming the latter may be. The dinner over, and the servants dismissed, the ladies sit for a short time at dessert and then retire; the youngest man in the room rises to open the door for them, and all the rest rise and stand by their chairs. Then comes the "drawing-round," and the conversation grows lighter and easier. But young men and old should beware of making it too light, or of running, as our barristers often do, into stories that are unfit for ladies' ears.

A true gentleman will be the same in ladies' society as he is out of it. A young man should not linger over his wine, and he may rise and leave the dining-room before the others go. But it remains with the host to offer to "join the ladies," which he should do whenever he sees any one growing warm over his port and talking too freely. Coffee and tea are both served up stairs, and both should be hot. Coffee is drunk without milk, and with sugar; tea, by those who know how to enjoy it, without either; but they are the *raræ aves* of society, men who know what is good and enjoy it quietly. A little green tea is necessary after wine, for it awakens and excites. No man should drink enough wine to make him feel too easy with the ladies. If he has done so without feeling its effects, he had better go home before he goes up to the drawing-room. In France the gentlemen come away with the ladies, and there is no wine-drinking. In England he custom is dwindling down to a mere form, and the shorter you remain after the departure of the ladies the better. But remember, that many meats require as much as four hours to digest, and that the best aid to digestion is lively, easy conversation. A dinner party breaks up

at about eleven. There should be a little music in the
evening ; but it is a great mistake to have a regular evening party after a dinner. At eleven you go home, and
having had a walk, put on your white neck-tie for the
next event of the evening, which is discussed in the thirteenth chapter.

CHAPTER XII.

WE have next to consider a lady in the all-important character of a hostess at a dinner party.

Her first duty in this capacity is to send out her invitations in due time and proper form. With regard to the time, it is necessary, during the height of the London season, to send an invitation three weeks before the dinner party ;abut, in the quiet season of the year, or in the country, it is neither essential to do so, nor usual. The best plan for persons who give many dinner parties, is to have a plate with their names and invitations printed thus : —

Mr. and Mrs. ——
Request the favor of
Mr. and Mrs. ——'*s*
Company at dinner on the ——
at —— *o'clock.*

In writing to persons of rank far above your own, or to clergymen of high dignity, such as bishops and deans, the word " honor" should be substituted for " favor."

These invitations should properly be sent by a servant, and not by the post, unless the distance be great.

Next comes the choice of guests, thus assembled, to sit in close contact for two hours or more.

This involves many considerations. If your guests do

not assimilate, no luxury of dinners, no perfection of
manners on your part, can avert a failure. Yet so little
is this understood, that there are persons who collect, as
it would seem, a party so discordant as to provoke a question whether they had not shaken them all in a bag together, and turned them out loose upon each other—the
man of easy principles with the serious doctor of divinity;
the man of talent with a rich and mindless merchant; the
quiet country family with the trashy London dashers,
and so on; and these solecisms in taste and discretion
occur frequently. Nor ought the worldly positions of
people to be the sole consideration. Many a nobleman
will assimilate far better with the poor author than with
the millionaire; wealth, simply because it is wealth, gains
little prestige in good circles; there is a prejudice against
the *nouveau riches* among the old families of England.
Neither is it desirable to club all your aristocratic or fashionable acquaintance together; you offend by so doing,
those who are left out; and many lose valuable friends
who, however conscious they may be of an inferior position, do not like to be reminded of it. It is something,
too, to avoid giving pain to the feelings of others.

The general rule, however, is to invite persons of nearly
the same standing in society to meet at dinner; taking
care that their general views and mode of life are not so
contrasted as to be likely to clash. In the country, difference of politics used to form a barrier; Whig and Tory,
even if they sat at table together, would scarcely drink
wine with each other. But all that inconvenience to host
and hostess has long since passed away, and to the facilities of forming a party the custom of no longer asking any
one to take wine has contributed.

Those who wish to form agreeable dinner-parties will avoid a class : a dinner composed of officers only and their wives recalls too forcibly barrack life; "talking pipe-clay," as they term it, is as fatiguing as "the ship," though not so vulgar. Wives of officers in marching regiments have generally travelled far, and seen nothing : they can tell you little but how bad their quarters were, and how they were hurried away from such and such a place. The gentlemen of the bar sprinkled about, make a charming spice to a dinner ; but, like all spices, one must not have too much of them : they want keeping down, otherwise you have your dining-room turned into Westminster Hall ; or you feel, if you venture to talk yourself, as if you were subjecting yourself to a cross-examination. Yet the late Lord Grenville remarked, that he was always glad to meet a lawyer at a dinner-party, for he was then sure that some good topic would be started. The title of doctor is against the fascination of a physician's manners ; his very attentions may seem to have an interested air, since the doctor's clients are in society. A conclave of doctors is even more formidable than one of lawyers, for the former have only to deal with the constitution of the state, and the latter are looking, perhaps, at your constitution, and privately condemning it. A whole party composed of clergymen is perhaps worse; delightful as companions, valuable as friends, as many clergymen are, when assembled they run naturally into topics we do not wish to have familiarized. Secular interests peep out from those we esteem sacred ; the pleasures of gastronomy, which are as fully appreciated by the clergy as by any other class, seem so little to accord with the spirit-stirring eloquence we heard last Sunday, that we regret

having met our "venerable rector" under such circumstances.

"Perhaps," says Dr. Johnson, "good-breeding consists
in having no particular mark of any profession, but a general elegance of manners." On this principle of gene-
ralizing should dinner-parties be formed.

In high English society, to quote that accomplished
member of society, Mr. Hayward, in his *Treatise on
Codes of Manners*, any calling was some few years since
derogatory to the perfect character of a gentleman ; it is
now otherwise. Yet the distinction of the aristocratic
professions, as opposed to other callings, is maintained,
and it will perhaps continue to be so. These are the
church, the bar, the higher walks of medicine, the army
and navy. The different members of these professions and
their wives and families are therefore fit for any society ;
there is no possible objection to their mixing at a dinner-
table with nobility, provided they be well-bred and agreeable. The literary man, if a gentleman by education and
manners, is always an agreeable addition ; and the highest
in rank have in this country set the example of inviting
artists, architects, and sculptors, but not always their families, to their tables.

Great eminence in talents sets aside distinctions ; and
"the first class of millionaires," Mr. Hayward assures us,
"rise superior to rules." But it is not in good taste to
follow out this last maxim, unless high personal character,
the good employment of vast wealth, and a gentlemanly
bearing, accompany riches. The lady, whose talk about
"bigotry and virtue" was the amusement of the clubs
some years since, had no right, in regard to her husband's
position and character, to be associated, as she was, with

women of high rank or of old patrician families; the var-
nish has since been taken off the picture, and it has sunk
down to its original value, after having been at a fabulous
estimation in the social mart.

The next points refer to the duties of a lady on the
arrival of the guests at the house. She remains in some
convenient part of her drawing-room, and too much cannot be said of the importance of her being dressed some
time before the party arrives. Want of attention in this
respect, though very much less thought of now than formerly, is a real breach of good manners. Neither should
her daughters, should she have any, come dropping in
one by one, but should be seated, ready to receive the
visitors.

Previously, however, to her going up to dress, the lady
of the house should have arranged, with some consideration, who is to take precedence.

1. With respect to persons of title. These take precedence according to their titles; but, should there be
diplomatic foreigners of the first class, they go out first;
or, should there be a bishop and his wife, precedence is
usually given to them by courtesy, even over dukes and
marquises; bishops ranking with earls.* The same courtesy is extended to all the dignified clergy; whilst the
wives of all the clergy take precedence of the wives of
barristers; and the wives of the esquires, without professions or trade, take precedence of both clergymen's and
barristers' wives. These distinctions are seldom, it is true,
rigorously to be pursued, but it is convenient to know
them; it is as well, also, especially to remember that the

* See Lodge's *Orders for Precedency.* An archbishop ranks with
a duke.

wives of clergymen and of barristers, by right, take precedence of the untitled wives of military and naval men.
There is no place specified for physicans, who, however,
are ranked in the households of the royal family next to
the knights, and whose wives, therefore, go out after those
of the barristers.

These seem to be worldly and unimportant rules; but
whatever prevents mistakes, ill-will, and the possibility of
doing a rude action without intention, comes under the
comprehensive head—" How to be civil with ease."   Besides, although in friendly society, as it is called, a breach
of etiquette might not signify, there is so much that is
unfriendly, so much in which criticism stalks among the
company seeking whose conduct he may challenge, that a
hostess should be perfectly armed with every defence
against comment.

As her guests enter she should advance half-way to
meet them.   This is a point of politeness; and a lady in
a county near London gave great offence once at her first
dinner, by standing with one arm on her mantle-piece,
waiting till her company came up to her.   All the chairs
should be ready, so that there should be no placing or
needless confusion ; but, should any change in the arrangements of the rooms be requisite, it should be made by the
butler or by the gentleman of the house.   The lady of
the house should do nothing but receive, converse, and
look as well as she can.   To this end her room and all
the minutiæ should be tastefully arranged.   A distribution of natural flowers adds greatly to the gaiety of a
drawing-room, how richly or poorly soever it may be furnished : people are apt to forget in England, what is never
forgotten in France, how greatly the style and arrange-

ment of furniture contribute to make a party go off well, and those engaged in it look well, of which pleasing fact people often have a sort of intuitive conviction, even without the aid of the looking-glass.

And now the test of good-breeding in a hostess is to be detected; it is often a severe one. Her guests may arrive all at once, she must not be hurried, yet each and all *must* feel that they have her individual attention. She must have something pleasing and cheerful to say to every one, but she must not say or do too much. Perhaps her guests are late, or perhaps, worst martyrdom of all, her servants are late in announcing dinner. She chafes inwardly; but still, feeling as if on a stage, with an army of observation around her, she bears up; strikes out new subjects; appears as if still expecting some one; no, nothing is to go wrong with her; be it ever really so wrong that day, she must not seem to notice it.

It may be argued that this implies a degree of self-restraint akin to dissimulation: but that is an error; self-restraint does not imply dissimulation. At length dinner is announced; perhaps a few minutes previously some reckless youth, or sexagenarian, but probably the former, since the being too late for dinner is not commonly the fault of age, comes breathlessly in. I am shocked to say I have seen married ladies look very much out of temper at the delinquent on such occasions, especially if he happened to be "some one we must ask"—a youth from college, or a country cousin—and I have heard the gentleman call out "dinner" to the servant before the door was closed. The French host and hostess would die rather. In a well-arranged party the butler should have a list of

the guests, so that he may know, as one after another
comes in, that he may be placing the silver dishes with hot
water in them on the table, arranging the lights, and doing
many little things that require time, and, if omitted, cause
delay.

The party being assembled, and dinner announced, the
gentleman of the house offers the lady of the highest rank
his arm, and, having previously arranged with the other
gentlemen which ladies they are to conduct, moves off
with the one he has chosen to the dinner-table, and places
her on his right hand, next to himself.

The gentleman appointed to conduct the lady of the
house almost simultaneously offers her his arm; they follow, and are followed in their turn by the whole of the
company, linked by previous arrangement.   As these various couples enter, the master of the house, already in
the dining-room, arranges where they are to sit.   Sometimes, however, and in certain houses, this is not done,
but, more gracefully I think, the party seat themselves as
they enter ; a due sacrifice to the rules of etiquette having
been made by the master and mistress of the house in their
own persons.

It is still customary, but not invariably so, as formerly,
for a lady to sit at the head of her own table.   Let us,
however, suppose her there, as being the most frequent
arrangement.

Henceforth she has nothing to do with the dinner, except
to partake of it.   In old times, the lady presiding was
expected to carve every dish before her, and to be perfect
in the art of carving.   Lady Mary Montague, presiding
at her father's table, was condemned, at fifteen, to perform

this feat whenever her father had a party. Had she lived now she need never have touched a spoon, *fork*, or knife, except those on her own plate; her lovely face might have beamed serenely on those around her; and her dawning powers of mind have been enhanced by conversation, which was in those days impossible. In the present era, whilst the hostess should, as it were, see everything that goes on, or does not go on, she should *look* at nothing, say nothing, and reserve all stricutres on failure and reproof, if needful, not until the time when guests shall have departed, but until the next day, when her servants, having recovered the fatigue of unusual exertion, will be more willing to listen without irritation and to good effect than on the previous evening.

Drinking much wine is vulgar, whether the sin be perpetrated by a duchess or a farmer's wife : all manifest self-indulgence tends to vulgarity. A lady, also, should not be ravenous at table; neither should she talk of eating or of the dishes. Whatever conversation takes place should be easy; if possible sensible, even intellectual, without pedantry. It may be personal, if with prudence; for nothing is so agreeable, for instance, as to hear public characters discussed at table; and there is a natural love of biography in the human mind that renders anecdote, without scandal, always agreeable. The conversation at dinner tables is usually carried on in an under tone, and addressed first to one neighboring gentleman, then to another. In large dinner-parties general conversation is impossible. It is only at that delightful form of social intercourse, a small party, that one may enjoy the luxury of an animated and general conversation.

It is now the custom for ladies to retire after the ice and dessert have gone round. They then retire, almost in the same order as they came, to the drawing-room. Here the province of the lady of the house is to maintain easy and cheerful conversation, and to make it, if possible, general. Her labors are often not well repaid, but, in modern times, are not of long duration.

One is tempted, however, sometimes to envy the French customs. At a Parisian dinner-party, each gentleman rises with his appointed lady neighbor, gives her his arm, and leads her into the drawing-room, where coffee comes in directly. Thus the evening begins. In some instances the gentlemen, and ladies also, soon take their leave; in others, remain till ten or eleven o'clock. But the dreary interregnum which still occurs in this country, whilst mine host is circulating the bottle below—and ladies are discussing their servants, the last tooth their baby cut, or the raging epidemic, in the drawing-room above—is unknown in the salons of Paris.

It must not be forgotten that all the comfort and part of the success of a dinner-party must depend on the previous arrangements; but the qualities which regulate a house, and the experience which is brought to bear upon the important knowledge of how to give a dinner-party, as far as the *material* part is concerned, is not in my province.

What Lord Chesterfield says is here to the purpose: "The nature of things," he remarks, "is always and everywhere the same, but the modes of them vary more or less in every country:" but good-breeding, he adds, consists in an easy and genteel conformity to them, or rather,

" the assuming of them at proper times and in proper places."

In conclusion, let us recal the advice of Napoleon the First, who duly respected the importance of dinner-parties as a social institution:

" *Tenez bonne table, et soignez les femmes.*"

CHAPTER XIII.

BALLS.

BALLS are the paradise of daughters, the purgatory of chaperons, and the Pandemonium of Paterfamilias. But when he has Arabella's ball-dresses to pay for; when mamma tells him he cannot have the brougham to-night, because of Lady Fantile's dance; when he finds the house suddenly filled with an army of upholsterer's men, the passage barricaded with cane-bottomed benches, the drawing-room pillaged of its carpet and furniture, and in course of time himself turned bodily out of his own library with no more apology than, " We want it for the tea to-night ;" when, if he goes to bed, there is that blessed—oh ! yes, blessed—horn going on one note all night long, and, if he stops up has no room to take refuge in, and must by force of circumstances appear in the ball-room among people of whom he does not know one quarter, and who will perhaps kindly put the final stroke to his misery by mistaking him for his own butler ; when Paterfam. undergoes this and more, he has no right to complain, and call it all waste of time and pure folly. Will he call it so when Arabella announces that she is engaged to the young and wealthy Sir Thysse Thatte. Bart., and that it was at one ball he met her, at another he flirted, at a third he courted. and at a fourth offered ? Will he call it so when he learns that it is the balls and parties—innocent amusements—which have kept

(378)

his son Augustus from the gaming-table, and Adolphus from *curaçoa*? Perhaps he will give them a worse epithet when they have killed Ada and worn out her mother. But then whose fault was that? *Est modus in rebus*, and balls in moderation are as different from balls in excess as gun-practice at Woolwich from gun-practice at Delhi.

There is not half enough innocent amusement in England, and, therefore, there is far too much vice. I should like to see dancing come in and drinking go out (as it would do) among our lower orders. I should like to see Clod clap his heels together on the village-green, instead of clogging his senses with bad beer at the village public-house. They do so in France, and the French are a sober race compared with the English. It would improve the health of the women and the morals of the men. But this is not my present affair. The advantage of the ball in the upper classes is, that it brings young people together for a sensible and innocent recreation, and takes them away from silly, if not bad ones, that it gives them exercise, and that the general effect of the beauty, elegance, and brilliance of a ball is to elevate rather than deprave the mind.

Balls can only be given often by the rich, but ball-goers are expected to turn ball-givers once a year at least, and your one dance, if well arranged, will cost you as much as your dinners for the whole season. It is not often then that people who have no daughters, and are too old to dance themselves, give a ball; and, as a rule, if you cannot afford to do it in good style, it is better to leave it alone. In London, however, no one will blame you for not giving a dance. The difficulty, then, is not to find balls enough to go to, but time enough to go to all.

When you have made up your mind to give a ball, and have succeeded in fixing a day when there will be no very grand affair, such as a court-ball, to take your guests away, the first thing to do is to send the invitations.

"How many shall we ask, Arabella?"

"Oh! at least two hundred, mamma. I do so like a large ball."

"Nonsense, my dear, our rooms won't hold eighty with comfort."

"Then there is the staircase."

"A pleasant prospect for late comers."

"And the hall."

"Where they will have the society of the footmen—very agreeable."

"And the conservatory," urges Arabella.

"No, my child, that is reserved for flirtations. In short, if we have more than a hundred, it will be a terrible crush."

"But, mamma, a crush is quite the fashion. I'm sure people here in London don't go to balls to dance."

"What for then, Miss Wisdom?"

"To say they have been there; to say it was a frightful crush at the Joneses; to see their neighbors, to be sure."

"And to be melted with the heat."

"Well, we can ice them, mamma."

However, Arabella is partly right. In London, and during the season, if a ball is given as a formality, and the rooms are not large, it is better to give up the hope of comfortable dancing, and have the *renommée* of a crush. All the gentlemen who failed to get into the drawing-room, and all the young ladies whose dresses were hopelessly wrecked, will execrate, but still remember you, and it is something to be remembered in London, whether well or ill. So that when you have called your guests together as close as sheep in a fold, allowed them to take an hour to climb the stairs, and half an hour to get down again, given them a supper from Gunter's, with champagne of the quality which induced impudent Brummell to ask for " some more of that cider; very good cider that," you have done the notorious if not the agreeable thing, and Mrs. Fitzjones' ball will be talked of and remembered. But there are better ways of achieving this highly desirable notoriety of three days' duration.

Any number over one hundred constitutes a " large ball," below that number it is simply " a ball," and under fifty " a dance." I have been at a ball of *ten thousand*, as large as the garrison of Paris itself, given by Madame Hausmann at the Hotel de Ville in that city, and yet, though it was not " the thing" to dance there, the rooms looked almost empty, so many and so large were they. On the other hand, I have been at the Tuileries when there was not a tenth of that number, and found the dancing confined to one little spot in the long gallery, about as large as an ordinary London drawing-room. In short, the numbers must be proportioned to the size of the rooms, with this proviso, that the more you have, the more brilliant, the fewer you have, tho more enjoyable it will be.

In making your list, you must not take in *all* your acquaintance, but only all those who are moveable—the marionettes, in fact. Middle-aged people think it a compliment to be asked to a ball about as much as the boa-constrictor in the Regent's Park would. Both he and they like to be fed, and after five-and-thirty, it is laborious not only to dance, but even to look at dancing.

"What *shall* we do for gentleman, mamma? I have counted up thirty-eight young ladies who dance, and only twenty-five partners for them."

In some places this is a question to which there is no answer but despair. Young men are at a premium in the ranks of Terpsichore as much as those of death, and they must be bribed to join by as large a bounty, in the shape of a good supper. "I shan't go to the Fitzjoneses," yawns De Boots of the Scotch Muffineers, "the champagne was undrinkable last year, and the *pâté de foie gras* tasted like kitten." How De Boots of the Muffineers comes to know the taste of kitten does not transpire.

"Well, my love," says mamma, "we must get some intimate friends to bring a young man or two."

Thereupon there is a casting up of who knows whom, and whom it would be best to commission as recruiting-sergeant. But mamma, Arabella. and the intimate *ami de la maison* may talk and write and labor. they will never make up the full war complement. and wall-flowers will flourish still. This system of "bringing a friend" is a very bad one, and should be avoided. It reminds me of a story of worthy Mrs. P—, who had Junot's house in Paris, and in its magnificent rooms gave some of the largest and most brilliant balls, but, owing to the "friend" system, very mixed. So much so that on one occasion a gentleman went up to her and told her that there was one of the swell mob present. Mrs. P—was deaf and amiable. "Dear me." she replied. "is there really? I hope he has had some supper." But the disciple of Fagan had taken care of himself; he had not only had supper, but when he had done using his fork and spoon, had, in the neatest manner, put them away in his pocket, so that the next time I went to Mrs. P—'s, I found a *mouchard* sitting near the door, behind a large book. I was asked my name and address, and doubtless my description was taken down too. I found that ladies as well as gentlemen were treated in this way.

Your best plan, therefore, is to invite only one-third more than your rooms will hold, for you may be sure that more than that number will disappoint you. The invitations should be sent out three weeks beforehand, and you need not expect answers, except from those who have an excuse for not accepting.

The requisites for an agreeable ball are good ventilation, good arrangment, a good floor, good music, a good supper, and good company. The arrangements are perhaps more important than any other item, and in this country they are little understood or greatly neglected. Yet the enjoyment of the dancers is materially increased by the brillance and elegance of the details, beauty and dress are enhanced by good lighting or proper colors, and the illusion of a fairy like scene may be brought up by judicious management, and the concealment of everything that does not strictly accord with the gaiety. In Paris, where balls, in spite of the absence of supper, are more elegant than anywhere else, a vast deal of effect and freshness is secured by the employment of shrubs, plants, and flowers, and these may be freely used without making your rooms fantastic. Thus that odious entrance from the kitchen stairs, which yawns upon the lobby of most London houses, should be concealed by a thick hedge of rhododendrons in pots; the balustrades of the staircase and gallery should be woven with evergreens, and all the fire-places should be concealed by plenty of plants in flower. In Paris, again, the musicians are unseen, and the strains of the piano, horn, flageolet, and violin proceed from behind a flowery bank, artfully raised in one corner of the ball-room.

It is a rare thing in London to find more than four or five rooms *en suite*, and often the number does nor exceed two. In the "flats" of the large French houses, you have often as many as seven or eight rooms opening one into another, and so much is the advantage of space recognized, that a bed-room even is opened at the end of the suite, if necessary. I have danced in a room where the grand bed was standing in an alcove, scarcely concealed by thin muslin curtains, and disguised with a coverlet of embroidered white satin. But in England any sacrifice should be made to secure a refreshment-room, if not a supper-room, on the same floor as the ball-room, nothing being more trying to ladies' dresses than the crush down and up the stairs. A cloak-room down stairs for the ladies, with one or two maids to assist them; a tea and coffee room, with at least two servants; and a hat-room for gentlemen, are indispensable. If the ball is a large one, numbered tickets should be given for the cloaks and hats.

Up stairs the color and lighting of the rooms is essential. The ball-room especially should be that which has the lightest paper; and if there be dark curtains, particularly red ones, they must be taken down and replaced by light ones. The best color for a ball-room is very pale yellow. The light should come from the walls, heightened by strong reflectors. Chandeliers are dangerous, and throw a downward shadow; at any rate, wax should always be replaced by globe lamps. After the Tuileries' balls, we often returned with complete epaulettes of wax-spots on our shoulders, if in moments of carelessness we had stood under the chandeliers. Gas is heating, and throws rather a sickly glare.

How can we dance well without a proper ground? It was all very well for nymphs and satyrs to "trip it on the light fantastic toe" over greensward and pebbly paths, but then they did not waltz *à deux temps*. A "carpetdance" is a bad dance, and the cloth drawn over the Kidderminster is seldom tight enough, and never so good as a floor. English people have as great a horror of taking up their carpets as Frenchmen are supposed to have of washing their necks. Probably the amount of dust which would meet their gaze is too appalling to think of. Then, again, English boards are of a wood which it is not easy to polish. Commend me to the old oak-floors, which, with a little bees'-wax, come out as dark as ebony, and help the unskilled foot to glide. However, a polished floor, whatever the wood, is always the best thing to dance on, and, if you want to give a ball, and not only a crush, you should hire a man who, with a brush under one foot, and a slipper on the other, will dance over the floor for four or five hours, till you can almost see your face in it. Above all, take care that there is not bees'-wax enough to blacken the ladies' shoes. It is the amount of rubbing which must give it the polish.

Four musicians are enough for a private ball. If the room is not large, do away with the horn; the flageolet is less noisy, and marks the time quite as well. A piano and violin form the mainstay of the band; but if the room

17

be large, a larger band may be introduced to great advan-tage. The dances should be arranged beforehand, and, for large balls you should have printed a number of double cards, containing on the one side a list of the dances; on the other, blank spaces to be filled up by the names of partners. A small pencil should be attached to each card, which should be given to each guest in the cloak-room. Every ball opens with a quadrille, followed by a waltz. The number of the dances varies generally from eighteen to twenty-four, supper making a break after the fourteenth dance. Let us suppose you have twenty-one dances; then seven of these should be quadrilles, three of which may be lancers. There should next be seven waltzes, four galops, a polka, a polka-mazurka, and some other dance.

We come at last to what some people of bad taste think the most important part,—the eating and drinking. As a first rule, it may be laid down that nothing should be *handed* in a ball. A refreshment-room is, therefore, indispensable. The ladies are to be first considered in this matter. The refreshments may be simple, comprising tea, lemonade, that detestable concoction called *negus*, iced sherbet, ices, wafers, cakes, and bonbons. In French parties they give you, towards the end of the evening, hot chocolate, and this is coming into fashion in England, and is certainly very refreshing. In the south of Germany a lady asks you to fetch her a glass of beer; in Munich, this is customary even in the court circles. There is a terrible prejudice against beer in England, but it is per-haps the best thing to drink after dancing. Fancy our pretty Misses quaffing their pint of Bass! Yet why not? In Germany and France, and now, too, in England, the favorite bonbon is a chestnut or slip of orange in a coat of candied sugar. I remember well at Munich a trick that was played on an old *geheim-rath*, who was known to have a violent passion for *oranges glacées*, and suspected of carrying them away in his pockets in large quantities. A number of young officers managed to stuff his coat-pockets with these bonbons without his discovering it, and then one of them, assuming great interest in the old gentleman, induced him to sit down for a little chat. When he got up again there was a stream of orange juice issuing from each coat-tail, and the old man pottered about quite unconscious of the amusement he excited.

The supper, of course, has a separate room, which must be well lit. Of its contents, as I am not a confectioner, I can say nothing. Two things I can say: Ice everything (in a London season) that can be conveniently iced, and let there be nothing that requires carving. The fowls and birds should, therefore, all be cut up. The supper hour in London is generally midnight, after which it goes on till the end of the ball. In England, it is usually served with much expense and display on a table, round which all the dancers stand : but in France, even at the Tuileries, it is arranged on long buffets, as in our public balls, the servants standing behind, and thus saving a vast deal of pushing about, and much trouble to the gentlemen. Another importation from France, is the custom of giving hot soup at supper, and a very good one it is. In fact, hot things are still to be desired for supper, and always will be acceptable. At a ball no one sits down to supper ; at a small dance the ladies sit, and the gentleman stand behind them. A lady should never drink more than one glass of champagne, nor a man more

than two.. There is a modern custom which saves the
pockets of ball-givers, and is most grateful to dancers,
that of giving the men bottled beer. No man of sense
will drink bad gooseberry when he can get good Bass.
The latter refreshes more, and intoxicates less; but until
we become sensible on this point, champagne will remain
as indispensable an element of the ball-supper as trifle,
tipsy-cake, and mayonnaise; which last, if made with
fish, is the best dish you can eat at this meal.

I now pass to the etiquettes of the ball-room.

In the days when bows were made down to an angle of
45°, and it took two minutes to sink and two to rise in a
curtsey, the givers of balls must have been punished for
their entertainment by a stiffness the next day quite as
trying as that of the young gentleman who has followed
the hounds for the first time in his life. As for the worthy
Préfect and Madame la Préf'ete de la Seine, they would
have been carried away lifeless with fatigue before the
half of the thousands had had their bow in the receiving-
room of the Hotel de Ville at Paris. In the present day
the muscles of the mouth are brought more into requisition, and for the time being the worst of Xantippes must
turn into an angel of amiability if she gives a ball. The
lady of the house must, in short, linger till supper-time
in the neighborhood of the door by which her guests enter
the rooms; she must have a pleasant smile for everybody;
and, if possible, she should know everybody's name, and
how many they are in family. To a large ball you ask a
great number of people with whom you have a slight acquaintance, and of course a number of gentlemen arrive
who may be your husband's or son's friend's or recruits
levied by an *ami de la maison*. To these a bow rather

more inclined than to your own friends, and a particularly
amiable smile, is necessary ; but in order to put them
quite at their ease, you should be able to come forward and
say some little polite phrase or other. " Are we not to
have the pleasure of seeing more of your party ?" perhaps
you ask, when a mamma and one daughter are announced
But if there are no more of them to come, how awkward
for you and them ! So too it is wise to avoid asking after
relations, unless you are quite sure about their existence.
What can the bereaved widower say or look, when in the
excess of your amiability you inquire " How is Mrs. — ?"
The master of the house, too, if he is not gone out of
town " on business," for that night, should be in the
neighborhood of his spouse, in order to introduce to her
any of his own recruits. The sons will hang about the
same quarter for the same purpose, but the daughters will
be otherwise occupied. It is their duty to see that the
dances are formed, and a well-bred young lady does not
dance till she has found partners for all the young ladies
or as many of them as can be supplied from the ranks of
the recruits present. Now and then you will see her dart
anxiously out upon the landing, to press into the service
those languid loungers who are sure to be hanging about
the doors. She has the right to ask a gentleman to dance
without having a previous acquaintance, but she must be
careful how she uses it. I have known a case where a
distinguished young man having declined her invitation to
dance, but being pressed by " I can't make up the Lancers
without you," somewhat reluctantly accepted, performed
his part so well, that his partner was quite *éprise* with
him, and even ventured on a little flirtation. You can
imagine her dismay, when later in the evening she saw her

charming acquaintance carrying up a pile of plates from
the kitchen to the supper-room. For the first time in her
life she had danced with an occasional waiter. The genus
wall-flower is one that grows well in every ball-room, but
a young lady, however plain, however stupid, can, if she
dances well always have some partners. The great thing
is to secure the first, who, on retiring, will say to some of
his friends, "I'll tell you who dances well: that girl in
pink, Miss A—, I advise you to get introduced to her."
The right of introducing rests mainly with the ladies and
gentlemen of the house, but a chaperon may present a
gentleman to her charge: or if you, being a man, are intimate with a young lady, you may ask her permission to
introduce some friend. It is in very bad taste to refuse
this permission. but if a lady has an insuperable objection
to the person in question. she may decline to dance altogether, or refer the applicant to her chaperon. In France.
as I have said, no introduction is needed, though English
young ladies generally expect it even at French parties.
At any rate, if a gentleman comes up to her and asks her
to dance, she must not reply, as a celebrated English
beauty once did at the Tuileries. "I have not the pleasure
of your acquaintance," by which she acquired the reputation of very bad breeding.

A young lady must be very careful how she refuses to
dance with a gentleman. Next to refusing an offer of
marriage, few things are so likely to draw upon her the
indignation of the rejected applicant. for unless a good
reason is given. he is apt to take it as evidence of a personal dislike. There is a great deal of polite (?) falsehood used on these occasions. "I am sorry that I am
engaged." "I have a slight headache, and do not intend

to dance;" but a lady should never be guilty even of a conventional lie, and if she replies very politely, asking to be excused, as she does not wish to dance ("with you," being probably her mental reservation), a man ought to be satisfied. At all events, he should never press her to dance after one refusal. The set forms which Turveydrop would give for the invitation are too much of the deportment school to be used in practice. If you know a young lady slightly, it is sufficient to say to her, "May I have the pleasure of dancing this waltz, &c. with you?" or if intimately, "Will you dance, Miss A—?" The young lady who has refused one gentleman has no right to accept another for that dance; and young ladies who do not wish to be annoyed must take care not to accept two gentlemen for the same dance. In Germany such innocent blunders often cause fatal results. Two partners arrive at the same moment to claim the fair one's hand; she vows she has not made a mistake; "was sure she was engaged to Herr A—, and not to Herr B—;" Herr B— is equally certain that she was engaged to him. The awkwardness is, that if he at once gives her up, he appears to be indifferent about it; while, if he presses his suit, he must quarrel with Herr A—, unless the damsel is clever enough to satisfy both of them; and particularly if there is an especial interest in Herr B—, he yields at last, but when the dance is over, sends a friend to Herr A—. Absurd as all this is, it is common, and I have often seen one Herr or the other walking about with a huge gash on his cheek, or his arm in a sling, a few days after a ball.

Friendship, it appears, can be let out on hire. The lady who was so very amiable to you last night, has a right to ignore your existence to-day. In fact, a ball-

room acquaintance rarely goes any farther, until you have
met at more balls than one.   In the same way a man cannot, after being introduced to a young lady to dance with,
ask her to do so more than twice in the same evening.
On the Continent, however intimate, he must never dance
twice with the same lady, that is, if she be unmarried.
Mamma would interfere, and ask his intentions if he did
so.   In England, a man of sense will select at most one
or two partners, and dance with them alternately the
whole evening.   But then he must expect comment thereupon, and a young lady who does not wish to have her
name coupled with his, will not allow him to single her
out in this manner.   However. a man may dance four or
even five times with the same partner without this risk.
On the other hand, a really well-bred man will wish to be
useful, and there are certain people whom it is imperative
on him to ask to dance—the daughters of the house, for
instance, and any young ladies whom he may know intimately; but most of all the well-bred and amiable man
will sacrifice himself to those plain, ill-dressed, dull-looking
beings who cling to the wall, unsought and despairing.
After all, he will not regret his good-nature.   The spirits
reviving at the unexpected invitation, the wall-flower will
pour out her best conversation, will dance her best. and
will show him her gratitude in some way or other.   So,
too, an amiable girl will do her best to find partners for
her wall-flower friends, even at the risk of sitting out
herself.

   The formal bow at the end of a quadrille has gradually dwindled away.   At the end of every dance you offer
you right arm to your partner (if by mistake you offer
the left, you may turn the blunder into a pretty compli-

ment, by reminding her that it is *le bras du cœur*, nearest the heart, which if not anatomically true, is at least no worse than talking of a sunset and sunrise), and walk half round the room with her. You then ask her if she will take any refreshment, and, if she accepts, you convey your precious allotment of tarlatane to the refreshment-room to be invigorated by an ice or negus, or what you will. It is judicious not to linger too long in this room, if you are engaged to some one else for the next dance. You will have the pleasure of hearing the music begin in the distant ball-room, and of reflecting that an expectant fair is sighing for you like Mariana—

> "He cometh not," she said.
> She said, "I am a-weary a-weary,
> I would I were in bed;"

which is not an unfrequent wish in some ball-rooms. A well-bred girl, too, will remember this, and always offer to return to the ball-room, however interesting the conversation.

If you are prudent you will not dance every dance, nor, in fact, much more than half the number on the list; you will then escape that hateful redness of face at the time, and that wearing fatigue the next day which are among the worst features of a ball. Again, a gentleman must remember that a ball is essentially a lady's party, and in their presence he should be gentle and delicate almost to a fault, never pushing his way, apologizing if he tread on a dress, still more so if he tears it, begging pardon for any accidental annoyance he may occasion, and addressing everybody with a smile. But quite unpardonable are those men whom one sometimes meets, who,

17*

standing in a door-way, talk and laugh as they would in a barrack or college-rooms, always coarsely, often indelicately. What must the state of their minds be if the sight of beauty, modesty, and virtue does not awe them into silence. A man, too, who strolls down the room with his head in the air, looking as if there were not a creature there worth dancing with, is an ill-bred man, so is he who looks bored; and worse than all is he who takes too much champagne.

If you are dancing with a young lady when the supper-room is opened, you must ask her if she would like to go to supper, and if she says "yes," which, in 999 cases out of 1000, she certainly will do, you must take her thither. If you are not dancing the lady of the house will probably recruit you to take in some chaperon. However little you may relish this, you must not show your disgust. In fact, no man ought to be disgusted at being able to do anything for a lady; it should be his highest privilege, but it is not—in these modern unchivalrous days—perhaps never was so. Having placed your partner then at the supper-table, if there is room there, but if not at a side-table, or even at none, you must be as active as Puck in attending to her wants, and as women take as long to settle their fancies in edibles as in love-matters, you had better at once get her something substantial, chicken, *pâté de foie gras, mayonnaise,* or what you will. Afterwards come jelly and trifle in due course.

A young lady often goes down half-a-dozen times to the supper-room—it is to be hoped not for the purpose of eating—but she should not do so with the same partner more than once. While the lady is supping you must stand by and talk to her, attending to every want,

and the most you may take yourself is a glass of champagne when you help her. You then lead her up stairs
again, and if you are not wanted there any more, you
may steal down and do a little quiet refreshment on your
own account. As long, however, as there are many ladies still at the table, you have no right to begin. Nothing marks a man here so much as gorging at supper.
Balls are meant for dancing, not eating, and unfortunately
too many young men forget this in the present day.
Lastly, be careful what you say and how you dance after
supper, even more so than before it, for if you in the
slightest way displease a young lady, she may fancy that
you have been too partial to strong fluids, and ladies
never forgive that. It would be hard on the lady of the
house if everybody leaving a large ball thought it necessary to wish her good-night. In quitting a small dance,
however, a parting bow is expected. It is then that the
pretty daughter of the house gives you that sweet smile of
which you dream afterwards in a gooseberry nightmare
of "tum-tum-tiddy-tum," and waltzes à *deux temps*,
and masses of tarlatane and bright eyes, flushed cheeks
and dewy glances. See them to-morrow, my dear fellow,
it will cure you.

I think flirtation comes under the head of morals more
than of manners; still I may be allowed to say that ball-
room flirtation being more open is less dangerous than any
other. But a young lady of taste will be careful not to
flaunt and publish her flirtation, as if to say, " See, I
have an admirer !" In the same way a prudent man will
never presume on a girl's liveliness or banter. No man
of taste ever made an offer after supper, and certainly

nine-tenths of those who have done so have regretted it
at breakfast the next morning.

Public balls are not much frequented by people of good
society, except in watering-places and country towns.
Even there a young lady should not be seen at more than
two or three in the year. County-balls, race-balls, and
hunt-balls, are generally better than common subscrip-
tion-balls. Charity-balls are an abominable anomaly.
At public balls there are generally either three or four
stewards on duty, or a professional master of ceremonies.
These gentlemen having made all the arrangements, order
the dances, and have power to change them if desirable.
They also undertake to present young men to ladies, but
it must be understood that such an introduction is only
available for *one* dance. It is better taste to ask the
steward to introduce you simply to a partner, than to
point out any lady in particular. He will probably then
ask you if you have a choice, and if not, you may be certain he will take you to an established wall-flower. Public balls are scarcely enjoyable unless you have your own
party.

As the great charm of a ball is its perfect accord and
harmony, all altercations, loud talking, &c., are doubly
ill-mannered in a ball-room. Very little suffices to disturb the peace of the whole company.

CHAPTER XIV.

MORNING AND EVENING PARTIES.

WHEN all the flower of Greece turned out at the cry of the Argive King, manned their heavy triremes and sailed away to Tenedos, do you imagine that one-fiftieth part of their number cared as much as a shield-strap for that lady of the white arms but black reputation, whom the handsomest man of his day had persuaded to "fly beyond her fate's control;" do you believe it was for fair false Helen that they resolved to sack Troy? Not a bit of it, it was only an excuse for "making a party." So, too, it was only for the party and the fun that all those helmeted, scarved, iron-cased knights, most *preux* and gallant, quitted the bowers of their lady-loves (which, to say truth, must have been rather dull in days when there were no cheap novels, no pianos, no crochet, no chess, no backgammon, and no newspapers to talk about), and trotted off to Palestine, determined to return with the scalp of a Saladin. Why, if you were to examine the consciences of nine-tenths of those same chivalrous gentlemen, you would find the motive probably made up of the following ingredients in the following proportions :—

Religion, - - -	1
Hatred of Turks, - -	2
The wish of my lady-love, -	3
Because it's the fashion, -	4
Love of bloodshed, - -	5
For the sake of the party, -	15

(397)

In other words, all the other motives together would not outbalance that prime consideration.

People will make a party for anything. "Make a party to see the sun set;" "make a party to take a walk;" "make a party to hear the nightingale;" "make a party to go to church;" "make a party to go nowhere near church, but to Hampstead Heath instead;" "make a party to ride a donkey;" "make a party to play at a new game;" "make a party to do nothing at all." There are people—very good people they think themselves too—who cannot even read their bibles without a party, and the very people who rail at balls and parties. and amusement of any kind, will most *un*ostentatiously make a party to see them give away a hundred cups of tea or fifty pinafores, which act then goes in the world by the name of "charity." I don't think the Pharisees were quite so bad as this, because if they did do their good deeds in public, they did not make a party to come and see them, unless indeed the sounding of a trumpet was the Hebrew way of sending out invitations.

However, this is not my present business. The system of gathering a little assembly to join in every pleasure. as long as it is free from ostentation and cant, only shows what sociable and sympathetic beings we are. For the real objects of these parties are not, believe me, the sunset, the walk, the nightingale's service, the donkey. the new game, and the dispensing of pinafores, but the entertainment of one another's society, so that all parties having the same ultimate aim may be governed by the same laws. I have made an exception for dinner and dances, because with many people the food and the waltz *are* the sole object. But in most other cases the excuse given for the gathering is precisely the kind of thing which could be enjoyed much more in solitude, or, at most, with one sympathetic companion. Take a pic-nic as an instance. We go miles, at a considerable outlay may be, only to enjoy some beautiful view, or to wander in some ancient ruin. Does the small gossip of the pic-nic aid us in the enjoyment of the former, or its noisy prattle hallow rather than disturb the memories of the past that haunt the latter?

So then the main difference in all kinds of parties lies in the selection of the guests, the dress they wear, and the peculiar tone of the conversation. Another great distinction lies, too, between town and country parties. Let us then divide parties under these two general heads.

Town-parties consist in conversaziones, private concerts, private theatricals, tea-parties, and matinées.

The first, which also go by the names of Receptions and "At Homes," have for principal object conversation only, so that in the selection of guests youth and beauty are less considered than talent, distinction, and fashion. An Indian prince, a great nobleman, a distinguished foreigner, or a celebrated statesman, are considered valuable attractions, but it must be a consolation to the lion-huntress to feel that if the presence of these curiosities increases the reputation of her assemblies, they do by no means add to, but rather diminish the general ease of the conversation. On the other hand, to assemble as many persons distinguished for talents or achievements as possible, must necessarily give them brilliance ; and, as I have said, the great behave better in the presence of rivals and compeers than where they are chief planets. The invitations should be sent out from a week to a fortnight beforehand. Tea must be served in a separate room, to which the guests are first conducted, and ices handed at short intervals throughout the evening. Sometimes in smaller receptions a supper is served, but this is by no means common, as from these meetings the ladies generally repair to a ball. The hour for meeting is between nine and ten, and the party breaks up before one in the morning. The lady and gentleman of the house both receive the guests, somewhere near the door of the principal room ; or if the reception is a small one, the lady joins in the conversation, and comes forward when a guest is announced. Two or three rooms must be thrown open, curiosities, good engravings, handsome books, rare miniatures, old china, photographs, stereoscopes, and so forth, laid out gracefully on the tables, and a liberal supply of ottomans, *dos à dos*, and sofas placed about in convenient positions, not, however, so as to impede a general movement about the rooms. In the larger receptions gentlemen should not sit down, and, above all, not linger close to the door, but come forward and talk sense—not ball-room chit-chat—to such people as they happen to know. Introductions are not here the order of the day, as they must be in balls, but the lady of the house will take care to introduce gentlemen to such ladies as seem to have none to talk to. On the other hand, strangers who enter your set for the first time must receive the greatest attention—the greater the stranger the greater the guest—and must be introduced to the principal people. The lady must take care to create circulation, and the guests themselves should not be pinioned to one spot or one chair.

The place occupied by music in these parties is a very

ridiculous one, because it is got up only to make a noise, and prevent people being frightened, like Robinson Crusoe, at the sound of their own voices. Sometimes a professional musician or two is introduced; sometimes young ladies are called upon to murder Italian or mouth out German; sometimes—not very often—there is some charming amateur singing, but unless the professionals are very great favorites, or the young ladies have very fine voices, or the guests—rarer still—can appreciate good melodious speaking music, the touch of the first notes is the signal for every one to find their ideas and their tongues. So far it must be confessed that the music inspires them, and the people who were stupidest before, suddenly shine out quite brilliantly; but it is curious that while the first two chords can effect this, the remainder, good or bad, is drowned and talked down in the most ungrateful manner. Nothing can be worse bred than this; and, therefore, in really good society, you will find that people know when to use their tongues and when their ears. As to the etiquette of music, it is the sole privilege of the lady of the house to ask a guest to sing or play; and when he or she *can* do so they will, if well bred, at once consent, without any palaver. A young lady must be led—poor victim—to the piano by some gentleman near at hand, who then offers to fetch her music for her; and there is one hint which I will venture to give to young ladies when they have got their music, and have *quickly* chosen their song or piece: never wait till the company is silent, do not go on playing introductory bars, and looking round as if you expected them to stop talking, for on the one hand, you will seldom succeed in making them do so; on the other, those who notice you

will think you are vain of your talents. Make up your
mind that you are to sing only for the sake of the conversation, and be consoled that those who can appreciate
your singing will draw near and listen. The gentleman
who has conducted you to the piano now stays to turn
over your pages for you; take care that he is able to follow you, or give him a sign at the proper moment, otherwise he will be turning too soon, and bring you both into
terrible confusion. The best way of giving receptions,
which cost very little, is to fix on some day of the week,
and repeat them every time it comes round. You then
issue invitations to a very much larger number than your
rooms will hold and for the whole course of receptions,
so that your friends can choose the weeks most convenient
to them. If at the first party you should only ·have a
dozen guests, do not be disheartened. If your rooms are
well lit up and well arranged, and yourself agreeable,
they will be filled to excess before the middle of the
season.

Private concerts and amateur theatricals ought to be
very good to be successful. Professionals alone should
be engaged for the former, none but real amateurs for the
latter. Both ought to be, but rarely are. followed by a
supper, since they are generally very fatiguing, if not
positively trying. In any case, refreshments and ices
should be handed between the songs and the acts. Private concerts are often given in the " morning," that is,
from two to six P. M.; in the evening their hours are
from eight to eleven. The rooms should be arranged in
the same manner as for a reception, the guests should be
seated, and as music is the avowed object. a general
silence preserved while it lasts. Between the songs the

col.versation ebbs back again, and the party takes the general form of a reception. For private theatricals, however, where there is no special theatre, and where the curtain is hung, as is most common, between the folding-doors, the audience-room must be filled with chairs and benches in rows, and, if possible, the back rows raised higher than the others. These are often removed when the performance is over, and the guests then converse, or sometimes even dance. During the acting it is rude to talk, except in a very low tone, and, be it good or bad, you would never think of hissing.

The tea-party is a much more sociable affair, and may vary in the number of guests from ten to thirty. The lighting is by ordinary lamps and candles; two rooms suffice, and tea should be either handed or set out on a side-table in one of them. The guests should be chiefly of one set, and known to one another; but if they are not so, they must be generally introduced. The ladies all sit down, and so may the gentlemen if they like, which they are, poor things, almost forbidden to do at receptions. The entertainment consists mostly of music and singing, by ladies and gentlemen present; but sometimes a few round games are got up for the torture of old bachelors like myself. If the singing is good, a tea-fight may be a pleasant thing, especially for curates and old maids; but in London it does not come under the head of "gaieties," and therefore the invitations to it must be given only a day or two before, either by word of mouth or a friendly note.

The *matinée* requires three things to make it successful, good grounds, a good band, and good weather. Money can command the first two, but, as we have no check over the clerk of the weather, *matineés* are as well left alone

in towns, where people will dress exorbitantly for everything of this kind.   However, if well arranged, and under
propitious skies, a matinée is a very good thing for Urba-
nus, who loves sunshine, flowers, and gay toilets.   The
company should be very numerous, comprising all the best
dressed people you know, for dress is everything on these
occasions.   In addition to a good brass-band, you would
do well to obtain the services of a glee club to sing in the
open air between the instrumental pieces; but then a matinée becomes a very expensive entertainment, and so, in
fact, it must be.   You invite your guests for one o'clock,
they arrive at two, and disperse in time to dress for dinner.
They content themselves with walking about, listening to
the music, and taking refreshments, or if you give it them,
a lunch, in the large marquée, which, of course, you have
had erected on the lawn.   You have no trouble with your
guests, and never dream of introducing them; you bring
them together under propitious circumstances, and they
must amuse themselves.   In matinées abroad they often
dance.   They are there very fashionable and much liked.
In these open-air parties, in large towns and their neighborhood, people who do not know one another remain in
that condition; they are rarely, if ever, introduced, and
they never dream of speaking to one another without an
introduction.   Very different, and much more sensible, is
the foreign custom.

For these town-parties, there are one or two general
rules: The hostess should not be too *empressé* nor bust-
ling in her welcome, she should receive every one alike
with amiable dignity, and above all, if she expects a lion
or a grandee, should dismiss him from her thoughts till
he comes, and then make no difference in his reception to

that of the other guests. If she does make a distinction, the latter will smile cynically at her toadyism, and contrast their own reception with that of "the favored guest." To make up for this restraint on her enthusiasm, she is not obliged to know much about the domestic affairs of her guests. In good company of this kind, the babies and nurserymaids, the son at the Cape, and the daughter in India, are forgotten for the time, or reserved for the smaller tea-party. In the conversazioni and receptions, you will hear none but public subjects,—every one's property—brought on the *tapis*. This knot you take for statesmen, for as you pass, each one of them is prophesying, with a shrewd look, what next step the Emperor will take. No, sir, they are simply fathers of families. Here you are certain you have lighted on a batch of critics, male and female; could ever any one else show such venom in the discussion of the last celebrated book? Nothing of the kind; critics are doves in company, and these are only educated men, with as little actual connexion with literature as a sailor on the mizenyard. Then these men who are scientifically discussing some recent discovery, and hanging profoundly over the fate of some engineering enterprise, are merely thinkers, by no means professional; while those who talk of Lord John as an intimate chum, and Pam. as a man they could clap on the shoulder, are not M. P.'s, but only club-loungers. Even the gossip takes a public character, and the scandal is about people known to the whole world of fashion. Then, again, the manner of the guests is calm and easy; there is no necessity to create mirth, the laughter is quiet, even the wit is received with a smile, and discussions are carried on with interest but not with excitement. All the company too, is for the time on an equality, and it is bad taste to recognize a man's rank in a marked manner. Precedence is best laid aside, and the curate may, if he likes, pass out of·the room before the bishop. In short, the reception is a kind of evening lounge.

Very different is the character of country-parties. If they are more sociable and friendly, because almost everybody is known to one another, if there is less formality and display about them, there is also less equality. If it is not necessary to light your rooms brilliantly, and secure the services of professional singers. in short, to supply some particular attraction, it is incumbent to bow to the local position held by each guest. Not indeed that this is good style, but that it is expected by people who very often have little more than their position to recommend them. The deputy-lieutenant may be a much duller man than the small squire, but in his own county he would take it very ill if you did not show him more attention than to the other. The vicar may. and often is far less agreeable than the curate, but the latter would never dream of making a move to go before the stately incumbent had risen. Then, too, the conversation always verges on local and rural topics. The two squires talk of crops, game, boundaries, and magisterial questions, and find them far more interesting than the fate of Europe. Their wives discuss the flower-show. the hunt-ball, the return of some family to the neighborhood. The young people get a step farther in year-long flirtations, and discuss with more or less acerbity the engagements of their mutual friends. In short, people. rather than things, are the themes of interest, and a stranger in a country-party finds himself almost a foreigner in the land. And woe to him if he does not know by what title your nearest pack of hounds is called, or is ignorant of the noble sport of hunting, for, heavy-headed after their huge dinners, he will find most of the gentlemen unable to exert their brains farther than to re-call "that splendid run," or speculate on whether the next "master" will be a light or a heavy weight.

However, in country-parties, the strangers in the land receive as a rule the greatest attention, and if you, coming from town, find the company heavy, and the conversation narrow, you will at least have the consolation of infusing new spirit into, and quickening the movement, of clogged brains.

Country-parties consist chiefly of small dances which are not balls; tea-parties; private fêtes, which are much the same as the matinées already described; and pic-nics. Sociability and easy mirth is the main feature in all of them. As you are among people whom you know for the most part, you may be more familiar in your general manners, and to be agreeable, you are expected to be merry, humorous, and ready for anything that may be proposed. On the other hand, as prejudices are always greater in proportion to the narrowness of the mind, and are some-times especially deep-rooted in the squires and clergymen whom you meet in these gatherings, you must be very careful how you approach the topics which most interest them. I have known a whole party, at one moment full of merriment and laughter, suddenly cast into the deepest gloom of horror and dismay, by the innocent allusion of a stranger to "M. B." waistcoats, the rector who was present being high-church. On the same principle it is wise to avoid speaking much of the church itself, the schools, the dispensary, the preserves, the poor, and so

forth, of. the village, as country people are somewhat
given to making these subjects matters for serious difference, and it is a rare case for the squire and the clergyman to be perfectly agreed on all points where their supposed rights can possibly clash.   I have known a village
divided into a deadly feud for ten years by nothing but
the pews in the church—one party wishing to keep them,
and another to pull them down; and, though these re-
ligious-minded people met perhaps once a month at various tea-parties and dinners, the church was never spoken
of, and a stranger who might have unconsciously mentioned the pews therein, would have thrown in a firebrand
which would have lit up the whole parish.

On entering a country party, you at once seek out the
lady of the house, and shake hands with her.   The same
process is then performed with those members of the
family whom you know, and any other of your acquaintance present.   In taking leave the same process is repeated, and a simple bow would generally be considered as an
impoliteness.   The invitations to these parties partake of
the same sociable character, and are made by friendly
notes sent a few days beforehand, or even on the very day
itself.   You have not the same liberty of declining them
as in town, nor can you have recourse to the polite formu-
la of a "previous engagement, since everybody knows
what is going on in the neighborhood, and who is to be
at any party.   You must therefore find a good excuse or
go.   For my part, I think we should be better Chris-
tians, and just as friendly, if we stated our real reasons:
"I regret that I have not the time to spare," "I do not
feel inclined for society," or, "I have no dress for the
occasion."   Such replies might create a little surprise

but people must admire their candor, and everybody could
sympathize with the writer's feelings. At any rate, you
must avoid a sneer such as that given by a too candid lady to a clergyman's wife who had invited her to a quiet
little discussion of muffins on Shrove Tuesday. "I regret," she wrote, "that I shall be unable to accept your
invitation, as the near approach of Lent would preclude
my joining in any festivities."

Country hours, again, are much earlier than those in
town. Except at great houses, where the dinner hour is
seven, eight o'clock is the usual time for a tea-party to
begin, and before twelve the last guest departs. It is necessary to be punctual in the country, whatever you may
be in town; and it would be considered as an unwarrantable assumption of fashion to arrive an hour after the
time stated in the invitation.

Tea is handed in the drawing-room, or, if the party be
a small one, so arranged that all may sit round. In the
latter case the tea-table must be plenteously spread with
cakes, fruit, &c. &c. Appetites flourish in the free air
of hills and meadows, and as a rule, country parties have
more of the feeding system about them than those of town.
Thus, unless dinner has been at a late hour, it is usual to
have a supper laid out, or at least sandwiches, jellies, and
trifle at a side-table. This, I must say, is a more agreeable feature of country entertainments than that of round
games. At these, however, you must not look bored;
you must really for the time believe yourself a child
again, allow yourself to be amused, and enter heart and
soul into it. Endeavor by every means in your power
to add to the general hilarity; talk without restraint, enter into innocent rivalry with the young ladies; or, if

18

one of them yourself, challenge the most youthful, especially the shy, of the other sex. You must find something to laugh at in the merest trifle, but never roar or
shriek. Never claim your winnings, but if they are
offered you must take them, except from a young lady,
and from her on no consideration.

While we are melting here under the dog-star, and
crushing up crowded staircases, and into ovens of rooms
in the tightest dress that is worn, our country cousins are
really enjoyiug themselves. They are now having tea
out on the lawn, with *bona fide* cream to it too, none of
our miserable delusions of calves' brains (beautiful satire
on those who credulously swallow them) or chalk and
water. Then when tea is done, they are positively going
to dance here on the lawn, or there in that large empty
out-house, resolved that nothing shall induce them to go
into that house again till night ; and if they do not dance,
they bring out every chair that is in it, and sitting round,
play at hunt-the-ring, post, turning the trencher, or Blind
Man's Buff. What dear children they are ! how pleasant
to see the old gentlemen dragged in by the young girls,
and made to play *nolentes volentes !* how charming the
laughter of these merry maidens, and the playful flirtation of the sturdy youths, who all day long have been
carrying a gun or breaking a new horse in ! Well, well,
if there is beauty enough to make us bless the excitement
which brings the color to some lovely cheek,—if the
young men can really help looking bored, and the old
ones sham delight (as we old ones can, let me tell you,
sir), why, then, these out-door gaieties may be fresh and
reviving and cheering to us dusty, withered, smoke-dried
townsmen. But then where is conversation ? Swamped

in *badinage* which, if I am not a young lover, I cannot possibly pump up. And where is that flow of thought and diversity of imagination which makes one hour with a clever man or a *femme d'esprit* worth twenty-four in the presence of a mere beauty and animal spirits? Not there.

So, then, they are matters of taste, these little parties, but not so the etiquette they require. You must be gay, you must laugh and chuckle and all that, but you must not overdo it; you must not let your merriment carry you away. In out-door games especially, you must be careful not to romp, not to rush and tear about, nor be boisterously merry. It may be difficult to steer between the Scylla of dullness and the Charybdis of romping, but you must always remember what dear fragile things the ladies are, and treat them tenderly. These games are, in fact, a severe test of politeness, grace, and delicacy, and if I wanted to discover your title to the name of gentleman or lady, I should set you to play at post or hunt-the-ring, or what not of child's sport.

Lastly, as to pic-nics, they are no longer the cheery gatherings of other days, when each person brought his quantum, and when on opening the baskets there were found to be three pigeon-pies but no bread, four contributions of mustard but no salt, dozens of wine but no beer, and so on. The only thing you are asked to bring in the present day is your very best spirits; and everybody is expected to contribute these, for you cannot have too much of them. A castle, a church, or something to see, about which to create an interest, is necessary to a successful pic-nic, much more so than champagne, which it is perhaps *safer* not to have, though it is always expected.

Servants ought, if possible, to be dispensed with, and a
free flow of the easiest merriment, not *free* in itself, it
will be understood, should be allowed and encouraged.

The collation, cold of course, is generally the first object after arriving at the rendezvous. It is of necessity
somewhat rough, for these same pic-nics are the happy
occasions when people *try* to forget that they are highly
civilized, but are scarcely ever allowed to do so. However, nothing is more justly ridiculous than that people
who come out to play the rustic should be accompanied by
a bevy of Mercuries, and that while we attempt to imitate
the simplicity of rural dryad life, spreading our viands
beneath the shady trees, we should have some half-dozen
stately acolytes of fashion moving about us with all the
solemnity of a London dinner-party. The servants then
should be driven away *à force d'armes*, and the gentlemen take their place. Then see how immensely it increases the general hilarity to watch Fitzboots of the
Muffineers sent about by the pretty misses, made of use
for the first time in his life, and with his hands so full
that he cannot even stroke out his splendid whiskers.

Certainly the barriers of society ought to be broken
down on these occasions. Everybody should be perfectly
at his ease, and if the people are really well-bred, the
liberty thus given will not be the least abused. A man
who drinks too much champagne, or a young lady who
strolls away for a couple of hours with a young man
among the ruins or in the wood, should scarcely be asked
to join a second pic-nic. Then, too, free as they are, gay,
laughing, and careless, they should not descend to noisy
romping. There ought to be a fair sprinkling of chaperons and elderly people, not to damp the gaiety but to

restrain the carelessness of the younger ones. After all, let youth be youth, and let it have its fling. If it be really innocent and well brought up, Miss Etiquette, prim old maid, will have nothing to say ; if otherwise, then she may preach in vain at a carnival. If our spirits are good (and I feel quite young again in talking of these things) let us enjoy them to the fullest, and be as silly and as wild as the youngest. Never shoot a skylark while soaring ; never curb young mirth in its proper enjoyment.

CHAPTER XV.

AT a time when our feelings are or ought to be most sus-
ceptible, when the happiness or misery of a condition in
which there is no medium begins, we are surrounded with
forms and etiquettes which rise before the unwary like
spectres, and which even the most rigid ceremonialists
regard with a sort of dread.

Were it not, however, for these forms, and for this
necessity of being *en règle*, there might, on the solemni-
zation of marriage, be confusion, forgetfulness, and even—
speak it not aloud—irritation among the parties most intimately concerned. Excitement might ruin all. Without a definite programme, the old maids of the family
would be thrusting in advice. The aged chronicler of
past events, or grandmother by the fireside. would have
it all her way; the venerable bachelor in tights, with his
blue coat and metal buttons, might throw everything into
confusion by his suggestions. It is well that we are independent of all these interfering advisers; that there is
no necessity to appeal to them. Precedent has arranged
it all; we have only to put in or understand what that
stern authority has laid down; how it has been varied by
modern changes: and we must just shape our course
boldly. " Boldly?" But there is much to be done before we come to that. First, there is the offer to be

(414)

made. Well may a man who contemplates such a step say to himself, with Dryden,

" These are the realms of everlasting fate ;"

for, in truth, on marriage one's wellbeing not only here but even hereafter mainly depends. But it is not on this bearing of the subject that we wish to enter, contenting ourselves with a quotation from the *Spectator :*

" It requires more virtues to make a good husband or wife, than what go to the finishing any the most shining character whatsoever."

England is distinguished from most of the continental countries by the system of forming engagements, and the mode in which they are carried on until terminated by marriage.

In France, an engagement is an affair of negotiation and business ; and the system in this respect greatly resembles the practice in England. on similar occasions, a hundred and fifty or two hundred years ago, or even later. France is the most unchanging country in the world in her habits and domestic institutions, and foremost among these is her *" Marriage de convenance,"* or *" Marriage de raison."*

It is thus brought about. So soon as a young girl quits the school or convent where she has been educated, her friends cast about for a suitable *parti.* Most parents in France take care, so soon as a daughter is born, to put aside a sum of money for her " *dot,*" as they well know that whatever may be her attractions, *that* is indispensable in order to be married. They are ever on the look out for a youth with at least an equal fortune, or more ; or, if they are rich, for title, which is deemed

tantamount to fortune; even the power of writing those
two little letters *De* before your name has some value in
the marriage contract. Having satisfied themselves they
thus address the young lady:—"It is now time for you
to be married; I know of an eligible match; you can see
the gentleman, either at such a ball or (if he is serious)
at church. I do not ask you to take him if his appearance is positively disagreeable to you; if so. we will look
out for some one else."

As a matter of custom, the young lady answers that the
will of her parents is hers; she consents to take a survey
of him to whom her destiny is to be entrusted; and let
us presume that he is accepted, though it does not follow,
and sometimes it takes several months to look out, as it
does for other matters, a house, or a place, or a pair of
horses. However, she consents; a formal introduction
takes place; the *promis* calls in full dress to see his future wife; they are only just to speak to each other, and
those few unmeaning words are spoken in the presence of
the bride-elect's mother; for the French think it most
indiscreet to allow the affections of a girl to be interested
before marriage, lest during the arrangements for the
contract all should be broken off. If she has no dislike,
it is enough; never for an instant are the engaged couple
left alone, and in very few cases do they go up to the altar
with more than a few weeks' acquaintance, and usually
with less. The whole matter is then arranged by nota-
ries, who squabble over the marriage-contract, and get all
they can for their clients.

The contract is usually signed in France on the day
before the marriage, when all is considered safe; the religious portion of their bond takes place in the church, and

then the two young creatures are left together to understand each other if they can, and to love each other if
they will; if not they must content themselves with what
is termed, *un ménage de Paris.*

In England formerly much the same system prevailed.
A boy of fourteen, before going on his travels, was con-
tracted to a girl of eleven, selected as his future wife by
parents or guardians; he came back after the *grande
tour* to fulfil the engagement. But by law it was imperative that forty days should at least pass between the
contract and the marriage; during which dreary interval
the couple, leashed together like two young greyhounds,
would have time to think of the future. In France, the
perilous period of reflection is not allowed. " I really am
so glad we are to take a journey," said a young French
lady to her friends ; " I shall thus get to know something
about my husband; he is quite a stranger to me." Some
striking instances of the *Marriage de convenance* being
infringed on, have lately occurred in France. The late
Monsieur de Tocqueville maried for love, after a. five
years' engagement. Guizot, probably influenced by his
acquaintance with England, gave his daughters liberty to
choose for themselves, and they married for *love**—" a
very indelicate proceeding," remarked a French com-
tesse of the old *régime,* when speaking of this arrangement.

Nothing can be more opposed to all this than our English system. We are so tenacious of the freedom of choice,
that even persuasion is thought criminal.

In France negotiations are often commenced on the la-

---

* Two brothers, named *De Witte.*

dy's side ; in England, never. Even too encouraging a
manner, even the ordinary attentions of civility, are occa
sionally a matter of reproach. We English are jealous
of the delicacy of that sacred bond, which we presume to
hope is to spring out of mutual affection. It is not here
our province to inquire what are the causes that have so
sullied the marriage tie in England ; what are the reasons
that it seldom holds out all that it promises ; we have only
to treat of the rules and etiquettes which preface the
union. A gentleman who, from whatever motives, has
made up his mind to marry, may set about it in two ways.
He may propose by letter or in words. The customs of
English society imply the necessity of a sufficient knowledge of the lady to be addressed. This, even in this
country, is a difficult point to be attained ; and, after all,
cannot be calculated by time, since, in large cities, you
may know people a year, and yet be comparative strangers ; and, meeting them in the country, may become intimate in a week.

Having made up his mind, the gentleman offers—wisely,
if he can in speech. Letters are seldom expressive of
what really passes in the mind of man ; or, if expressive,
seem foolish, since deep feelings are liable to exaggeration.
Every written word may be the theme of cavil. Study.
care, which avail in every other species of composition.
are death to the lover's effusion. A few sentences, spoken
in earnest, and broken by emotion, are more eloquent than
pages of sentiment. both to parent and daughter. Let
him, however, speak and be accepted. He is in that case
instantly taken into the intimacy of his adopted relatives.
Such is the notion of English honor, that the engaged
couple are henceforth allowed to be frequently alone to-

gether, in walking and at home. If there be no known obstacle to the engagement, the gentlemen and lady are mutually introduced to the respective relatives of each. It is for the gentleman's family to call first ; for him to make the first present ; and this should be done as soon as possible after the offer has been accepted. It is a sort of seal put upon the affair. The absence of presents is thought to imply want of earnestness in the matter. This present generally consists of some personal ornament, say, a ring, and should be handsome, but not so handsome as that made for the wedding-day. During the period that elapses before the marriage, the betrothed man should conduct himself with peculiar deference to the lady's family and friends, even if beneath his own station. It is often said : " I marry such a lady, but I do not mean to marry her whole family." This disrespectful pleasantry has something in it so cold, so selfish, that even if the lady's family be disagreeable, there is a total absence of delicate feeling to her in thus speaking of those nearest to her. To her parents especially, the conduct of the betrothed man should be respectful ; to her sisters kind, without familiarity ; to her brothers, every evidence of good-will should be testified. In making every provision for the future, in regard to settlements, allowance for dress, &c., the *extent* of liberality convenient should be the spirit of all arrangements. Perfect candor as to his own affairs, respectful consideration for those of the family he is about to enter, mark a true gentleman.

In France, however gay and even blameable a man may have been before his betrothal, he conducts himself with the utmost propriety after that event. A sense of what is due to a lady should repress all habits unpleasant to her: smoking, if disagreeable; frequenting places of amusement without her; or paying attention to other women. In this respect, indeed, the sense of honor should lead a man to be as scrupulous when his future wife is absent as when she is present, if not more so. These rules of conduct apply in some respects to ladies also. Nothing is so disgusting or unpromising for the future as the flirtations which engaged young ladies permit themselves to carry on after they have pledged themselves to one person alone. This display of bad taste and vanity often leads to serious unhappiness, and the impropriety, if not folly, should be strongly pointed out to the young lady herself.

The attitude assumed by a flirt is often the impulse of folly more than of boldness. It is agreeable to her vanity, she finds, to excite jealousy, and to show her power. Even if the rash and transient triumph produce no lasting effect on the peace of mind before marriage, it is often recalled with bitterness after marriage by him who was then a slave, but is now a master.

In equally bad taste is exclusiveness. The devotions of two engaged persons should be reserved for the *tête-à-tête*, and women are generally in fault when it is otherwise. They like to exhibit their conquest; they cannot dispense with attentions; they forget that the demonstration of any peculiar condition of things in society must make some one uncomfortable; the young lady is uncomfortable because she is not equally happy; the young man detests what he calls nonsense; the old think there is a time for all things. All sitting apart, therefore, and peculiar displays, are in bad taste; I am inclined to think that they often accompany insincerity, and that the truest

affections are those which are reserved for the genuine
and heartfelt intimacy of private interviews. At the same
time, the airs of indifference and avoidance should be
equally guarded against; since, however strong a mutual
attachment may be, such a line of conduct is apt need-
lessly to mislead others, and so produce mischief. True
feeling, and a ladylike consideration for others, a point in
which the present generation essentially fails, are the best
guides for steering between the extremes of demonstration on the one hand, and of frigidity on the other.

During the arrangement of pecuniary matters, a young
lady should endeavor to understand what is going on, receiving it in a right spirit. If she has fortune, she
should, in all points left to her, be generous and confiding,
at the same time prudent. Many a man, she should remember, may abound in excellent qualities, and yet be
improvident. He may mean to do well, yet have a passion for building; he may be the very soul of good nature, yet fond of the gaming-table; he may have no
wrong propensities of that sort, and yet have a confused
notion of accounts, and be one of those men who muddle
away a great deal of money no one knows how; or he
may be a too strict economist, a man who takes too good
care of the pence, till he tires your very life out about an
extra queen's-head; or he may be facile or weakly good-
natured, and have a friend who preys on him, and for
whom he is disposed to become security. Finally, the
beloved Charles, Henry, or Reginald may have none of
these propensities, but may chance to be an honest merchant, or a tradesman, with all his floating capital in
business, and a consequent risk of being one day rich, the
next a pauper.

Upon every account, therefore, it is desirable for a young lady to have a settlement on her; and she should not, from a weak spirit of romance, oppose her friends who advise it, since it is for her husband's advantage as well as her own. By making a settlement there is always a fund which cannot be touched—a something, however small, as a provision for a wife and children; and whether she have fortune or not, this ought to be made. An allowance for dress should also be arranged; and this should be administered in such a way that a wife should not have to ask for it at inconvenient hours, and thus irritate her husband.

Every preliminary being settled, there remains nothing except to fix the marriage day, a point always left to the lady to advance; and next to settle how the ceremonial is to be performed is the subject of consideration.

Marriage by banns is confined to the poorer classes; and a license is generally obtained by those who aspire to the " habits of *good society.*" It is within the recollection of many, even middle-aged persons, that the higher classes were, some twenty years ago, married only by special license—a process costing about £50 instead of £5: and therefore supposed by our commercial country especially to denote good society. Special licenses have, however, become unfashionable. They were obtained chiefly on account of their enabling persons to be married at any hour, whereas the canon prescribes the forenoon: after mid-day it is illegal to celebrate a marriage. In some instances, during the Crimean war, special licenses were resorted to to unite couples—when the bridegroom-elect had been ordered off, and felt, with his bride, that it were happier for both to belong to each other even in death. But the ordinary couples walk up to the altars of their respective parish churches.

It is to be lamented that previously to so solemn a ceremony, the thoughts of the lady concerned must necessarily be engaged for some time upon her *trousseau*. The *trousseau* consists, in this country, of all the habiliments necessary for a lady's use for the first two or three years of her married life; like every other outfit there are always a number of articles introduced into it that are next to useless, and are only calculated for the vain-glory of the ostentatious. A *trousseau* may, in quiet life, be formed upon so low a sum as £60 or £70; it seldom costs, however, less than £100, and often mounts up to £500. By which useless extravagance a mass of things that soon cease to be fashionable, or that wear out from being laid by, is accumulated.

The *trousseau* being completed, and the day fixed, it becomes necessary to select the bridesmaids and the bride-groom's man, and to invite the guests.

The bridesmaids are from two to eight in number. It is ridiculous to have many, as the real intention of the bridesmaid is, that she should act as a witness of the marriage. It is, however, thought a compliment to include the bride's sisters and those of the bridegroom's relations and intimate friends, in case sisters do not exist.

When a bride is young the bridesmaids should be young: but it is absurd to see a "single woman of a certain age," or a widow, surrounded by blooming girls, making her look plain and foolish. For them the discreet woman of thirty-five is more suitable as a bridesmaid. Custom decides that the bridesmaids should be spinsters, but there is no legal objection to a married woman being a bridesmaid should it be necessary, as it might be abroad, or at sea, or where ladies are few in number. Great care should be taken not to give offence in the choice of bridesmaids by a preference, which is always in bad taste on momentous occasions.

The guests at the wedding should be selected with similar attention to what is right and kind, with consideration to those who have a claim on us, not only to what we ourselves prefer.

In London, for a great wedding breakfast, it is customary to send out printed cards from the parents or guardians from whose house the young lady is to be married.

Early in the day, before eleven, the bride should be dressed, taking breakfast in her own room. In England we load a bride with lace flounces on a rich silk, and even sometimes with ornaments. In France it is always remembered, with better taste, that when a young lady goes up to the altar, she is " *encore jeune fille ;*" her dress, therefore, is exquisitely simple ; a dress of tulle over white silk, a long wide veil of white tulle, going down to the very feet, a wreath of maiden-blush-roses interspersed with orange flowers. This is the usual costume of a French bride of rank, or in the middle classes equally. In England, however, one must conform to the established custom, although it is much to be wished that in the classes who can set the example, the French usage should be adopted. A lace dress over silk is generally worn in England. The lace should be of the finest quality. Brussels or Honiton is the most delicate and becoming : the veil should be of the same sort of lace as the dress. A wreath of roses and orange flowers is worn round the head, not confining the veil. The silk ought to be plain ; glacé, not

moiré, if the bride be young, as the latter is too heavy ;
if she is no longer young, nothing is so becoming as moiré
silk, either white or silver grey. Widows and ladies not
young are usually married in bonnets, which should be of
the most elegant description, trimmed with flowers or
feathers, according to the taste of the wearer.

The gentleman's dress should differ little from his full
morning costume. The days are gone by when gentlemen
were married—as a recently deceased friend of mine was
—in white satin breeches and waistcoat. In these days
men show less joy in their attire at the fond consummation
of their hopes, and more in their faces. A dark-blue
frock-coat—black being superstitiously considered ominous
—a white waistcoat, and a pair of light trousers, suffice
for the " happy man." The neck-tie also should be light
and simple. Polished boots are not amiss, though plain
ones are better. The gloves must be as white as the linen.
Both are typical—for in these days types are as important
as under the Hebrew lawgivers—of the purity of mind
and heart which are supposed to exist in their wearer.
Eheu ! after all, he cannot be too well dressed, for the
more gay he is the greater the compliment to his bride.
Flowers in the button-hole and a smile on the face show
the bridegroom to be really a " happy man."

As soon as the carriages are at the door, those bridesmaids, who happen to be in the house, and the other
members of the family set off first. The bride goes last,
with her father and mother, or with her mother alone, and
the brother or relative who is to represent her father in
case of death or absence. The bridegroom, his friend, or
bridegroom's man, and the bridesmaids ought to be waiting
in the church. The father of the bride gives her his arm,

and leads her to the altar. Here her bridesmaids stand near her, as arranged by the clerk, and the bridegroom takes his appointed place.

It is a good thing for the bridegroom's man to distribute the different fees to the clergyman or clergymen, the clerk, and pew-opener, before the arrival of the bride, as it prevents confusion afterwards.

The bride stands to the left of the bridegroom, and takes the glove off her right hand, whilst he takes his glove off his right hand. The bride gives her glove to the bridesmaid to hold, and sometimes to keep, as a good omen.

The service then begins. During the recital, it is certainly a matter of feeling how the parties concerned should behave ; but if tears can be restrained, and a quiet modesty in the lady displayed, and her emotions subdued, it adds much to the gratification of others, and saves a few pangs to the parents from whom she is to part.

It should be remembered that this is but the closing scene of a drama of some duration—first the offer, then the consent and engagement. In most cases the marriage has been preceded by acts which have stamped the whole with certainty, although we do not adopt the contract system of our forefathers, and although no event in this life can be certain.

I have omitted the mention of the bouquet, because it seems to me always an awkward addition to the bride, and that it should be presented afterwards on her return to the breakfast. Gardenias, if in season, white azalia, or even camellias, with very little orange flowers, form the bridal bouquet. The bridesmaids are dressed, on this occasion, so as to complete the picture with effect. When there are six or eight, it is usual for three of them to dress in one color, and three in another. At some of the most fashionable weddings in London, the bridesmaids wear veils—these are usually of net or tulle : white tarlatan dresses, over muslin or beautifully-worked dresses, are much worn, with colors introduced—pink or blue, and scarves of those colors ; and white bonnets, if bonnets are worn, trimmed with flowers to correspond. These should be simple, but the flowers as natural as possible, and of the finest quality. The bouquets of the bridesmaids should be of mixed flowers. These they may have at church, but the present custom is for the gentlemen of the house to present them on their return home, previous to the wedding breakfast.

The register is then signed. The bride quits the church first with the bridegroom, and gets into his carriage, and the father and mother, bridesmaids, and bridegroom's man, follow in order in their own.

The breakfast is arranged on one or more tables, and is generally provided by a confectioner when expense is not an object.

Flowers, skilfully arranged in fine Bohemian glass, or in *epergnes* composed of silver, with glass-dishes, are very ornamental on each side of the wedding-cake, which stands in the centre. When the breakfast is sent from a confectioner's, or is arranged in the house by a professed cook, the wedding-cake is richly ornamented with flowers, in sugar, and a knot of orange-flowers at the top. At each end of the table are tea and coffee. Soup is sometimes handed. Generally the viands are cold, consisting of poultry or game, lobster-salads, chicken or fish à *la Mayornaisses ;* hams, tongues, potted-meats, prawns, and game-pies ; raisins, savory jellies, sweets of every description—all cold. Ice is afterwards handed, and, before the healths are drunk, the wedding-cake is cut by the nearest gentleman and handed round.

The father then proposes the health of the bride and bridegroom. The latter is expected to answer, and to propose the bridegroom's man. The bridegroom's man returns thanks, and pledges the bridesmaids, who answer through the bridegroom. All other toasts are optional, but it is *de rigueur* that the health of the clergyman or clergymen who tied the knot, if present, should be drunk.

After these ceremonials have been duly performed, and ample justice has been done to the breakfast, the bride retires, and the company usually take leave of her in the drawing room and depart.

It must be borne in mind that the wedding-breakfast is not a *dinner*, and that the gentlemen do not stay behind to take wine when the party breaks up and the ladies go up stairs.

A few words before this sometimes gay, sometimes sad scene is dismissed.

The good sense of several personages in the higher ranks has broken through the customary appearance of the bride at the breakfast, or indeed if she breakfast at all. In France. the friends assembled to witness a wedding do not follow the bride home. A ball or soiree generally follows in the evening. Most people, one would suppose, would be gladly released from the unnatural repast at an unusual hour ; the headache that makes the rest of the day miserable ; the hurry of the morning : the lassitude of the afternoon ; the tearful, stumbling speeches of " dear papa" after champagne ; the modest, shy, broken sentences of the victimized bridegroom; the extremely critical situation of his bachelor friend, expected to be in love with all the bridesmaids; the sighs of the mother, and prognostics of maiden aunts; the heat, the disgust to those articles which look so well by candlelight, but do not bear daylight—creams, whips, jellies, and all that tribe of poisons; and, worst of all, the vast expense to those who pay, and slight degree of pleasure to those who do not—these are among the miseries of the wedding-breakfast.

Then the peculiar situation of the bride, tricked out with finery like the *bœuf-gras* on Shrove-Tuesday, every one staring at her to see how she looks; her sensitive nature all excited by the past solemnity; her inmost feelings crushed or raked up, as may be, by congratulations. To subject a lady to such torture seems an act of cruelty in cold blood. Suppose her joy is too great for utterance, that there has been opposition in delay, why stick her up on a pedestal, so that all may read the emotions of that throbbing heart beneath its encasement of Brussels lace? Suppose that heart does not go along with the joy, and the compliments and the hopes of ever-constant felicity; " let the stricken deer go weep ;" do not parade what now had better be forgotten. To some heart in that over-dressed assembly of smiling friends there will be a touch, in whatever is said, to give pain ; on occasions also where the feelings form the *actual* theme, the less said the better.

The bride has, however, retired, and we will follow. Her travelling-dress is now to be assumed. This should be *good* in quality, but plain, like a handsome dress for morning calls. An elegant bonnet, not too plain, a handsome shawl or mantle, and colored gloves, form the suitable costume, of which it is impossible to define the component parts, but we merely recommend that the colors of the dress, and shawl, and bonnet, should as nearly as possible assimilate; that the style should be of the very best, so that the impression left may be suitable, agreeable and elegant.

One more word about fees to servants. These form a very varying point on a marriage, and depend on the condition in life of the parties. A considerable sum is expected from a nobleman, or a commoner of large fortune, but a much more modest calculation for a professional man, or a son whose father is still living, and who receives merely an allowance to enable him to marry.

Presents are usual, first from the bridegroom to the bridesmaids. These generally consist of jewelry, the device of which should be unique or quaint, the article more elegant than massive. The female servants of the family, more especially servants who have lived many years in their place, also expect presents, such as gowns or shawls; or to a very valued personal attendant or housekeeper, a watch. But on such points discretion must suggest, and liberality measure out the *largesse of* the gift.

CHAPTER XVI.

FIRST let us consider who are entitled to this honor, since there are regulations on the point which it is both unwise and ill-bred to overlook.

It is almost useless to refer to the nobility, their wives and daughters, who are of course eligible for presentation, as are all persons of title of *good character* in society.

The wives and daughters of the clergy, of military and naval officers, of physicians and barristers, can be presented. These are the aristocratic professions; but the wives and daughters of general practitioners and of solicitors are not entitled to a presentation. The wives and daughters of merchants, or of men in business (excepting bankers), are not entitled to presentation. Nevertheless, though many ladies of this class were refused presentation early in this reign, it is certain that many have since been presented, whether by accident, or by a system of making the Queen more accessible, does not appear.

No *divorcée*, nor lady married, after having lived with her husband or with any one else before her marriage, can be received, although probably many upon whose conduct rests some stain less notorious *are* presented. The late Queen Adelaide felt the insult very severely, when the *ci-devant* cook-maid, of no good repute but a countess by marriage, was brought into the presence-chamber. Queen

Adelaide, it is said, could with difficulty restrain tears of vexation. The countess's name was called out in vain. The Queen turned on one side, and suffered her to pass on unheeded, the King simply bowing to her ladyship as she passed on. At the same time, the Dowager-Countess of Essex, once a public singer, but highly respectable, has always been received with marked respect.

In seeking for a lady to present another lady at Court (the first step), the higher the rank and the more unexceptionable the character the better. In asking this, it must be remembered that it is a favor of great delicacy to require from any one except a relation. It is necessary also for the lady who presents to be at the drawing-room on the day when the presentation takes place. If a lady of rank cannot be found, the wife of a county member, or of a man high in office, or of a military man of standing, or of a barrister's wife whose husband is of high standing, can be resorted to. Generally speaking, ladies in the Queen's household, unless of high position, do not like to present other ladies, not relations. *Any* lady who has been presented at Court may present in her turn.

These arrangements having been been made, and a suitable dress prepared, the next step is to consult the regulations specified and published by the Lord Chamberlain. They are as follows :—

THE QUEEN'S LEVEES OR DRAWING-ROOMS.

REGULATIONS

To be observed with regard to the Queen's Levees at St. James's Palace.

The Noblemen and Gentlemen, who propose to attend

Her Majesty's Levees, at St. James's Palace, are requested to bring with them two large cards, with their names *clearly written* thereon, one to be left with the Queen's Page in attendance in the corridor, and the other to be delivered to the Lord Chamberlain, who will announce the name to the Queen.

PRESENTATIONS.

Any Nobleman or Gentleman who proposes to be presented to the Queen must leave at the Lord Chamberlain's Office, *before twelve o'clock*, two clear days before the Levee, a card with his name written thereon, and with the name of the Nobleman or Gentleman by whom he is to be presented. In order to carry out the existing regulation that no presentation can be made at a Levee excepting by a person actually attending that Levee, it is also necessary that a letter from the Nobleman or Gentleman who is to make the presentation, stating it to be his intention to be present, should accompany the presentation card above referred to, which will be submitted to the Queen for Her Majesty's approbation. It is Her Majesty's command, that no presentations shall be made at the Levees, except in accordance with the above regulations.

It is particularly requested, that in every case the names be *very distinctly written* upon the cards to be delivered to the Lord Chamberlain, in order that there may be no difficulty in announcing them to the Queen.

The state apartments will not be open for the reception of the company coming to Court until half-past one o'clock.

These regulations apply equally to ladies and gentle

19

men. Directions at what gate to enter, and where the carriages are to set down, are always printed in the newspapers.

It is desirable to be early, in order to avoid the great crowd, which, of late years, has rendered attendance at the drawing-room a great effort, even to the strongest. On getting out of the carriage, everything in the shape of a cloak, or scarf, even of lace, must be left behind; the train is folded carefully over the left arm, and the wearer enters the long gallery at St. James's, where she waits until her turn comes for presentation: she then proceeds to the Presence-Chamber, which is entered by two doors; she goes in by that indicated to her, and, on finding herself in the Presence-Chamber, lets down her train, which is instantly spread out by the Lords-in-waiting with their wands, so that the lady walks easily forward to the Queen. The card on which the lady's name is inscribed is then handed to another Lord-in-waiting, who reads the name aloud to the Queen. When she arrives just before Her Majesty, she should curtsey very low, so low as almost, but not quite, to kneel to the Queen, who, if the lady presented be a peeress, or a peer's daughter, kisses her forehead; if merely a commoner, holds out her hand to be kissed by the lady presented, who, having done so, rises, and making another curtesy to Prince Albert, and also severally to any members of the Royal Family present, and then passes on, keeping her face towards the Queen, and backing out to the door appointed for those who go out of the Presence-Chamber.

In this transient scene, habitual elegance and dignity of carriage, presence of mind, coupled with the respectful demeanor proper on such occasions, are requisite, and nervousness and diffidence are as much out of place as a bold and careless deportment.

THE END.

NEW BOOKS

And New Editions Recently Published by

RUDD & CARLETON,

1 3 0 GRAND STREET, NEW YORK,

(BROOKS BUILDING, COR. OF BROADWAY.)

N.B.—RUDD & CARLETON, UPON RECEIPT OF THE PRICE, WILL
SEND ANY OF THE FOLLOWING BOOKS, BY MAIL, *postage free*, TO
ANY PART OF THE UNITED STATES. THIS CONVENIENT AND
VERY SAFE MODE MAY BE ADOPTED WHEN THE NEIGHBORING
BOOKSELLERS ARE NOT SUPPLIED WITH THE DESIRED WORK.

NOTHING TO WEAR.

A Satirical Poem. By WILLIAM ALLEN BUTLER. Profusely and elegantly embellished with fine illustrations on tinted paper, by Hoppin. Muslin, price 50 cents.

THE KELLYS AND THE O'KELLYS.

A New Novel, from the pen of ANTHONY TROLLOPE, Author of "Doctor Thorne," &c. Reprinted from the English edition. One vol., 12mo., muslin, price $1 25.

ALEXANDER VON HUMBOLDT.

A new and popular Biography of this celebrated *Savant*, including his travels and labors, with an introduction by BAYARD TAYLOR. One vol., steel portrait, price $1 25.

HUMBOLDT'S PRIVATE LETTERS.

The Correspondence of Alexander Von Humboldt with Varnhagen Von Ense, and other contemporary celebrities. From the German. Muslin, price $1 25.

CESAR BIROTTEAU.

A Novel, by HONORE DE BALZAC.   The first of a Series of Translations from standard Works of this celebrated French novelist.   One vol., 12mo., muslin, price $1 00.

ADVENTURES OF VERDANT GREEN.

By CUTHBERT BEDE, B.A.   The best humorous story of College Life ever published.   80th edition, from English plates.   Nearly 200 original illustrations, price $1 00.

LIFE OF HUGH MILLER.

Author of "Schools and Schoolmasters," "Old Red Sandstone," &c.   Reprinted from the Edinburgh edition. One large 12mo., muslin, new edition, price $1 25.

LOVE (L'AMOUR).

By M. JULES MICHELET.   Author of "A History of France," &c.   Translated from the French by J. W. Palmer, M.D.   One vol., 12mo., muslin, price $1 00.

WOMAN (LA FEMME).

A sequel and companion to "Love" (L'Amour) by the same author, MICHELET.   Translated from the French by Dr. J. W. Palmer.   12mo.   Muslin, price $1 00.

DOCTOR ANTONIO.

A Love Tale of Italy.   By RUFFINI, author of "Lorenzo Benoni," "Dear Experience," &c.   Reprinted from the London copy.   Muslin, new edition, price $1 25.

DEAR EXPERIENCE.

A Tale.   By G. RUFFINI, author of "Doctor Antonio," "Lorenzo Benoni," &c.   With illustrations by Leech, of the London Punch.   12mo., muslin, price $1 00.

THE GREAT TRIBULATION ;

Or Things coming on the Earth. By Rev. JOHN CUMMING, D.D., author of "Apocalyptic Sketches," &c. From the English edition. FIRST SERIES. Muslin, price $1 00.

THE GREAT TRIBULATION.

SECOND SERIES of the new work by Rev. DR. CUMMING, which has awakened such an excitement throughout the religious community. 12mo., muslin, price $1 00.

BOOK OF THE CHESS CONGRESS.

A complete History of Chess in America and Europe, with Morphy's best games. By D. W. FISKE, editor of *Chess Monthly* (assisted by Morphy and Paulsen). Price $1 50.

BEATRICE CENCI.

A Historical Novel. By F. D. GUERRAZZI. Translated from the original Italian by LUIGI MONTI. Muslin, two volumes in one, with steel portrait, price $1 25.

ISABELLA ORSINI.

A new historical novel. By F. D. GUERRAZZI, author of "Beatrice Cenci." Translated by MONTI, of Harvard College. With steel portrait. Muslin, price $1 25.

WOMAN'S THOUGHTS ABOUT WOMEN.

The latest and best work by the author of "John Halifax, Gentleman," "Agatha's Husband," "The Ogilvies," &c. From the London edition. Muslin, price $1 00.

AFTERNOON OF UNMARRIED LIFE.

An interesting theme admirably treated. Companion to Miss Muloch's "Woman's Thoughts about Women." From London edition. 12mo., muslin, price $1 00.

THE CULPRIT FAY.

By Joseph Rodman Drake. A charming edition of this world-celebrated Faery Poem. Printed on colored paper. 12mo., muslin, with frontispiece. Price 50 cts.

THE HABITS OF GOOD SOCIETY.

A valuable handbook for Ladies and Gentlemen; with thoughts, hints, and anecdotes, concerning social observances, taste, and good manners. Muslin, price $1 25.

LECTURES OF LOLA MONTEZ.

Including her "Autobiography," "Wits and Women of Paris," "Comic Aspect of Love," "Gallantry," &c. A new edition, large 12mo., muslin, price $1 25.

CURIOSITIES OF NATURAL HISTORY.

By Francis T. Buckland. Interesting and instructive illustrations and sketches in Natural History. From the London edition. One vol., muslin, price $1 25.

VERNON GROVE;

By Mrs. Caroline H. Glover. "A Novel which will give its author high rank among the novelists of the day."—*Atlantic Monthly.* 12mo., muslin, price $1 00.

MOTHER GOOSE FOR GROWN FOLKS.

Humorous rhymes based upon the famous "Mother Goose Nursery Melodies." Attractively printed on tinted paper, with frontispiece. Muslin price, 75 cts.

EDGAR POE AND HIS CRITICS.

By Mrs. Sarah H. Whitman. Embracing a sketch of the life, and many incidents in the history and family of Edgar Allan Poe. 12mo., muslin. Price 75 cents.

BALLAD OF BABIE BELL,

And other Poems. By THOMAS BAILEY ALDRICH. The first selected collection of verses by this author. 12mo. Exquisitely printed, and bound in muslin, price 75 cents.

THE COURSE OF TRUE LOVE

Never did run Smooth. An Eastern Tale in verse. By T. B. ALDRICH, author of "Babie Bell." Elegantly printed on colored plate paper. Muslin, price 50 cents.

ROMANCE OF A POOR YOUNG MAN.

From the French of OCTAVE FEUILLET. An admirable and striking work of fiction. Translated from the Seventh Paris edition. 12mo., muslin, price $1 00.

DOESTICKS' LETTERS.

A compilation of the Original Letters of Q. K. P. DOE-STICKS, P. B. With many comic illustrations by McLenan. 12mo., muslin, new edition, price $1 25.

PLU-RI-BUS-TAH.

A song that's by-no-author. *Not* a parody on "Hia-watha." By DOESTICKS. 150 humorous cuts by McLenan. 12mo., muslin, new edition, price $1 25.

THE ELEPHANT CLUB.

An irresistibly droll volume. By DOESTICKS, P.B., assisted by KNIGHT RUSS OCKSIDE, M.D. Profusely illustrated by McLenan. Muslin, new edition, price $1 25.

THE WITCHES OF NEW YORK.

A New humorous work by DOESTICKS ; being particular and faithful Revelations of Black Art Mysteries in Gotham. 1 vol. 12mo., muslin, new edition, price $1 25.

MILES STANDISH ILLUSTRATED.

With exquisite *Photographs* from Original Drawings by JOHN W. EHNINGER, illustrating Longfellow's new Poem. Bound in elegant quarto, morocco covers, price $6 00.

TWO WAYS TO WEDLOCK.

A popular Novellette. Reprinted from the columns of Morris & Willis' *New York Home Journal.* One vol. 12mo. Handsomely bound in muslin, price $1 00.

THE NEW AND THE OLD;

Or, California and India in Romantic Aspects. By J. W. PALMER, M.D., author of "Up and Down the Irrawaddi." Abundantly illustrated. Muslin, 12mo. $1 25.

UP AND DOWN THE IRRAWADDI;

Or, the Golden Dagon. Being passages of Adventure in the Burman Empire. By J. W. PALMER, M.D., author of "The New and the Old." Illustrated, price $1 00.

SOUTHWOLD.

By Mrs. LILLIE DEVEREUX UMSTED. "A spirited and well drawn Society novel—somewhat intensified but bold and clever." One vol. 12mo., muslin, price $1 00.

THE VAGABOND.

A volume of Miscellaneous Papers, treating in colloquial sketches upon Literature, Society, and Art. By ADAM BADEAU. Bound in muslin, 12mo., price $1 00.

RECOLLECTIONS OF THE REVOLUTION.

A private manuscript journal of home events, kept during the American Revolution by the Daughter of a Clergyman. Printed in unique style. Muslin, price $1 00.

AN ANSWER TO HUGH MILLER.

By THOMAS A. DAVIES. An argument in opposition to the Geological Theories and Biblical Exegesis of the Hugh Miller school. 12mo., muslin, price $1 25.

HAMMOND'S POLITICAL HISTORY.

A History of Political Parties in the State of New York. By JABEZ B. HAMMOND, LL.D. 3 vols. octavo, with steel portraits of all the Governors. Muslin, price $6 00.

HARTLEY NORMAN.

A New Novel. "Close and accurate observation, enables the author to present the scenes of everyday life with great spirit and originality." Muslin, 12mo., price $1 25.

BROWN'S CARPENTER'S ASSISTANT.

The best practical work on Architecture; with plans for every description of Building. Illustrated with over 200 Plates. Strongly bound in leather, price $5 00.

ERIC; OR, LITTLE BY LITTLE.

A Tale of Roslyn School. By F. W. FARRAR (Fellow of Trinity College, Cambridge). An admirable picture of inner school life. Muslin, 12mo, price $1 00.

THE SPUYTENDEVIL CHRONICLE.

A sparkling Novel of Fashionable Life in New York; introducing a Saratoga Season; Flirtations, &c. Companion to the "Potiphar Papers." Muslin, price 75 cts.

WALTER ASHWOOD,

A Novel. By PAUL SIOGVOLK. Author of "Schediasms." The Scenes laid chiefly at Niagara Falls, Chamouni, Interlachen, and Wiesbaden. Muslin, price $1 00.

ETHEL'S LOVE-LIFE.

By Mrs. M. J. M. SWEAT.   A Novel.   "Rarely has any
recent work expressed the intenseness of a woman's love
with such hearty *abandon.*"   1 vol. 12mo., price $1 00.

BORDER WAR.

A Tale of Disunion.   By J. B. JONES, author of " Wild
Western Scenes."   One of the most popular books ever
published in America.   Muslin, 12mo., price $1 25.

A BACHELOR'S STORY.

By OLIVER BUNCE.   Upon the thread of a pleasant story
the author has strung a wampum of love, philosophy,
and humor.   One vol. 12mo., muslin, price $1 00.

FOLLOWING THE DRUM ;

Or, Glimpses of Frontier Life.   Being brilliant Sketches
of Recruiting Incidents on the Rio Grande, &c.   By
Mrs. EGBERT L. VIELÉ.   12mo., muslin, price $1 00.

EMELINE SHERMAN SMITH.

Poems and Ballads.   Embracing many favorite contributions to the leading journals, together with several un-
published poems.   One large octavo, muslin, price $2 00.

K. N. PEPPER PAPERS.

Containing the Verses and Miscellaneous Writings of one
of the first humorous contributors to the " *Knickerbocker
Magazine.*"   One vol. 12mo., muslin, price $1 00.

THE STORY OF THE TELEGRAPH.

A careful and Authentic History of Telegraphy and the
Atlantic Cable; with Biographies, Maps, Steel and
Wood Engravings, Portraits, &c.   Muslin, price $1 00.

9 783744 665216